A Defence
of the
Bible
Second Edition

By
Dr Gary Baxter

First edition September 2010
Second edition October 2011
Second printing April 2013

Cover art and design: Rachel Davison:rach.jd@gmail.com

Cover imagery: Whirlpool Galaxy courtesy NASA, ESA, S. Beckwith (STScI) and Hubble Heritage Team (STScI/AURA); historic portraits and Hebrew Scriptures courtesy Wikimedia Commons; additional imagery by Rachel Davison.

Contents

Chapter	Page
Introduction	1
1 – Is There Any Truth in Other Religions?	2
2 – Is There Scientific Support for the Theory of Evolution?	17
3 – Is There Any Scientific Support for Biblical Creation?	54
4 – Can the Bible Withstand Scientific Scrutiny?	90
5 – The Bible and Prophecy	123
6 – Did Jesus Really Live, Die and Rise from the Dead?	151
7 – Summary	169
Appendix 1 – A Summary of the Bible	174
Appendix 2 – Tacitus' Comments on Nero's Treatment of Christians	176
Appendix 3–Pliny the Younger's Letter to Emperor Trajan	177
Index	179

Notes to readers

This book comprises a compilation of six talks and a conclusion (chapter 7). Consequently, each chapter is complete within itself and can be read independently of the other chapters.

All scripture references are taken from the New King James Bible unless otherwise stated.

All photographs, images and sketches in this book are supplied courtesy of Wikimedia Commons or by our graphic designer, unless credit is ascribed to another source.

Our website: www.adefenceofthebible.com, shows where copies of this book may be purchased

Acknowledgements

In chronological order

Pastor Robert Gunter's suggestion that I should consider conducting a series of talks within our church that would encourage people to believe the Bible led to the publication of this book, as people and other churches requested copies of the talks. His discussions and encouragement and the time taken to review the crude manuscript are greatly appreciated. **Pastor Ernie Veszely** as Senior Pastor approved the talks, and his suggestion that they should take place at our evening service in order that they may reach a larger group of people is acknowledged with thanks.

Dr Carl Wieland, Managing Director, Creation Ministries International (creation.com.) provided helpful advice on certain aspects of the book, which is much appreciated. Also, he gave permission to include the work of Dr Russell Humphreys: *Evidence for a Young World*.

Mr. John W de Silva has written a number of books and he ably assisted me with the setting out of this second edition. His help is gratefully acknowledged.

Dr Kristi Baxter, my daughter-in-law, kindly devoted many hours to editing the crude manuscript of the first edition. Her work is acknowledged with gratitude.

Mrs. Rachel Davison used her creative talents in designing the cover as well as her editing skills; both to this second edition as a service to her Lord. This is much appreciated.

Mr. Tony Williams has been of great assistance in compiling the index along with his knowledge of Microsoft Word in solving seemingly intractable problems. Many thanks.

Mr Darren Grey used his skills to create a new and improved website. For this, I am very appreciative.

Mr Alexander Silva has translated chapter four of this book into Portuguese as a service to his Lord and for the benefit of his family and friends in Brazil.

A number of people assisted with the preparation of this book in a smaller but still significant way. Appreciation is expressed to Dr Don Batten of Creation Ministries International (technical advice), to Miss Emma Lloyd (document assistance) and to my son Mr Craig Baxter (Hebrew words).

Many thanks and appreciation is extended to the people who kindly gave their time to proof-read the manuscripts. These people are: Mr. Kevin Glassenbury, Mr. Ray Pugh, Mr. Neil Parker, Mr. Ian McColl, Mr. Bill Metcalfe, Cheryl Baxter (my sister) and Mr. and Mrs. Richard and Helen Jenkin.

My wife Larissa has always been a source of encouragement to me when I have served our Lord even in the smallest way. As with everything in a marriage, this book has come about through a partnership, without which it would not have even begun.

Introduction

The following is a compilation of six talks composed in defence of the Bible, which I was asked to give to our church by Pastor Robert Gunter, to whom I am eternally grateful, for the Lord has used this simple act of service. The talks were based upon a situation I faced. After teaching the Bible to a group of young people (late teens) for 12 months, and knowing that our time together was coming to an end, I was concerned that they were going into a world that was largely antagonistic to the scriptures and that their fledgling faith might fall victim to its relentless pressure. So, literally on the back of an envelope, I jotted down five compelling reasons to believe in the God of the Bible, and spoke for about three minutes on each. The five reasons were: the impossibility of evolution, the uniqueness of the Bible, the person of our Lord Jesus Christ, the Jewish people and the testimony of the martyrs.

Although these five subjects were changed and ultimately became six, the message is still the same; Christians have an abundance of evidence to believe. And the Christian faith is unique in this regard. Believers are not required to put their brains into neutral when they enter a church. In fact, the best defence of the scriptures comes about when people are challenged to investigate and think.

My own walk with the Lord began at the age of about six or seven. A faithful servant of the Lord, a Mr. Morrison or Morris, I'm not sure of his exact name, had bench seats put into his Vanguard panel van and on a Sunday morning drove around the neighborhood picking up children and taking them to Sunday school. This would not be possible in today's highly regulated and decadent society. I can very clearly recall writing on the front page of my workbook, "Jesus is my Savior." I am sure that I would have copied my teacher's writing, but it was enough for me to want to follow Jesus.

As the years passed, I would diligently say my prayers every night, in the form of the Lord's Prayer. At the age of seventeen I met my future wife and we would attend church together. However, we had never heard of personal salvation and our devotion stagnated. Some church leaders will have a lot to answer for. As I went through university and completed my PhD in synthetic organic chemistry, I assumed that the Theory of Evolution was fact, so I tried to marry this theory with Christianity and as a consequence, embraced theistic evolution—I even spoke in a church about it. Then one day, praise God, I read a booklet by Sylvia Baker called *A Bone of Contention*. The author very methodically demolished each pillar on which the Theory of Evolution stood. The scales fell from my eyes and I could see clearly. I then devoured Josh McDowell's classic book *Evidence That Demands a Verdict*, followed by many books from Creation Ministries International (creation.com).

I now read scientific articles and magazines in the light of a young earth created by God. In this way they make more sense.

Gary J Baxter, January 2012

Chapter 1

Is There Any Truth in Other Religions?

Sometime ago someone said to me, "How do you know that you Christians are right? There are some 900 million Hindus—how do you know that they are not right? Or what about all of the Buddhists—are they wrong also?" I have heard it said that all religions are equally valid, and that it's a bit like climbing a mountain—it doesn't matter where you start, we all get to the same place in the end. Another ploy of those who oppose Christianity is to refer to it by the all-embracing term, 'religion.' As such, what applies to one, such as strange worship practices, fanatical behavior, or belief in the illogical, applies to all.

Before we look closely into some aspects of the Bible and in order to respond to these statements, it would be profitable to scan some of the world's major religions and cults, and to ascertain how they came about and what their adherents actually believe.

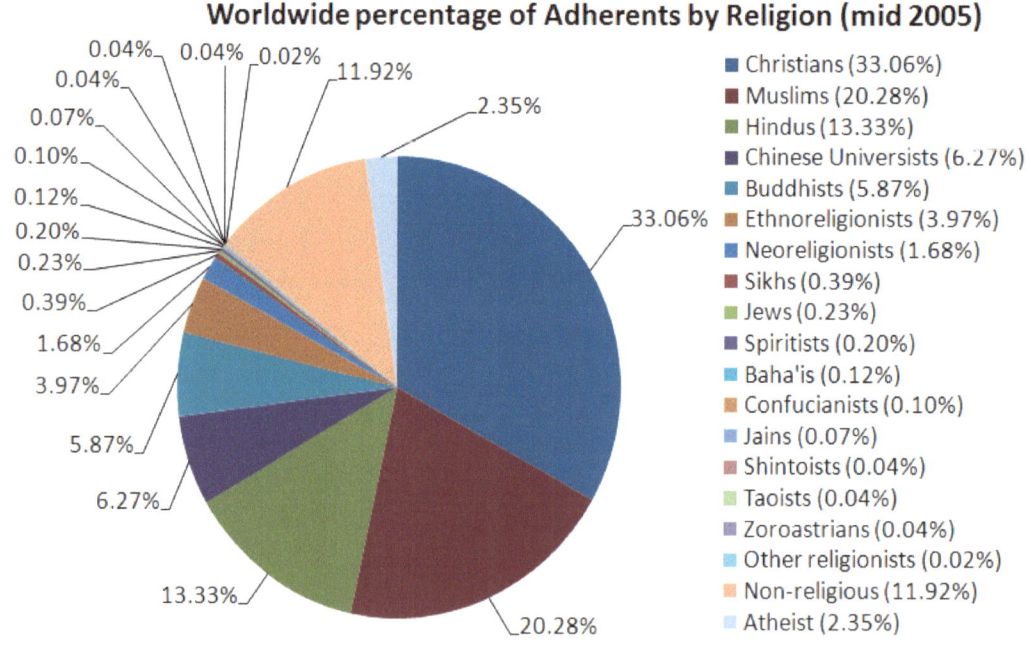

The pie chart above shows the major religions of the world ranked by the number of adherents.[1]

The significance of Hinduism, Islam (the religion of Muslims) and Buddhism is clear from the chart. A review of the basic beliefs of these three major non-Christian religions is presented. This is followed by a brief analysis of the cults of Mormons, Jehovah Witnesses, Christian Science and Christadelphians, and then an overview of Christianity.

---

[1] Source: wikipedia.org/wiki/Major_religious_groups, retrieved October 18, 2008.

1   Is There Any Truth in Other Religions?

Hinduism

Hinduism has no single founder, no single scripture, and no commonly agreed set of teachings. Throughout its extensive history, there have been many key figures teaching different philosophies and writing numerous holy books. For these reasons, writers often refer to Hinduism as 'a way of life' or 'a family of religions' rather than a single religion.[2] It is based around one central and impersonal god, Brahman (also known as 'Brahma'), who is held to be infinite, eternal, and the cause, source, material and effect of all creation. Essentially, god is everything and everything is god. There is no single founder, no specific theological structure and no central religious organisation.[3]

The following historical information on Hinduism has been taken from *A Spectator's Guide to World Religions* by John Dickson.[4]

Hinduism is based upon three overlapping groups of historical writings:

> **Vedas:** 1500–500 BC
> **Upanishads:** 1000–300 BC
> **Smriti (Manu Smriti):** 500 BC–AD 300

Vedas (1500–500 BC)
There are four foundational books, which, if published, would fill a bookshelf. These books basically dictate a ritualistic practice involving animal sacrifices and fire offerings, as well as the priest drinking of a hallucinogenic plant juice.

The Vedas require a belief in many and varied gods and among them is the god Soma, which is associated with the plant juice the priest drinks.

The Indian religion that developed out of the Vedas and belief in these writings is still central to Hinduism.

Upanishads (1000–300 BC)
These writings came about when Indian gurus began to reflect on their religion and sought to make sense of the world in the light of that tradition. These writings, in terms of theology, far outweigh the Vedas.

The Upanishads introduce the concept (the corner stone of Hinduism), that there is a mysterious background force known as *Brahman*. To Hindus, Brahman is the ultimate and only reality in the universe. From Brahman everything in the universe came and to Brahman everything in the universe will return. Everything originates from Brahman: creation, human beings, the gods, etc. All these things flicker for a while and then return to their source where they are absorbed in the ultimate and only true reality.

Connected with the idea of Brahman is the concept of the 'Atman' or soul. This is the 'inner you,' the real life-force that exists in every living creature. It is that part of you that is from Brahman.

---

[2] Source: bbc.co.uk/religion/religions/hinduism/ataglance/glance.shtml, retrieved April 27, 2011.
[3] Source: *Religions of the World Passport*, Insight for Living; oneplace.com, April 24, 2011.
[4] J. Dickson, *A Spectator's Guide to World Religions*, Blue Bottle Books, 2004.

1. Is There Any Truth in Other Religions?

Every Hindu wants his soul to return to Brahman. However, his soul may be caught up in an endless cycle of reincarnation that is, dying and then being reborn as some other creature. This, they believe, happens to all living creatures, including insects.

Smriti (500 BC–AD 300)

These writings reveal the Great Epic of the Bharata Dynasty. At the center of this massive mythological epic is the battle between cousins, after which almost the entire race is destroyed. Just before the battle, a long and detailed conversation breaks out between the hero of the story, Prince Arjune, and his advisor, Krishna, who turns out to be an incarnation of the god Vishnu. In this conversation, which is known as the *Bhagavad-gita*, the good god Krishna endorses the hierarchical view of humanity consisting of four levels of people or castes:

1. **Priests**— they form the top level in Indian society with nearness to the ultimate life-principle of the universe, which is Brahman.
2. **Warrior kings**—in contemporary Indian society, these people belong to what we would call the upper–middle class.
3. **Common people**— these make up the bulk of the Indian society and are involved with industry and commerce.
4. **Servants (Sundras)** — their role is simply to serve the three upper castes. A servant can only hope that his or her karma, i.e. the good things they do in life (see discussion below); will cause a promotion to the above order in the next life.

There are only three possible ways of escaping the endless cycle of birth and rebirth so that the person can return to Brahman.

1. **Path of Duties**— that is, to faithfully continue one's duties. And ones' 'duties' depend on which caste the person belongs to.
2. **Path of Knowledge** —this can be attained by contemplation and religious realisation of the soul's oneness with Brahman.
3. **Path of Devotion** —this requires devoting one's self completely and utterly to one of the many gods.

Within Hinduism, there is an exceedingly wide variety of gods to potentially worship, each with its own characteristics, statues and symbols before which to pay homage. If, for example, one wants to pray for knowledge and understanding, one would pray to the god *Sarasati*. One might pray to the god *Moksha* to obtain grace. Many Hindus worship their own village god or goddess. However, to say that Hinduism is a polytheistic religion with an unknown and unnamed number of gods would not be entirely correct. Many Hindus view their religion as monotheistic, with only one Supreme Being (Brahman) who is formless and impersonal. All other gods and goddesses are simply facets of this one god. This Supreme Being is viewed as the god of all other religions and equal to all existence or the ultimate reality.

Even though the Hindu faith could be viewed as monotheistic, it does embrace within it, a trinity of three gods: Brahma, Vishnu and Shiva.

Karma

Karma is the concept that all of a person's actions in life stick to his soul in such a way as to determine his soul's re-existence in his next incarnation. For example, good karma means that the

1 Is There Any Truth in Other Religions?

person goes up the order in the next life and bad karma means he goes down. The ultimate goal of a Hindu is not to come back as something better the next time round, rather it is to escape the need to come back at all by going into Brahman.

Whilst karma is the entrapment of one's soul in this endless cycle, Moksa is the release from it so that one can enter into the reality of Brahman, the source of true existence.

Hindus believe that the universe appears and disappears every twenty-four million years—twelve million years of existence and twelve million years of non-existence. This raises the question of how non-existence, or *nothing*, is able to bring about existence, that is, *something*.

Below are some of the major deities of the Hindu faith.[5]

Lord Brahma symbolises the aspect of the Supreme Reality that brings forth the creation. For this reason, Hindus call Lord Brahma creator of the universe. He is the first member of the Hindu trinity that also includes Lord Vishnu and Lord Shiva. His divine consort is Saraswati, the goddess of learning and knowledge. Goddess Saraswati provides Lord Brahma with knowledge that is necessary for the process of creation.

The four faces of Brahma represent the sacred knowledge of the four Vedas and this is the most prominent feature of any image of Brahma. The four faces, therefore, symbolise that Brahma is the source of all knowledge necessary for the creation of the universe. The four arms represent the four directions and thus represent the omnipresence and omnipotence of Lord Brahma.

Lord Vishnu or Krishna represents the aspect of the Supreme Reality that preserves and sustains the universe. Although there are variations in images and pictures of Lord Vishnu, he is generally symbolised by a human body with four arms. In his hands he carries a conch (shankha), a mace (gada), and discus (chakra). He wears a crown, two earrings, a garland (mala) of flowers, and a gem around the neck. He has a blue body and wears yellow clothes. Lord Vishnu is shown standing on a thousand-headed snake (named Shesha Nag), and the snake stands with its hoods open over the head of the lord.

Lord Shiva represents the aspect of the Supreme Being (Brahman of the Upanishads) that continuously dissolves to recreate in the cyclic process of creation, preservation, dissolution and re-creation of the universe.

A statue of Lord Shiva

---

[5] Source: Wikipedia.org/wiki/Hinduism, retrieved May, 2011.

1   Is There Any Truth in Other Religions?

Other major deities are Goddess Durga, Lord Ganesha and Goddess Saraswati.

Goddess Durga   Lord Ganesha   Goddess Saraswati

This has been a very brief overview of Hinduism. It is a very complex religion devised over many hundreds of years, and for those who are unfortunate enough to have been born into the servant class from which there is no escape, it is very repressive.

Buddhism

Buddhism is virtually atheistic; the concept of a god is ignored. All reality is regarded as an illusion. Truth is based on experience and personal enlightenment.[6]

This religion is thought to have been started by an Indian prince who was raised on Hinduism. His name was Siddhartha Gautama and he belonged to the 'warrior king' caste of Indian society. Historical records about his life are not plentiful. He may have lived during the period 500–400 BC. He is reported to have lived to 80 years of age. His teachings were passed down verbally and finally written about 300–400 years after his death.

Gautama's father was a Raja and tradition has it that at 29 years of age, Gautama went outside his palace and was overcome by grief when he saw the suffering around him. He decided to abandon his life of privilege, along with his wife and young son, and set out alone to discover for himself the secret of serenity in a world of pain. He wandered the Ganges River area studying Hinduism and speaking to Gurus. But the presence of suffering and evil still troubled him. One day, while sitting under a fig tree, he discovered why people were suffering and found a way to overcome suffering. From then on, he was known as Buddha, 'the enlightened one'.[7]

He rejected the idea of an eternal soul; in fact, he believed that there was no individual identity at all. A key to Buddhist thinking is that ultimately, we do not exist.

The reasoning behind such a belief goes something like this:

The thing that I call 'me' is really a combination of ever-changing physical and mental activities going on in the same space (that is, my body and brain). These activities are the result of physical

---

[6] *Religions of the World Passport*, Insight for Living; see also: oneplace.com.
[7] J. Dickson, *A Spectator's Guide to World Religions,* Blue Bottle Books, 2004, pages 50-51.

1 Is There Any Truth in Other Religions?

and mental activities that occurred a moment earlier. These, in turn, are the result of the ones that occurred the moment before that, and so on. There is no 'me' arising from this chain of cause and effect. There is just the chain itself—merely physical and mental activities causing further physical and mental activities. Thinking of me as an individual is just a fantasy—a mere illusion.

The goal of Buddhism is to help people to realise that they ultimately do not exist, because the notion of self is the root of all suffering. It is your desire for self-satisfaction, self-existence, and self-advancement that creates the experience of pain. Remove the 'self', by realizing there never was such a thing, and suffering will evaporate.[8]

In order to achieve the removal of desire and the mental pain of suffering, the Buddha gave his followers four beliefs and eight habits to memorise and practise.

The Four Noble Truths
1. The recognition that suffering exists in many forms.
2. The origin of suffering—suffering arises because of desires or cravings.
3. The end of suffering—suffering is overcome by the elimination of human cravings; Buddha called this state *Nirvana*.
4. The path to end suffering—this leads to the eight habits:
    a. Right Understanding—the need to study Buddhist texts.
    b. Right Aim—the need to aspire to Buddhist ideals.
    c. Right Speech—the need to speak in such a way as to remove any desires and eradicate the idea of self.
    d. Right Action—the need to negate all desires, to refrain from killing or injuring any living creature, and to abstain from alcohol.
    e. Right Livelihood—the need to find employment that does no harm to other creatures.
    f. Right Effort—the need to engage daily in an energetic decision to put an end to false thoughts and unwholesome states of mind.
    g. Right Mindfulness—Buddhists must strive to be aware of everything around them.
    h. Right Concentration—meditation is an essential aspect of a Buddhist's life.

The eight-fold path has nothing to do with prayer, worship of a god or religious ceremonies.[9]

There are many statues of Buddha and they are used for different purposes. For example, the veneration of Medicine Buddha, the Supreme Healer (*Sangye Menla* in Tibetan) is considered a powerful method not only for healing and increasing healing powers both for oneself and others, but also for overcoming the inner sickness of attachment, hatred and ignorance. It is believed that meditating on the Medicine Buddha can help decrease physical and mental illness and suffering.[10]

Medicinal Buddha

Karma

The Buddha adopted the Hindu idea of karma and Buddhists believe that we do not choose our rebirth but are born solely in accordance with our karma. If good karma ripens, we are reborn in a

---

[8] J. Dickson, *A Spectator's Guide to World Religions,* Blue Bottle Books, 2004 page 56.
[9] *ibid* page 69.
[10] Source: religionfacts.com/buddhism/.../medicine_buddha.htm, retrieved April 28, 2011.

fortunate state; either as a human being or a god, but if negative karma ripens we are reborn in a lower state, as an animal, a hungry ghost, or a hell being. It is as if we are blown by the winds of karma to our future lives, sometimes ending up in higher rebirths, sometimes in lower rebirths.[11]

The ultimate aim of the Buddhist is to attain the state of *Nirvana*. Here, the person has escaped the world of cause and effect, all suffering has ceased, and they are free from the cycle of birth and rebirth. This is achieved by following the eight-fold path.

Buddhism essentially teaches works-based salvation—that you must strive unceasingly and overcome all desire in order to have any hope of reaching *Nirvana*. It is a man-made religion and offers a man-made solution.

The final words attributed to Buddha before his death says it all:

Work hard to gain your own salvation.[12]

Islam

The religion of Islam was started by a man from the Arabian tribe of Quraysh who later became known as simply as Muhammad. He was born in Saudi Arabia in AD 570. The first biography of Muhammad's life was written 125 years after his death in AD 632, by a Muslim scholar named Ibn Ishaq, and was further revised in the ninth century (some 250 years after Muhammad's death). It came to be regarded as the official account of his life and is known as the *Sirah*, which means life.[13]

The second source of knowledge of Muhammad is the *Hadiths*, which are a vast collection of individual reports about the words and deeds of Muhammad, collected two to three centuries after his death.[14]

From the above sources, it is determined that Muhammad was born in Mecca, which was the geographic focal point of religious beliefs throughout pagan Arabia. In the center of Mecca was a huge box-shaped building called the *Kaba*, which housed 360 idol-gods of Arabia.

As Muhammad grew, he married a wealthy widow who became the first of his eleven wives. The second and youngest wife was Aisha, who was reported to have been only six years old when he married her and only nine when the marriage was consummated. He is believed to have been 53 years old at the time.[15] He is said to have been a contemplative man who loved to leave the hustle and bustle of the city and go up into the mountains to a cave where he could ponder the mysteries of life.

According to Muslim tradition, while he was in the cave, the 40-year-old Muhammad heard the voice of the archangel Gabriel, who claimed that he had been chosen as a messenger of god to restore the world to the truth about creation. Over the next 22 years until his death in AD 632, it is claimed that he received frequent revelations of this type. After each encounter he would commit

---

[11] Buddhist website; aboutbuddhism.org/buddhism-beliefs.php, retrieved April 29, 2011.
[12] buddhanet.net/e-learning/buddhism/lifebuddha/2_31lbud.htm, retrieved April 15, 2011.
[13] J. Dickson, *A Spectator's Guide to Religions of the World*, Blue Books, 2004, page 181.
[14] *Ibid*, page 181.
[15] Source: Wikipedia.org/wiki/Muhammad's_wives, retrieved April 29, 2011.

1   Is There Any Truth in Other Religions?

the message to memory, as he was thought to have been illiterate.[16] His followers memorised his revelations. From time to time, different sections were written on bits of stone, leather, palm leaves and scraps of paper.[17] In about AD 650 (after his death), his revelations were collected and combined to form what is known as the Koran (Qur'an). These writings are central to Islam.[18]

Muhammad was impressed by Jewish and Christian monotheism. His teachings were rejected in Mecca, so he moved to Medina some 400 kilometers away. Here, he established a small group of followers, which grew until he was elevated to the position of civil ruler—thus was born the first Islamic state. This time marks the beginning of the Muslim calendar. Here the people's faith was centered on two things: that Allah was the one true god and Muhammad was Allah's messenger.

Tensions between Muslims in Medina and 'pagans' in Mecca increased and Muhammad's army won an outstanding victory against the numerically superior army of Mecca. The citizens of Mecca readily converted to Islam and through the persuasion of the sword, Islam quickly spread throughout the Middle East.[19]

Muhammad came across many Jews and Christians and consequently, it is not surprising that the Koran includes parts of the Bible, which predates the Koran by many hundreds of years. The Koran contains biblical themes and represents a corruption of the original (the Bible). A few of these deviations are listed below, in order to give the reader a sense of their nature:

- Abraham's blessing was passed down to Ishmael, not Isaac, and it was Isaac whom Abraham expelled from the camp.
- Jesus was not killed, but with the help of Allah, He escaped and Judas was crucified in his place.
- Man was created in paradise, not on earth; the first couple was later banished to earth.
- Jesus Christ was a created being.
- No genealogies are given prior to the Flood.

The Koran is arranged by chapter size, with the largest chapter coming first and the smallest, last. Events are not in chronological order.

Interestingly, most Muslims have not read the Koran. Officially, it cannot be published in any language other than Arabic.

After Muhammad's death, there were disputes about who would be his successor and this led to the two divisions of Islam: *Sunni* and *Shiite*.

The *Sunnis* (traditionalists) may be regarded as those who follow the orthodox path. About 85 percent of Muslims are *Sunni*. The final authority in *Sunni* Islam rests with a special group of men who interpret the law (sharia) of Islam.

---

[16] submission.org/muhammed/illiteracy.html, retrieved May, 2011.
[17] *The Koran*, Translated by N. J. Dawood, Penguin Classics, 2004, Introduction, page 1.
[18] J. Dickson, *A Spectator's Guide to World Religions,* Blue Bottle Books, 2004 page 184; Isaac ben Abraham, *Islam, Terrorism and Your Future,* Cedar Hill Press, 2002 page 17; *The Koran*, Trans. N. J. Dawood, Penguin Classics, 2004.
[19] *The Koran*, Translated by N. J. Dawood, Penguin Classics, 2004, Introduction, page 1.

1 Is There Any Truth in Other Religions?

The *Shiites* are in the minority (15 percent); however, they are in the majority in Iraq and Iran. They are passionate about the fact that their leaders should come from descendants of Muhammad's family; these men are called Imams. They also believe in the glory of martyrdom. They venerate past Imams and believe that they can have salvation 'credits' passed on by the faithful deceased Imams, whereas *Sunnis* believe a person is responsible for his or her own salvation.[20]

Both groups believe in the five pillars of Islam –

1. The declaration: 'There is no God but Allah and Muhammad is his prophet'.
2. Pray five times a day, always facing Mecca.
3. Alms to the poor by way of giving two percent of one's salary.
4. Making a hajj (pilgrimage) to Mecca at least once in a lifetime.
5. Fasting during the month of Ramadan.

Salvation

There is no guarantee of salvation in Islam. Muhammad taught that he had no way of knowing his own eternal destiny. Islam teaches that there will be a Judgment Day, at which a man's good works will be weighed against his bad works. If the outcome is deemed positive, he will be allowed to enter Paradise. However, the only sure way to enter into Paradise is to die a martyr, at which point he will also receive riches and a harem.[21]

Women

Islam teaches that women are inferior to men in all aspects of life and that women are to be submissive to men to the extent that they become the man's property (Koran 2:223[22], 2:228, 2:282, 4:11, 4:34). Women automatically lose all rights to their children under Islamic law.[23] The testimony of one Islamic man carries weight equal to that of two women (Koran 2:282) and a man has double the inheritance rights of a woman (Koran 4:11). A man may have many wives including slave girls (Koran 4:2-4). Beatings are required for disobedient wives (Koran 4:34-35).

Apostasy

The right of religious freedom, including the right of individuals to change their religion, is taken for granted by most people in the West. But in Islam, people are only free to change from a non-Islamic faith to Islam; they are not free to change in the opposite direction. All schools of sharia (Islamic law) agree that adult male Muslims who leave their faith should be killed.[24]

Jihad

The term *jihad* literally means struggle. There are three types of *jihad* commonly recognised by Muslim scholars: the *jihad* of self-discipline, the *jihad* of Satan and the *jihad* of infidels—that is,

---

[20] J. Dickson, *A Spectator's Guide to World Religions,* Blue Bottle Books, 2004 pages 195-196.
[21] Isaac ben Abraham, *Islam Terrorism and Your Future,* Cedar Hill Press, 2002 page 61.
[22] Note: 2:223 is an abbreviation for The Koran, chapter, (Surah or Sura in Arabic) 2 and verse 223.
[23] answering-islam.org/Woman/index.html, retrieved May 2010.
[24] *Barnabasaid*, January/February 2009, page 11.

the fight against all who reject or stand in the way of the advancement of Islam.[25]

The Koran teaches that Muslims should fight and destroy the infidel (non-Muslims). Some excerpts from the Koran,[26] which advocates such activity, are given below:

But when the sacred months are over, slay the Idolaters wherever you find them. Arrest them, besiege them, and lie in ambush everywhere for them. If they repent [change to Islam] *and take to prayer and render alms levy, allow them to go their way. God is forgiving and merciful.* (9:5)

Fight against such of those to whom the scriptures were given as believe in God [Jews and Christians], *nor the Last Day, who do not forbid what God and His apostles have forbidden, and do not embrace the true faith, until they pay tribute* [a tax which non-Muslims must pay] *out of hand and are utterly subdued.*(9:29)

God revealed His will to the angels, saying: 'I shall be with you. Give courage to the believers. I shall cast terror into the hearts of the infidels [non-Muslims]. *Strike off their heads, strike off the very tips of their fingers!'* (8:12)

Believers, make war on the infidels who dwell around you. Deal firmly with them. Know that God is with the righteous. (9:123)

There are those who claim that Islam means peace, but as shown above, it only means peace through submission. This stands in stark contrast to the words of Jesus:

Love your neighbor as yourself. (Matthew 22:39)

Love your enemies, bless them that hate you, and pray for them who despitefully use you, and persecute you. (Matthew 5:44)

Statements contained in Islamic writings which have been proven incorrect in the light of modern knowledge are listed on pages 111-113

The Cults

There are a large number of cults. Some of the major ones are examined below briefly, with a summary of their main beliefs. All have perverted the scriptures, mostly to further the ends of their founders and/or senior leaders. A defining feature of cults is their denial of the Lordship of Christ.

The Church of Jesus Christ of Latterday Saints (Mormons)

The Mormon Church commenced when Joseph Smith (1805–1844, pictured right) was supposedly told by an angel to dig up a set of gold plates, which he did, after which he translated the writings on them to give the book of Mormon. Having done this, unfortunately he lost the gold plates, and nobody has been able to find them since. Although the writings were purported to be the inspired word of God and entirely correct, there have been some 4,000 changes from 1830 to the modern version.[27]

---

[25] Isaac ben Abraham, *Islam, Terrorism and Your Future,* Cedar Hill Press, 2002.
[26] *The Koran*, Trans. N. J. Dawood, Penguin Classics, 2004.
[27] ccgm.org.au/articles/Articles/ARTICLE-0131.htm.

1 Is There Any Truth in Other Religions?

The Mormons believe that there are trillions of planets scattered throughout the cosmos, all inhabited by gods who were once human. The two eldest sons of one god, whose name is Elohim, both wanted to become the savior of mankind. The son named Jesus won his father's approval and his brother Lucifer, in a jealous rage, took one third of the angels to join his campaign against Jesus.

They claim to use the Bible (King James Version) and the book of Mormon for their doctrine. Polygamy is allowed—Joseph Smith had 12 wives and all good Mormon men can become gods. For Joseph Smith taught: *As man is, God was; as God is man may become.*

The final say on which men becomes gods, however, is determined by the greatest of all prophets, Joseph Smith, the judge who will determine who will enter into the celestial kingdom. The women who make it will spend the rest of eternity having babies to populate planets.

Jehovah's Witnesses

Jehovah's Witnesses consider themselves to be the only true Christians. However, their organisation, the *Watchtower Bible and Tract Society*, denies and/or contradicts several of the essential doctrines of the Christian faith.

Charles Taze Russell (1852–1916, pictured right) founded this religious movement. As a teenager he rejected his Presbyterian roots, joined a more liberal Congregational church, and then left this group as well. He denied the deity of Christ and the biblical teachings on Hell and eternal punishment. Russell had no formal Bible training, but built upon various teachings that were popular at the time. In the 1880s he founded a non-profit corporation now known as the *Watchtower Bible and Tract Society*. The name Jehovah's Witnesses was adopted in 1931.

Jehovah's Witnesses deny many of the teachings of Christ and have become known for their various prophecies of when the great and final battle of Armageddon will occur—allegedly 1914, 1915, 1918 and 1975. Of course, all of these dates proved incorrect.

Their doctrine comes from their own version of the Bible and is a distortion of the true word of God. They believe the 144,000 redeemed souls of Revelation chapter 14 are all Jehovah's Witnesses. Since the actual number of Jehovah's Witnesses exceeds that number, they believe that the top 144,000 people in the organisation will go directly into heaven and all the 'other sheep' must become Christ's earthly subjects by keeping His laws and obeying His commands.

They believe that Jesus is the angel Gabriel. They are not allowed to receive another person's blood and there is much heartbreak when they prefer that their infant children die rather than receive a lifesaving blood transfusion. This idea comes from a distortion of God's prohibition on the Children of Israel from eating blood. There are 14 million 'Witnesses' worldwide.

Christian Science

The founder of this movement was Mary Baker (1821–1910, pictured next page), who was born in 1821 in the USA. In her middle years, she was in constant pain caused by a spinal weakness. She became involved with the practice of spiritualism and clairvoyance. After divorce from her second husband, she met Phineas Quimby. He was a metaphysician, and practised a form of mind-over-matter healing, which he called Christian Science. Mary believed he cured her back pain, although

1   Is There Any Truth in Other Religions?

the pain later returned. After Quimby's death, Mary took up this metaphysical healing and she wrote:

'In the year 1866, I discovered the Christ Science or divine laws of Life, Truth and Love and named my discovery Christian Science.'[28]

In 1877 she married her third husband, Asa Eddy. She published many books, but the one that has become the standard for the movement is *Science and Health with Key to the Scriptures*. The followers of Christian Science believe that the Bible can only be read in conjunction with Mrs. Eddy's book.

Christadelphians

The religion of the Christadelphians was started by Dr John Thomas (pictured right), who was born in London, the son of a minister. As a young man, he studied medicine and published articles in the medical journal *The Lancet*. In 1832 he emigrated to America. During the voyage, a ferocious storm almost broke the ship. Dr Thomas prayed but realised his lack of Bible knowledge. Consequently, on arrival in New York he studied the Bible and attended church. Over the years, he came to reject orthodox Christianity and in 1848 he established *The Royal Association of Believers* in New York, now known as the Christadelphians.

The Christadelphians openly deny almost every essential doctrine of Christianity, including the Trinity, the deity of Christ, the substitutionary atonement of Christ and salvation by grace through faith. They also deny the immortality of the soul and the reality of eternal conscious punishment for those who reject God. Despite their rejection of orthodox Christian doctrines, they claim to be the one true church, the remnant of faithful disciples left over from a partial apostasy.

Christianity

Christianity is based solely on the Bible, to the extent that anything brought into the practice of Christianity from outside the Bible is false. The God of creation has revealed Himself to mankind through the Bible, apart from the testimony of creation itself that points people to the existence of a Creator. The reader is invited to compare the origins of the Bible with the writings of the religions discussed on the previous pages and make up his or her mind as to which is more believable.

The Bible is unique in all literature. About 40 writers including kings, farmers, prophets, fishermen, a tax collector, a doctor, a Rabbi, a cupbearer, a military General, and others, wrote it over a period of 1,600 years. It was written on three continents (Asia, Africa[29] and Europe) and in three languages (Hebrew, Aramaic and Greek)—but it is one coherent story from start to finish with salvation through faith in Jesus Christ as its theme.

It starts with the omniscient, omnipresent and omnipotent Supernatural Being who created everything and desired to have a relationship with the pinnacle of His creation: mankind. The

---

[28] Source: Christian Science website: endtime.org/intro/cs.html, retrieved April 29, 2011.
[29] Moses would have written the first five books of the Bible while he was in the Sinai desert which is regarded as being part of Africa, see: wikipedia.org/wiki/Geography_of_Africa, retrieved June 18, 2011.

1   Is There Any Truth in Other Religions?

relationship was based on the condition that if mankind obeyed God and worshipped Him only, He would bless them. This formed the foundation of the old covenant or Old Testament. Mankind failed to keep their part of the agreement. This is known as sin. God still wanted to have the relationship but sin caused a separation that man could not overcome.

God, in an act of unfathomable grace, sent His own Son, the Lord Jesus Christ (God the Son), who was and is sinless, to take the penalty for the sins of everybody upon Himself, and to pay that penalty, which is death. This He did on the cross of Calvary, so that all who put their faith in Him could have that original relationship with God restored, and be with Him for all eternity. This redemptive action of God is known as the new covenant or New Testament.

Among the world's major belief systems, only Christianity includes the doctrine of eternal salvation by grace—that is, God's unmerited mercy, freely extended to sinners, made possible by Christ's atoning work on the cross. Grace sets Christianity apart from the man-made religions, which invariably teach salvation by works.

A very brief summary of the Bible is contained in Appendix 1.

The Bible has been read by more people and published in more languages than any other book.

All of the New Testament, with the exception of John's letters and possibly his gospel, Revelations and Jude, was written before AD 70. These remaining books were completed and in circulation within the next 30 years. This is affirmed by the book of Matthew, which records Jesus prophesying the destruction of the Temple, and yet makes no mention of the fulfillment of that prophecy.[30] Thus, we can safely assume that the document was written before the Temple was destroyed, which was in AD 70. Recent archeological research supports first century dates for early gospel authorship.[31]

Even during the time of the apostles there is evidence that believers treated their writings as special. In his second letter, Peter equates the writings of Paul with scripture[32] and Paul equates the writings of Luke[33] with scripture.[34] By the end of the second century, as evidenced by the writings of Justin Martyr, Clement of Alexandria, Tertullian and others, Christians regarded the writings of the apostles, including Paul, the four gospels and the book of Acts, as divine scripture. They read them when they met and they established the Jewish scripture as the Old Testament and the apostles' writings as the New Testament. However, dispute remained over Hebrews, James, 2 Peter, 2 and 3 John, Jude and Revelations. Much heresy abounded and the early church was very careful in discerning what was truly inspired. Two criteria were used:

    1. Were the writings of apostolic[35] origin?

---

[30] Matthew 24:1-2; see also Mark 13:2 and Luke 21:5-6.

[31] Dts,edu/read/Wallace-new-testament-manuscript-first-century, retrieved May, 2012.

[32] 2 Peter 3:16.

[33] Luke 10:7.

[34] 1 Timothy 5:18.

[35] In this context, the word 'apostolic' is a reference to the men who were eyewitnesses of the earthly activity of Jesus and hence testified that Jesus was the risen Lord. Both Matthew and John were disciples of Jesus and as a consequence, were eyewitnesses. Mark wrote Peter's testimony and Luke used interviews of eyewitnesses and existing

1 Is There Any Truth in Other Religions?

2. Were the writings made use of in the church?

Even though the writings (letters and books) were held up as inspired scripture and circulated among the churches from the time of the apostles, it was not until AD 367 that the Bishop of Alexandria, Athanasius, compiled the first canon of scripture. He did this in his Easter Letter in an effort to protect his flock from the heretical writings circulating at the time. This contained the 27 books of the New Testament. His compilation was confirmed by the councils at Hippo in 393 and at Carthage in 397, and thus the books of the New Testament were settled.[36]

Parts of the New Testament have been preserved in more manuscripts than any other ancient work, having over 5,800 complete or fragmented Greek manuscripts, 10,000 Latin manuscripts and 9,300 manuscripts in various other ancient languages including Syriac, Slavic, Gothic, Ethiopic, Coptic and Armenian.[37] The historical veracity of the gospel writings compares well with other historical documents that people have no trouble believing, as shown in the table below.

Author	Date Written	Earliest Manuscript	Time Span	Number of Manuscripts
Caesar	100-44 BC	AD 900	1,000 years	10
Plato	427-347 BC	AD 900	1,200 years	7
Thucydides	460-400 BC	AD 900	1,300 years	8
Tacitus	AD 100	AD 1,100	1,000 years	20
Suetonius	AD 75-160	AD 950	800 years	8
Homer (Iliad)	900 BC	400 BC	500 years	643
New Testament	AD 40-100	AD 125	25-50 years	>24,000

*Source of table: J. Sarfati, *Creation*, 2011, 33(1), page 33

No other book has been so viciously attacked, with many of its translators imprisoned, tortured and/or murdered, and many millions of copies destroyed. Yet the Bible remains a global best-seller, now available in over 2,000 language groups, covering over ninety percent of the world's population.

An illustration of the reality of the God of the Bible can be found in the book of Isaiah, chapters 36 and 37. This passage gives an account of the events of 701BC, where the all-conquering Assyrian king Sennacherib, having laid waste to the walled cities of Samaria and Judea, now lays siege to Jerusalem. He sends a list of demands to the godly king Hezekiah, which state, in effect: *what makes you think that your God can save you when the gods of all of the surrounding people could not save them?*[38] In great fear and anguish, Hezekiah goes into the temple, lays the letter before the

---

documents to obtain his information. Paul refers to himself as being an apostle because of his encounter and call to ministry by Jesus on the road to Damascus (Acts 9:1-19).

[36] J. Hill and L. Hudson, *The New Lion Handbook: the History of Christianity,* Lion Hudson, 2007 page 68; A. K. Curtis, J. S. Lang and R. Petersen, *The 100 Most Important Events in Christian History,* Fleming H Revell, 1991, pages 36-38.

[37] wikipedia.org/wiki/Biblical_manuscript. Retrieved December 16, 2012.

[38] Isaiah 36: 18-20.

1 Is There Any Truth in Other Religions?

Lord and prays for deliverance because this tyrant has blasphemed the name of the true God. In the morning Hezekiah's prayer is answered as 185,000 Assyrian soldiers lie dead. Sennacherib then packs up and goes back to Assyria where he is murdered by his sons while praying to his god.[39] This event is confirmed outside of scripture by the Greek historian Herodotus who refers to it in his manuscript; *Histories* which he wrote in approximately 450 BC[40] and is also alluded to by Sennacherib himself, who had recorded on the Taylor Prism (see page 115) that he, had captured 46 cities but not Hezekiah's Jerusalem where he settled for booty instead.

The historical authenticity of the New Testament and its origin in early antiquity is supported by hard scientific evidence. A fragment of John's gospel is dated by experts at AD 125–150.[41] On one side is John chapter 18, verses 31–33, and on the other side are verses 37–38. The fragment contains Pilate's famous question: *What is truth?* With Jesus replying: *Everyone who is of the truth hears my voice*. The fragment resides in the John Ryland's Library, Manchester, England.

Robert Chapman (1803–1902) of Devon, England, has blessed and encouraged many with his description of the Bible:

This Book contains: The mind of God, the state of man, the way of salvation, the doom of sinners, and happiness of believers. Its doctrines are holy, its precepts are binding, its histories are true, and its decisions are immutable. Read it to be wise, believe it to be safe, and practice it to be holy. It contains light to direct you, food to support you and comfort to cheer you. It's the traveler's map, the pilgrim's staff, the pilot's compass, the soldier's sword and the Christian's charter. Here paradise is restored, Heaven opened, and the gates of Hell disclosed.

Christ is its grand subject, our good its design, and the glory of God its end. It should fill the memory, rule the heart, and guide the feet. Read it slowly, frequently, prayerfully. It is a mine of wealth, a paradise of glory, and a river of pleasure. It is given you in life, will be opened at the Judgment and be remembered forever. It involves the highest responsibility, rewards the greatest labor, and condemns all who trifle with its contents.

The Apostle John's tomb at Ephesus

Conclusion

People worship all types of gods, but there is only one true God and He is the great all-powerful, all-knowing and ever-present triune God of the Bible. This book aims to show that the Bible is true in every respect and can be trusted.

---

[39] 2 Kings 19:37.
[40] wikipedia.org/wiki/Sennacherib, retrieved May 16, 2011.
[41] P. Masters, *Heritage of Evidence in the British Museum*, Tephens and George, 2004.

Chapter 2

Is There Scientific Support for the Theory of Evolution?

Of the seven chapters of this book, this one is necessarily the most technical, because we need to confront evolution with real science. As a consequence, some words may not be familiar to the reader, although the points being made can be easily understood. If, however, the reader does not want to read through this information, he or she may simply turn to page 50 and read under *Conclusion* what Christian and non-Christian scientists say about the bankrupt state of the theory.

The commonly held view, and one strongly supported by the Western media, is that evolution is science and that biblical creation is religion. In fact, evolution is a hypothesis of what happened in the past to bring about our existence. It is unprovable, unrepeatable and not able to be confirmed by experiments. Scientists can only deal with the present, and although evolutionary theory comes couched in scientific language, this is only an attempt to give it scientific credibility. It still remains a hypothesis—a mere idea and something people believe by faith. The outstanding attribute of the Theory of Evolution and one that kept it from being discarded when it was first conceived is that it presents an alternative to our existence without invoking creation by a Supernatural Being, namely the God of the Bible.

A Brief Overview of the Theory of Evolution

It is important to understand exactly what modern-day evolutionists actually believe, which is an extension of what Darwin initially proposed.

The theory posits that approximately 13.7 billion years ago, a small and very dense ball of matter/energy, which arose from nothing, exploded. As the immense heat from this explosion dissipated, all 92 naturally occurring elements and all of the heavenly bodies were formed.

Some of these elements combined to form simple compounds and on earth these compounds combined to form the molecules of life, such as amino acids, deoxyribonucleic acids (DNA), ribonucleic acids (RNA), proteins, sugars and other carbohydrates, fatty acids etc. A mixture of DNA, RNA, proteins and other compounds managed to wrap itself in a membrane, which became the basis of a cell wall.

Such a structure became immensely more complex and single cell species came into existence. Hence sustainable life with the ability to reproduce itself appeared. Some single cell species joined together to become multi-cellular species, which in turn formed themselves into marine creatures, some of which became fish. Some of the fish grew legs from their fins and crawled out of the water to become reptiles. Some reptiles became dinosaurs and some of these creatures grew feathers and became birds. While all of this was happening, some other reptiles became mammals, which became the ancestors of monkeys and apes and some of these changed into human beings.

In summary, all it took for mankind to come into existence was an explosion, time and the fortuitous combining of elements and molecules.

2 Is There Scientific Support for the Theory of Evolution?

The Theory of Evolution: a Timeline

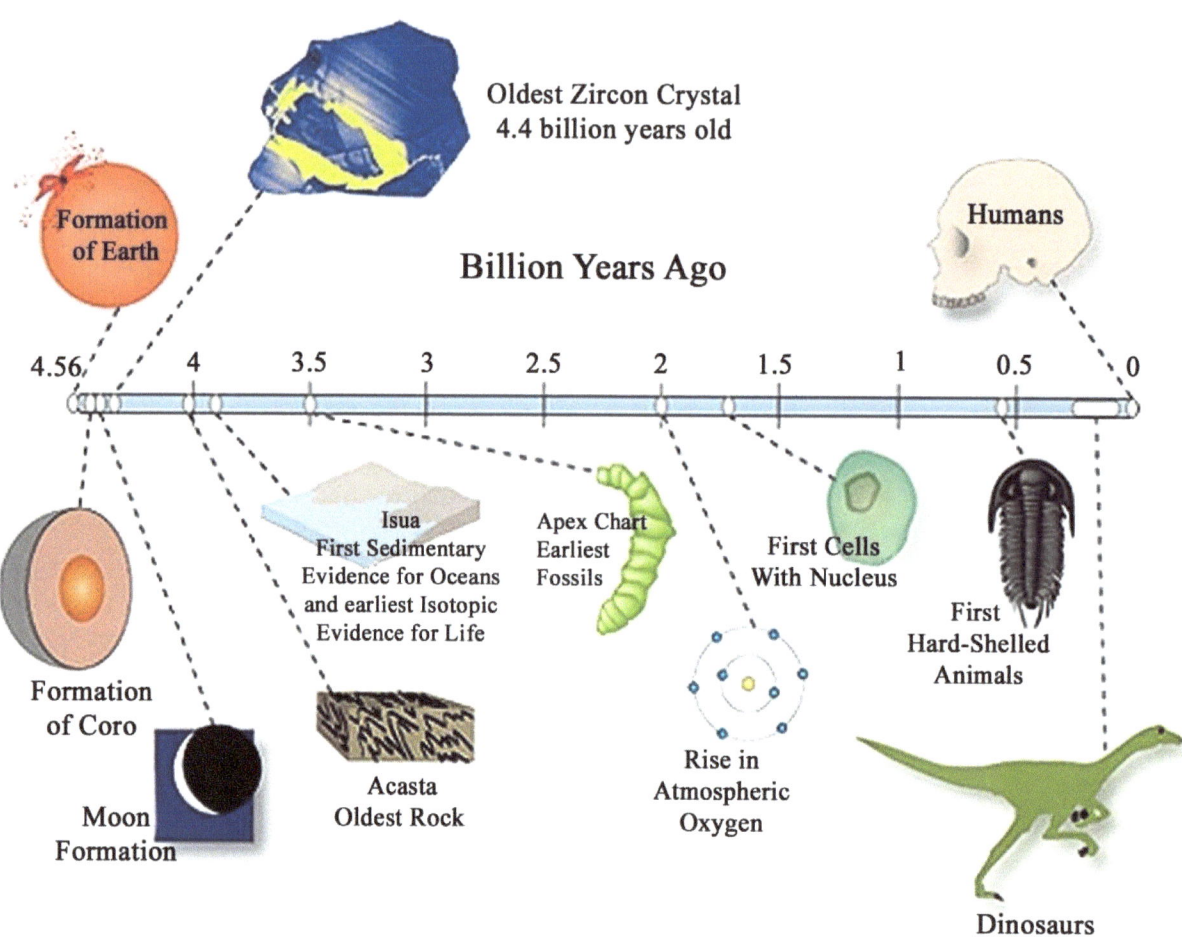

This schematic is compliments of Creation Wiki Pool

A Detailed Examination of the Theory of Evolution

Part 1: From an Explosion to Living Cells

The Big Bang
As stated previously, in the beginning there is thought to have been a dense ball of matter/energy. For the theory to be consistent, it had to have come from nothing in order to eliminate the need for a creator. In fact, cosmologists actually state that it came from nothing.

Take for example, a statement from Dr Arno Penzias, Physics Nobel Prize winner and co-discoverer of the cosmic microwave background radiation:

2   Is There Scientific Support for the Theory of Evolution?

Astronomy leads us to a unique event, a universe which was created out of nothing.[42]

And theoretical physicist Lawrence Krauss of Arizona State University, presented in a recent book, his claim that the laws of physics could have created the universe from nothing.[43]

Cosmologist and Massachusetts Institute of Technology professor Alan Guth had this to say:

The universe burst into something from absolutely nothing—zero, nada. As it got bigger, it became filled with even more stuff that came from absolutely nothing.[44]

The theory postulates that for some unknown reason, this ball exploded, and hence the name. Those who subscribe to this theory believe that, due to the tremendous forces and heat involved in the explosion, some of the hydrogen produced by the explosion condensed through nuclear fusion to give the range of elements present today. And as the system cooled, stars formed; as did galaxies. Planets and other heavenly bodies came into being by the agglomeration of debris left over from the initial explosion and subsequent expansion. But in opposition to this theory, we observe that the whole cosmos is uneven, lumpy and contains clumps of galaxies.[45] All of these bodies are rotating in perfect symmetry and harmony. This is certainly not what would be expected from an explosion. In order to explain the rotation of all of the components of the universe, it is necessary for the initial dense ball to have been rotating. However, this raises another problem for Big Bang supporters, and that is, due to the conservation of angular momentum, all of the components emitted from the dense ball have to rotate in the same direction about their axis. What we observe is some moons, planets, suns and galaxies are rotating clockwise and others anticlockwise.

The theory predicts that the galaxies with the greatest red shifts, that is, those furthest from us, should be young. Recent observations have shown that all galaxies have the same spread of ages.[46] Furthermore, the Big Bang theory requires the clumping together of matter to form the heavenly bodies, but they are much more likely to have bounced off each other as do billiard balls when they collide. In order to explain why galaxies do not fly apart due to their rapid rotation and to retain the theory, cosmologists have invoked the idea of dark matter, whereby >80% of all matter in the universe has to be dark matter.[47] It is called dark matter because it cannot be seen or detected. The Big Bang theory seems to have many inconsistencies. Even the weekly journal, *New Scientist*, has discarded it.[48] One cosmologist, Eric Lerner, who is president of Lawrenceville Plasma Physics in West Orange, New Jersey, is reported as saying:

This is not science. Big Bang predictions are constantly wrong and are being fixed after the event.

---

[42] Margenau and Varghese, *Cosmos, Bios and Theos*, La Selle, Il, 1992, page 83.
Note: Dr Penzias is a believing Jew and later commented that his discovery is completely consistent with the scriptures in that God created everything from nothing. Significantly, Jews and Christians believe that it was God who did the creating, whereas atheists believe that nothing created everything, which is clearly absurd.
[43] Krauss, L. *A Universe from Nothing*. New York: Free Press, 2012.
[44] *Discover*, April 2002.
[45] *New Scientist*, October 18, 2008, page 11.
[46] *New Scientist*, July 2, 2005.
[47] *New Scientist*, February 5, 2011, Dark *Matter* insert.
[48] *New Scientist*, July 2, 2005.

2 Is There Scientific Support for the Theory of Evolution?

Another, Joao Magueijo, of Imperial College, London, says:

The standard model is ugly and embarrassing; I hope it will soon come to breakdown point.

The situation is so serious that 50 astronomers and physicists met in Port Angeles, Washington, USA, on September 7–11, 2008, to discuss an alternative to the theory. All agreed that it needed to be replaced, but nobody could devise a satisfactory alternative.[49]

These men are top scientists and leaders in their profession. For evolutionists, the cherished Big Bang theory has been shown to be more fiction than fact. And they have nothing to replace it with except the fact that everything was created. Other theories such as the Oscillating theory and the Steady State theory proposed by the late Sir Fredrick Hoyle were discarded on the basis that they did not fit the observable evidence. In fact they were replaced by the Big Bang theory.

And try as they might, cosmologists cannot think of a way around the need for a beginning[50] which has theological overtones. *New Scientists* expressed the problem in its editorial very succinctly:

If you have an instant of creation, don't you need a creator?[51]

Darwin's Theory of Evolution

The hypothesis put forward by Charles Darwin in his book *On the Origin of Species*, which was published in 1859, postulates that all the various forms of life arose from single cell species through a process of gradual change. The mechanism for driving the changes was natural selection operating on randomly occurring variation. He had observed natural selection taking place with finches on the Galapagos Islands as drought conditions favored finches that had longer and stronger beaks, and were thus able to survive by cracking drought-toughened nuts.[52]

His hypothesis basically starts with living single cell species—he seemingly gave little thought to how these organisms came about in the first place. The fact that his driving force, natural selection, does not add to a species' genetic information (which is required for single cell species to evolve into human beings) but instead reduces it, will be addressed, along with the role that mutations play, on pages 46- 48. In Darwin's day, cells were thought of as being simple lumps of jelly-like substance. With the aid of modern means of investigation, scientists have uncovered the awe-inspiring and amazing complexity of cells, to the extent that their formation by natural processes defies explanation.

Note: The full title of Darwin's book is as follows: *On the Origin of Species by Means of Natural Selection, or the Preservation of Favored Races in the Struggle for Life*. Proponents of his theory never mention the full title because of its racist overtones, which of course are in complete harmony with Darwin's hypothesis.

---

[49] Source: John Hartnett, creation.com, retrieved November 8, 2008.
[50] *New Scientist*, January 14, page 6.
[51] *New Scientist,* editorial, January 14, 2012.
[52] wikipedia.org/wiki/Darwin's_finches, retrieved May 5, 2011.

2   Is There Scientific Support for the Theory of Evolution?

Darwin's Tree of Life

Most students will be familiar with Darwin's Tree of Life. It is a pictorial representation of how one species can grow into many, with the base of the trunk composed of single cell organisms which become multi-cellular species, with each branch representing a single species. The branching points are where one species becomes two. Thus, the tree gives rise to all the forms of life which have ever existed, including those still present today. In Darwin's time it helped carry the day for evolution, for it visually depicted the central premise of the Theory of Evolution. However, the modern technique of DNA sequencing has shown it to be totally without scientific support, like almost everything else about Darwin's hypothesis.

In 2009, the front-page display of the pro-evolution and anti-creationist weekly periodical *New Scientist*[53] carried the headline, 'Darwin was wrong: cutting down the tree of life.' On page 34 the article states:

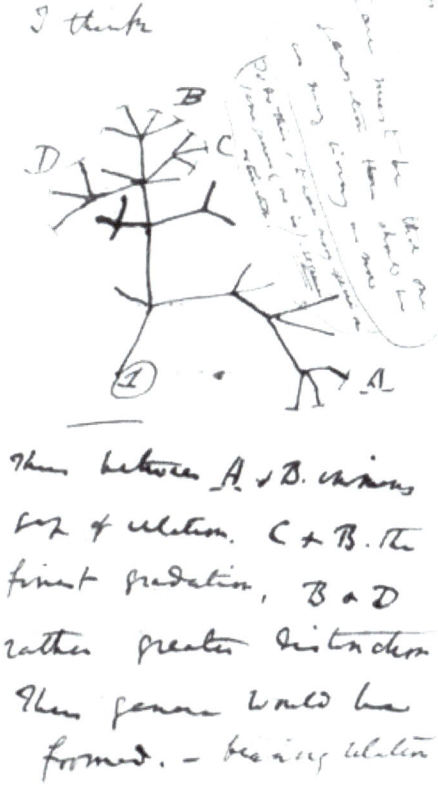

This page from Darwin's notebook shows his first sketch of an evolutionary tree from around July 1837.

For the past 150 years, biology has concerned itself with filling in the details of the tree. 'For a long time the holy grail was to build a tree of life,' says Eric Bapteste, an evolutionary biologist at the Pierre and Marie Curie University in Paris, France. A few years ago it looked as if the grail was in reach. But today the project lies in tatters, torn to pieces by an onslaught of negative evidence. Many biologists now argue that the tree concept is obsolete and needs to be discarded. 'We have no evidence at all that the tree of life is a reality,' says Bapteste.

DNA sequencing became possible in the early 1990s and this showed that many species closely related on Darwin's Tree of Life are not genetically related at all, hence the demise of Darwin's tree, and with it, the underpinning of his hypothesis. For example, scientists at the University of Bath have discovered that flies and moths are most closely related to beetles and more distantly related to bees and wasps.[54] And Japanese researchers have shown that bats are more closely related to horses than are cows.[55] In fact, another investigation of their genes has shown that bats are more closely related to horses than are cows or dogs, which is evidence against a gradual changing of one species into another.[56]

---

[53] *New Scientist*, January 24, 2009.
[54] *The Hindustan Times*, October 27, 2006.
[55] *The Hindustan Times*, June 26, 2006.
[56] *New Scientist,* June 24, 2006, page 23.

2   Is There Scientific Support for the Theory of Evolution?

Chemical Evolution

In living organisms, proteins are formed by the joining together of amino acids (like beads on a string) by means of a very intricate biochemical pathway, through the use of, among other things, enzymes as catalysts. However, enzymes are proteins themselves. In other words, it is necessary to have proteins in order for proteins to be made biochemically.

Dr John Marcus, who holds a PhD in biochemistry, makes the following comment:

The process of converting DNA information into proteins requires at least 75 different protein molecules. But each and every one of these 75 proteins must be synthesized in the first place by the process in which they themselves are involved. How could the process begin without the presence of all the necessary proteins? Could all 75 proteins have arisen by chance in just the right place at just the right time? Could it be that a strand of DNA with all the necessary information for making this exact same set of proteins just happened to be in the same place as all these proteins? And could it be that all the precursor molecules also happened to be around in their energized form so as to allow the proteins to utilize them properly?

Needless to say, without proteins life would not exist; it is as simple as that. The same is true of DNA and RNA. It should be clear that DNA, RNA and proteins must all be present if any of them are going to be present in a living organism. Life must have been created completely functional, or it would be a meaningless mess. To suggest otherwise is plain ignorance or perhaps desperation.[57]

Since the first proteins could not have been formed biochemically, the only other possible means for their formation is by the chance coming together of the appropriate chemicals. This is known as chemical evolution and it is the process in which evolutionists put their faith.

In the 1960s biologist Dr Dean Kenyon of San Francisco State University set himself the task of piecing together all of the processes that would have been involved in the evolution of a single cell. He realised that in any theory postulating the chemical formation of cells, it would be necessary to establish how proteins, which are long chains of amino acids, could have formed chemically, since they are integral to cell structure and function. He was optimistic that this would be a straightforward process and, in 1969, he and Dr Gary Steinman published a book titled *Biochemical Predestination*. In the book, they proposed that the very structures of amino acids predestined them to form the proteins of life.

Dr Kenyon was the leading figure in chemical evolution during the 1960s, 70s and into the 80s. However, about five years after the publication of his book; Kenyon began to reflect on his material. He realised that in no way could it explain the evolution of proteins, and he rejected the notion of chemical evolution. There are in excess of thirty thousand distinct proteins in living cells and these are formed biochemically by a very complex mechanism involving the reading of the various codes, that is, the arrangement of base pairs which are assembled along the deoxyribonucleic acid (DNA) backbone (see pages 44 and 45). This reading of the base pairs is then used to join the amino acids together in the prescribed order to form a biologically active protein. No DNA (and the hundreds of supporting mechanisms), no proteins. Kenyon then sought

---

[57] J. F. Ashton, *In Six Days, Why 50 Scientists Choose to Believe in Creation*, Strand Publishing, Australia, 2004.

to determine the source of the biological information in DNA that enabled it to dictate the biosynthesis of the thousands of proteins and further, to direct and to bring about the formation of the complete species, be it maize, mackerel, mouse or man. The only logical conclusion Dr Kenyon could arrive at is that behind the very basis of life, there is design. Thenceforth, he became a proponent of the Intelligent Design movement.[58]

Some of the problems of Chemical Evolution

Chemical evolution is the idea that all of the chemicals necessary for life formed themselves from their constituent elements and/or molecules and then arranged themselves into pre-cellular entities, which, over time, became fully functioning cells capable of reproducing themselves. Hence life came about from chemicals over a long time. This may seem fanciful, but it is what evolutionists believe. However, there are insurmountable problems with this thesis. We will focus predominantly onto some of the problems related to the formation of proteins.

The formation of chemicals of life

The Theory of Evolution dictates that life started mainly from the chemicals: methane, ammonia, hydrogen and water, in some type of primordial soup. In fact, in 1953, Stanley Miller, under the supervision of Dr Harold Urey at the University of Chicago, set up an experiment to test Alexander Oparin and JBS Haldane's hypothesis that conditions on the primitive earth favored chemical reactions that synthesised organic compounds from inorganic precursors. The experiment consisted of an electrical discharge which gave off significant amounts of ultraviolet light, in the presence of a mixture of methane, water, hydrogen and ammonia (see diagram). After this was allowed to proceed for one week, he analysed the solution and found that some amino acids were produced, as well as carbon monoxide and carbon dioxide, among other compounds. This was, and still is, hailed as the break-through experiment that 'proved' evolution. Interestingly, he had to use his intelligence to design an experiment, which attempted to show that life started without intelligence. He had to exclude oxygen, because some of the chemicals would react with it. As well, he had to isolate the amino acids as soon as they were produced or else they would decompose. He produced five times more chain ending compounds as he did amino acids. Chain ending compounds would terminate the growing polypeptide chain and prevent proteins from being formed. In the end, he finished up with a small number of amino acids, which were a mixture of both left-handed and right-handed with respect to their stereochemistry,[59] whereas all naturally-occurring amino acids are exclusively left-

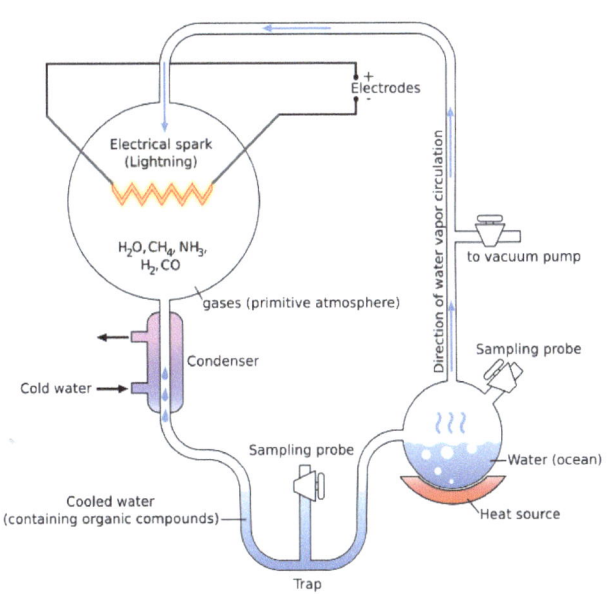

---

[58] Source: *Unlocking the Mystery of Life* (DVD), Illustra Media, 2010.

[59] For an explanation of stereochemistry, see page 28.

2 Is There Scientific Support for the Theory of Evolution?

handed (with the exception of glycine which has no chirality).

A follow-up paper reported on a repeat analysis of the original vials from this experiment, only this time the aqueous solution was analysed using very sensitive instruments and 22 amino acids were found to be present in minute quantities.[60] However, the comments made above still apply, whether there are 22 or 5 amino acids found. All attempts to meld these amino acids into sophisticated proteins or to create long, complex molecules such as DNA and RNA—the sorts of components that underlie even the simplest single-celled life forms, just resulted in a tarry mess. Though influential at the time, this work is now generally regarded as too simplistic.[61]

Amino acids to proteins

Evolutionists propose that amino acids which formed by the process described above, or one similar, came together to form proteins in some 'primordial soup.' For this reaction to have proceeded, it would have been necessary to have all, or nearly all, of the 20 various amino acids that make up natural proteins to have been present and exclusively left-handed with respect to their stereochemical orientation, and for them to be in a pure form, because many side reactions would have taken place, rather than protein formation, if they were not pure. Even if this were the case, they certainly would not have combined to form proteins, for several reasons. First, a catalyst would be required to initiate the chemical reaction. The other reasons follow.

The problem of hydrolysis

A chemical reaction with water is called hydrolysis. In order to synthesise proteins from amino acids in a laboratory, special precautions need to be taken to remove the water which is formed when an amino acid is joined onto the growing protein chain, or else the reaction will revert back to the original amino acids. So for proteins to be formed in the environment, water must be excluded and quickly removed once it has been formed from the chemical reaction—a very unlikely scenario for the pre-biotic earth. However, current evolutionary theory requires water to have been present for the initial synthesis of amino acids, as mentioned on the previous page.

The problem of stability

The amino acid cytosine, one of the 20 amino acids which are essential to life, has a biological half-life of 340 years at 25° C, making the idea of these compounds lying around in some type of primordial soup for thousands of years, waiting for some reaction to take place, highly implausible.

The problem of biological activity

In order for proteins to be biologically active, the constituent amino acids must be added to each other in a very precise order. In living cells, the DNA contained in the cell's nucleus uses the *information* it holds in its structure to achieve this correct ordering (see pages 46-47 for a fuller explanation). There are millions of ways in which amino acids can be joined together, but only a very few ways produce proteins that are biologically active.

---

[60] Johnson *et al*, *Science News*, October 16, 2008.
[61] *New Scientist*, January 29, 2011, pages. 32-35.

2 Is There Scientific Support for the Theory of Evolution?

The importance of amino acid ordering

The precision of the order of the amino acids in the protein is such that one out of order can have serious consequences. The problems come from mutations in the genes and are then expressed in the proteins that are made from these genes. Three examples follow that show what can happen if this order is not right.

1. **Sickle cell anemia.** With this malady, **one amino acid out of the 146** in the protein beta globin, which is a sub-unit of the hemoglobin molecule, is in the wrong place. Valine is in place of glutamic acid and this small mutation in the protein causes the whole shape of the blood cell to be greatly distorted when oxygen is not bound to the heme molecule. Sufferers of this disorder have a reduced life-expectancy.

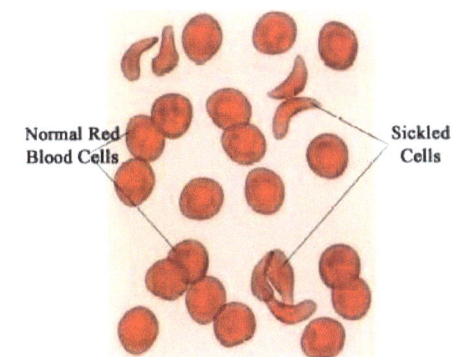

2. **Type 1 hemochromatosis** is a hereditary disease characterized by excessive intestinal absorption of dietary iron resulting in a pathological increase in total iron body stores.[62] The defective hemochromatosis (HFE) protein has been found to be due to any one of more than 20 mutations in the HFE gene which produces the HFE protein. Two particular mutations are responsible for most cases of this disorder. One mutation replaces the amino acid cysteine with the amino acid tyrosine at position 282 in the protein's chain of amino acids. The other mutation replaces the amino acid histidine with the amino acid aspartic acid at position 63 of the protein's chain.[63] As a consequence of just **one amino acid being wrong out of a total of 348** amino acids the whole complex and interrelated biochemical pathway malfunctions.

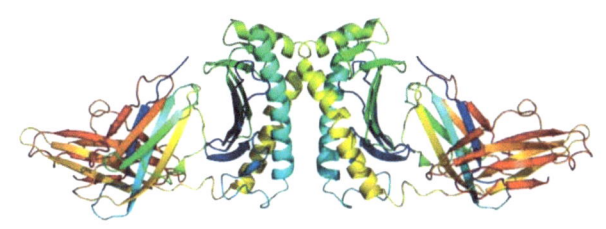

A representation of the Hemochromatosis protein

3. **Cystic fibrosis** is an extremely debilitating and eventually fatal hereditary disorder. It has been shown to be due to a defective protein in lung cells known as cystic fibrosis transmembrane regulator (CFTR). The most common mutation causing this defect is the loss of the amino acid phenylalanine at position 508 on the 1,480 amino acid long chain of protein CFTR. That is, **one amino acid missing from a protein chain of 1,480** amino acids causes the failure of the protein to shuttle chloride ions in and out of lung and other cells, which in turn causes lungs to clog up with mucus.[64]

A representation of the CFTR protein

---

[62] wikipedia.org/wiki/Iron_overload, retrieved June 6, 2011.
[63] ornl.gov/sci/techresources/Human_Genome/posters/chromosome/hfe.shtml.
[64] Source: *New Scientist*, March 5, 2011, page 18.

2. Is There Scientific Support for the Theory of Evolution?

The problem of chirality

Some chemical compounds can exist in two forms which are mirror images of each other, just as our two hands are mirror images; they are not superimposable as shown in the diagram below for amino acids. Each form is known as an enantiomer from the Greek word meaning opposite. This feature of being able to have two spatial orientations which are either left hand or right hand is known as chirality.

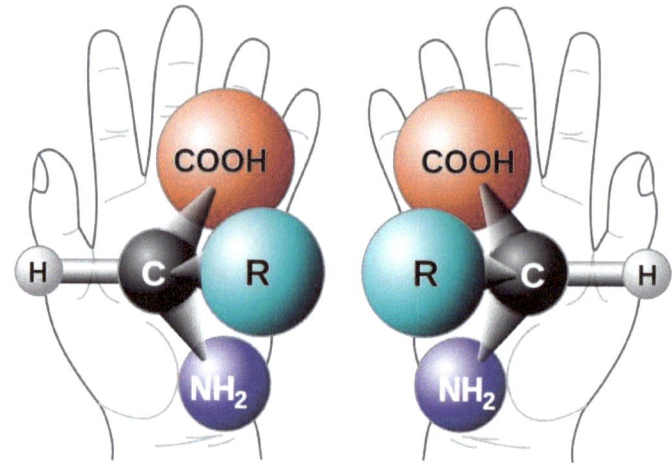

In compounds from living organisms where chirality exists, only one form of the enantiomer is present exclusively. However, if the same compounds were made in a laboratory there is always a 50:50 mixture of both enantiomers produced. This is called a racemic mixture.

For compounds containing only one chiral centre, the naming of enantiomers is based on the stereochemistry of D glyceraldehyde. If the enantiomer has the same spatial configuration as D glyceraldehyde it has the prefix D. If its configuration is the opposite, it has the prefix L. All naturally occurring amino acids, except glycine which has no chirality, are in the L (left hand) form and all naturally occurring sugars are in the D (right hand) form. If it was not for this fact, life as we know it, would not exist because there are some proteins that catalyse biological reactions (known as enzymes) and this ability comes from the way the protein is folded. If some D amino acids were present, the folding would be different, the enzyme would be inactive and biological reactions would not take place. Similarly, DNA and RNAs incorporate the sugars deoxyribose and ribose respectively, which are in the D form exclusively and this exclusivity gives the structure its double helical shape. The presence of one L sugar would perturb the helical structure, yet if the sugars were produced by the random joining of the constituent atoms as evolutionists propose, then there would be a 50:50 mixture of sugars and life would not be possible.

Over time, all chiral compounds racemise, that is, they proceed to a 50:50 mixture of both enantiomers (left and right hand) and for biological compounds the functions they perform start to breakdown. Racemisation is part of the aging process. A tragic example of this is with thalidomide which was produced in the left hand form exclusively from a natural precursor and prescribed for treating morning sickness in pregnant women. However, the right hand form has been found to possess teratogenicity that is, it can disrupt fetal development. When taken internally or even when stored, the left hand form slowly racemised and produced horrific deformities in children.[65]

Only one form of optical isomers could not have evolved over time because over time, they racemise; that is, they go from being only one type to both types. This fact alone, completely rules out the possibility of chemical evolution.

---

[65] wikipedia.org/wiki/Thalidomide.

2   Is There Scientific Support for the Theory of Evolution?

The probability of biologically active proteins forming by chance

Sir Fredrick Hoyle (astronomer) and Dr Chandra Wickramasinghe (mathematician) calculated the chances of biologically active proteins forming purely by chance from their constituent chemicals, which is what the Theory of Evolution, in its broad sense requires. In their 1981 book *Evolution from Space*, they calculated that the chance of obtaining the required set of enzymes (proteins which catalyse biochemical reactions) for even the simplest living cell was one in $10^{40,000}$. Since the number of atoms in the known universe is infinitesimally tiny by comparison (10^{80}), Hoyle argued that even a whole universe full of primordial soup wouldn't have a chance. He claimed:

The notion that not only the biopolymer (protein) *but the operating program of a living cell could be arrived at by chance in a primordial organic soup here on the Earth is evidently nonsense of a high order.*[66]

He compared the random emergence of even the simplest cell to the likelihood that *a tornado sweeping through a junkyard might assemble a Boeing 747 from the materials therein* and towards the end of his life, he came to the conclusion:

If one proceeds directly and straightforwardly in this matter, without being deflected by a fear of incurring the wrath of scientific opinion, one arrives at the conclusion that biomaterials with their amazing measure or order must be the outcome of intelligent design. No other possibility I have been able to think of.[61]

Professor Richard Dawkins, a very vocal and vociferous opponent of creation, has proposed a cumulative multi-step model involving random sequences and selection. This, he states, when applied to 28 random letters (simulating DNA base pairs), will produce the desired outcome by computer calculation in 30 minutes. He implies that such a procedure when applied to amino acids will produce a functioning protein in a reasonable time. There are many problems that rule out this idea. For example, the program requires the same amino acid sequence to have been replicated hundreds or thousands of times, then a few such strands being subjected to a mutation, which sustains a beneficial advantage over the others, with its concentration being increased through some selection procedure. After this happens many millions of times, a functioning protein is produced. It is nonsense to think that some natural process in the primordial earth would produce millions of the same amino acid sequence, say 100 units long, under anhydrous conditions (required because the polypeptide would hydrolyse back to its constituent amino acids if water were present), and then that one mutant sequence would have a selective advantage over the others. It is highly implausible that any selection process could operate on a host of lifeless chemicals lying around in some primordial soup. It is vastly more plausible that they would decompose. For a thorough examination of Dawkins' computer simulation, see creation.com/search and insert 'weasel.'

These are some of the enormous problems evolutionists have to address and this is only the very start; the formation of biologically active proteins. It can be likened to travelling the first millimeter on a trip to the moon.

---

[66] wikipedia.org/wiki/fred_hoyle, retrieved July 16, 2011.

2   Is There Scientific Support for the Theory of Evolution?

Nucleic Acids

At the same time that proteins are being formed from amino acids, evolution requires DNA and RNA to be formed from a mixture of the sugars ribose and deoxyribose, organic bases and phosphate. We have just seen how delicately balanced and specific the process for the formation of biologically active proteins (enzymes) is; deoxyribonucleic acid, which constitutes our genes, is many times more specific.

DNA itself is the most complex information storage mechanism in the universe. Each human cell's DNA contains in excess of 3 billion letters or pieces of information, which is equivalent to the information contained in 100,000 books. A two-millimeter length of DNA contains the same amount of information as a stack of CDs 1,600 kilometers high. In fact, scientists at Australia's CSIRO[67] and around the world are trying to develop a computer that uses biomolecules such as DNA as memory storage units. These are called DNA Computers. Information like this could not have come about by chance; it must have been created.[68]

The Human Genome Project has revealed several more layers of the complexity of functioning DNA (see also, pages 44-45), as discussed in a *New Scientist* article by Michael Page:[69]

Once, it all seemed so beautifully simple. Our DNA, we thought, consisted of a set of recipes, or genes, for making proteins, and once we had identified them all and worked out what they do, we would be a long way to understanding what makes us what we are.

If only. One of the big shocks that emerged from the Human Genome Project was that we have only around 23,500 genes—barely more than a nematode worm. But in many other ways our genome is turning out to be dizzyingly complex.

"It is very difficult to wrap your head around how big the genome is and how complicated," says Ewan Birney of the European Bioinformatics Institute near Cambridge, UK, who is part of a major project to uncover the workings of the genome. "It's very confusing and intimidating."

"For starters, rather than each gene coding for one protein, they often code for many. The coding parts of genes come in pieces, like beads on a string and by splicing out different beads, or exons, after RNA copies are made, a single gene can potentially code for tens of thousands of different proteins, although the average is about five. Recent studies suggest up to 95 per cent of our genes may be alternatively spliced in this way. Even more astonishingly, in at least one case in human beings, RNA copies of different genes are spliced together. If this were commonplace, it would vastly multiply the potential number of different proteins."

For evolutionists, the same problems exist here as they do for amino acids, only more so. Sugars, like amino acids, can exist in both left-handed and right-handed forms. However, on this occasion, the sugar ribose is entirely in the right-handed form. Again, the component chemicals of DNA and RNA don't wait around for thousands of years for the right chemicals to come along for them to

---

[67] Commonwealth Scientific and Industrial Research Organisation.
[68] *Creation*, 2007, vol. 29 No 2, page 48.
[69] *New Scientist*, June 19, 2010, page 34.

2   Is There Scientific Support for the Theory of Evolution?

react with—they degrade. Evolution requires a continual building up of complexity so that these molecules of life then wrap themselves in some type of pre-cellular protective sheath. This then leads onto a single cellular species capable of reproducing itself—and amazingly, we have life. We have life from non-life, and all that was required for the faithful was matter/energy, a big explosion, time and fortuitous chance.

Single Cells

Single celled (eukaryote) species are immensely complicated, as shown opposite and most forms of life use DNA to store genetic information and RNA to execute the the instructions encoded in the DNA. A video animation showing part of the inner workings of a cell, produced by Harvard University, can be seen online.[70] It attempts to show the almost incomprehensible complexity of a living cell. Hundreds of synthetic pathways and hundreds of nano-machines would have to function simultaneously for the component parts of the cell to come together to enable the cell to function and reproduce (via cell division).

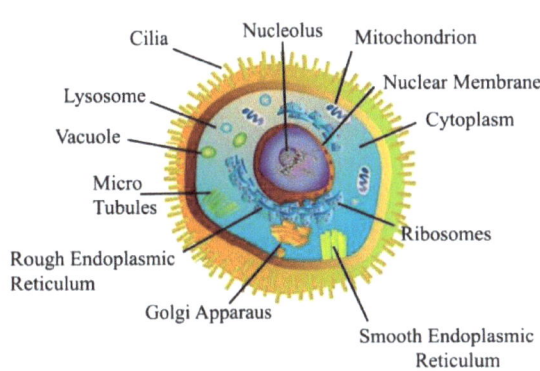

Part 2: From Living Cells to Human Beings

The Theory of Evolution postulates that this process of building up continues from single-celled species to multi-cellular species and then onto marine creatures and reptiles, which diverge to produce both birds and mammals. The mammals proceed through a common ancestor to monkeys and man. Here, another major problem exists for evolutionists: the need to demonstrate the spontaneous abandonment of biological imperative. What would be the driving force for a group of single cells of a particular species, actively living and reproducing, to surrender a different part of their function so that they could join together with other cells that have lost other parts of their functions in such a way as to become a living, replicating and fully functioning species? Of course, while all these partly disabled and non-functioning cells are lying around waiting to join together with others, they would simply decompose. Yet, this is what evolutionists believe.

Transitional Forms

Fossils of deceased creatures are not evidence of evolution. It is only the evolutionists and their artists who concoct the story. There have been many hoaxes in the name of evolution; some are mentioned below:

- **Feathered dinosaur** (*Archaeoraptor liaoningensis*): National Geographic[71] sensationalised the find of a transitional species between dinosaurs and birds complete with an illustration. It turned out to be a hoax.

---

[70] multimedia.mcb.harvard.edu/anim_innerlife.html, retrieved April 29, 2011.
[71] *National Geographic*, 1999, 196 (5), pages 98–107.

Is There Scientific Support for the Theory of Evolution?

- **Piltdown man** (*Eoanthropus dawsoni*): In 1912 a fossil of a human-like skull was discovered at Piltdown in England. It was hailed as the 'missing link' that showed humans had evolved from apes. Forty one years later in 1953, Dr Kenneth Oakley exposed it to be a fraudulent composite comprising a human skull and the jaw of an orangutan.
- *Homo pongoides*: The complete body of an 'ape man' toured the show circuit in the US during the late sixties. It was taken to be genuine and written about as such.[72] It was later shown to be a hoax.
- **The horse series**: Often cited as 'proof of evolution,' the horse series starts with the tiny four-toed *Hyracotherium*, sometimes called *Eohippus*, and moves by way of a smooth progression to the large single-toed horse of today. It looked good, but further investigation has shown it to be merely a construction to accommodate Darwinism.[73]
- **Haeckel's stages of human embryos**: Ernst Haeckel promoted Darwin's theory in Germany from 1866 by a series of sketches showing how a human embryo goes through various animal stages in the womb as it develops into a human being, such as fish gills and a monkey's tail. Haeckel's drawings were declared fraudulent by Professor His in 1874 and Haeckel confessed to their fabrication in a letter to *Münchener Allgemeine Zeitung*, January 9, 1909. Unfortunately, his drawings continue to be shown in textbooks even today and are used as an argument in support of abortion.

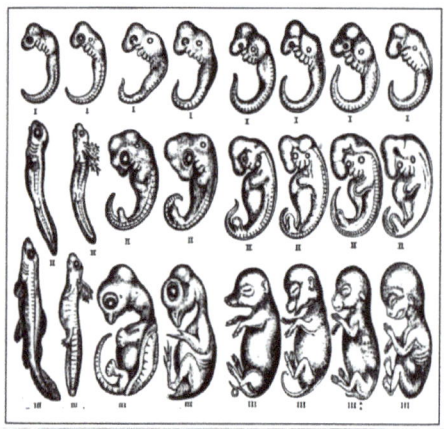 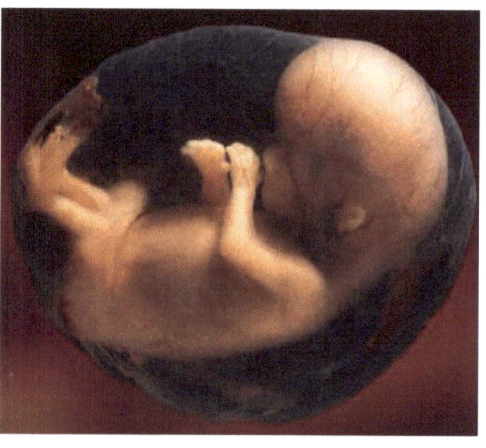

Above: Haeckel's drawings of 1874 depicting similarities of embryos of different species which he had published in *Anthropogenie*, in Germany in 1874. Above right: Human embryo at about 12 weeks and approximately 60 mm (2.25 inches) long.

When Darwin put forward his theory, he expected that paleontologists would find millions of intermediate species. In fact he wrote:

Geology assuredly does not reveal any such finely graduated organic chain; and this, perhaps, is the most obvious and gravest objection which can be urged against my theory. The explanation lies, I believe, in the extreme imperfection of the geological record.[74]

---

[72] *Natural Sciences of Belgium*, 45 (4), February 10, 1969.
[73] J. Safarti, *Creation*, 1999, 21 (3), pages 28–31.
[74] Darwin, C. (1859) *The Origin of Species* (Reprint of the first edition) Avenel Books, Crown Publishers, New York, 1979, page 292.

2 Is There Scientific Support for the Theory of Evolution?

Over 150 years later there are only a handful of hotly disputed candidates, of which *Archaeopteryx* is the best example. It is claimed to be an intermediate between a reptile and a bird because it has some skeletal characteristics similar to a small dinosaur and it had teeth as well. However, many extinct birds had teeth.

Archaeopteryx fossil   Archaeopteryx model

There is no doubt that it is a bird; for one thing, it was fully feathered and had a wishbone for the attachment of muscles for the downward stroke of its wings. Its bones were hollow, which enables all birds to fly. In fact, Dr Alan Feduccia, professor and former Head of Biology at the University of North Carolina and an evolutionist himself, stated:

Paleontologists have tried to turn Archaeopteryx into an earth-bound dinosaur. But it's not. It is a bird, a perching bird. And no amount of paleobabble is going to change that.[75]

There are enormous anatomical and physiological differences between fish, reptiles and birds. Let us simply consider what is really being suggested and taught as fact. The fins of fish, which are used for propulsion and maneuvering and are connected to the body by ligaments, supposedly changed into the legs of a tetrapod (four legs), which enabled it to walk and run and to support its weight. In order for it to do this, the legs had to become an integral part of the animal's skeleton. Next, the front legs turn into feathered wings. As seen from Mendel's groundbreaking work (page 80), if the creature does not possess the gene to code for feathers, then feathers will not be

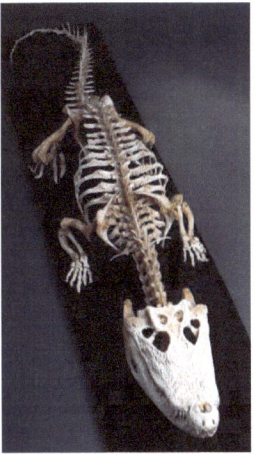 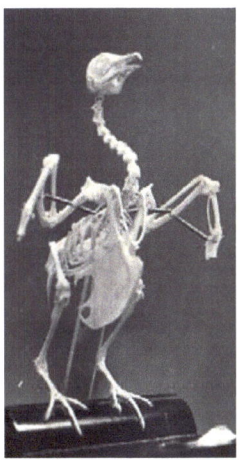

produced. As well, the whole bone structure of the animal had to change drastically from a composition of great strength that supports weight to one that does not need to support weight but must be light enough to enable the bird to fly. Consequently, the bones of a bird are hollow and amazingly light, yet still strong enough for the purpose for which they were designed. From the three images of the skeletons above, the reader is asked to consider the plausibility of the fish to reptile to bird transition.

---

[75] V. Morell, Archaeopteryx: Early Bird Catches a Can of Worms, *Science*, February 1993, 259 (5096), pages 764-5.

2 Is There Scientific Support for the Theory of Evolution?

The breathing mechanism is entirely different for fish, reptiles and birds. Fish are very active and as a consequence they need plenty of oxygen, but seawater contains only about one twentieth of the oxygen content of air, so fish have a very efficient way of extracting oxygen from water. As they swim or remain stationary in a stream of water, water enters through their mouth, flows over their gills and then out. The fish's blood flows through minute blood vessels in the feathery gills in an opposite direction and as it does, oxygen from the water is exchanged with carbon dioxide from its blood. In this way fish get all the oxygen they need. However, reptiles receive their oxygen quite differently. They have lungs which operate like bellows, whereby air is drawn into sacs called alveoli which are flushed with blood. It is here that oxygen is exchanged and spent carbon dioxide is expelled with the air the same way it came in.

Birds have a totally different mechanism—a complicated system of air sacs, which even involve their hollow bones. This system keeps air flowing in one direction through special tubes called parabronchi, located in their lungs. Blood moves through the lungs' blood vessels in the opposite direction for efficient oxygen uptake. See the diagrams below.

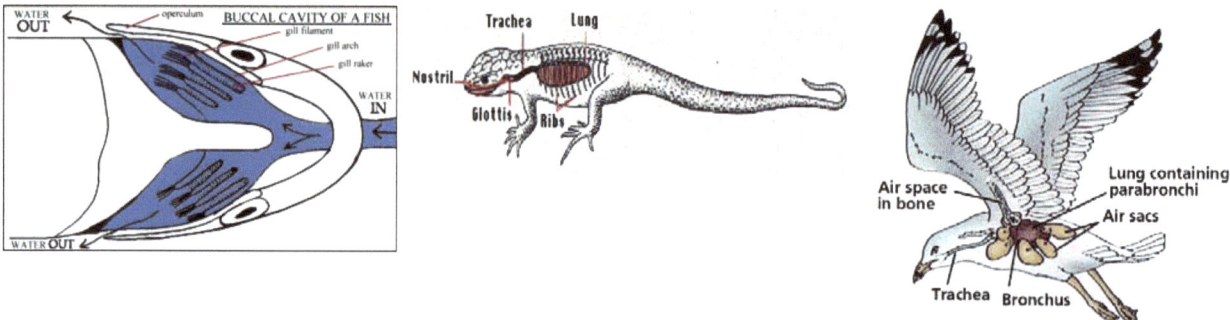

We have only considered two aspects of the three creatures under discussion yet we find that each possesses complex features that are unique to it. It is utterly implausible that one beautifully designed feature could convert into another. We have not even considered the scientific impossibility that some intermediate species could function with something halfway between fins and legs or between legs and wings and yet be better at survival than the species immediately before it on the evolutionary tree.

It is apparent that fish have always been fish, reptiles have always been reptiles and birds have always been birds, just as the Bible tells us. Each was uniquely and magnificently created for a specific purpose by the Master Creator.

Dr Colin Patterson makes the following point in response to a question regarding the lack of transitional species in his book, *Evolution*:[76]

I wrote the text of my book four years ago. If I were to write it now, I think the book would be rather different. Gradualism is a concept I believe in, not just because of Darwin's authority, but because my understanding of genetics seems to demand it. Yet Gould and the American Museum people are hard to contradict when they say there are no transitional fossils. As a paleontologist myself, I am much occupied with the philosophical problems of identifying ancestral forms in the fossil record. You say that I should at least show a photo of the fossil from which each type of

---

[76] C. Patterson, *Evolution*, Routledge and Kegan Paul, 1978.

2 Is There Scientific Support for the Theory of Evolution?

organism was derived. I will lay it on the line; there is not one such fossil for which one could make a watertight argument.[77]

The power of this statement is compounded by the fact that at the time Dr Patterson was in charge of possibly the largest collection of fossils in the world.

The renowned evolutionist Stephen Jay Gould wrote:

The absence of fossil evidence for intermediary stages between major transitions in organic design, indeed our inability, even in our imagination, to construct functional intermediates in many cases, has been a persistent and nagging problem for gradualistic accounts of evolution.[78]

Gould even said in another place:

The extreme rarity of transitional forms in the fossil record persists as the trade secret of paleontology. The evolutionary trees that adorn our textbooks have data only at the tips and nodes of their branches ... in any local area, a species does not arise gradually by the gradual transformation of its ancestors; it appears all at once and 'fully formed.'[79]

Forty years of research led Professor N Heribert Hilsson of Lund University, Sweden, to write:

It is not even possible to make a caricature of evolution out of palaeobiological facts. The fossil material is now so complete that the lack of transitional species cannot be explained by the scarcity of the material. The deficiencies are real; they will never be filled[80]

Living Fossils

Since evolutionists are hard-pressed to come up with even one genuine transitional species, does the fossil record show any change within species? The answer appears to be no, for there is an abundance of 'living fossils' that survive today and they are exactly the same as they have always been. They are a living testimony that contradict the evolutionists' claim that living creatures were changing into other species. Of course, there are changes within species.

In 1938, Marjorie Courtenay-Latimer was curator of a small museum situated in a port town near Cape Town, South Africa. A local seaman, Captain Hendrick Goosen of the trawler *Nerine,* would allow her to peruse his catch to see if there was anything of interest for the museum. On December 23, 1938, she noticed a fish, which she later described as: *the most beautiful fish I had ever seen, five feet long, and a pale mauve blue with iridescent silver markings.* She had no idea what it was and contacted her friend, Professor J L B Smith at Rhodes University, Grahamstown, some 80km (50 miles) away, with a description of the fish. He identified the fish from fossils as being a coelacanth (pronounced see-la-canth). The fish was described as; *the most important zoological find of the century. A living dinosaur ... would be no more amazing than this incredible discovery.*

---

[77] Personal letter written 10 April 1979, from Dr. Colin Patterson, Senior Palaeontologist at the British Museum of Natural History in London, to Luther D. Sunderland; as quoted in *Darwin's Enigma* by Luther D. Sunderland (Master Books, San Diego, USA, 1984, page 89.
[78] S. J. Gould, *Evolution Now: A Century After Darwin*, ed. John Maynard Smith, Macmillan, 1982, page 140.
[79] S. J. Gould, Evolution's Erratic Pace, *Natural History,* 86 (5):14, May 1977.
[80] Cited by Scott M. Huse, *The Collapse of Evolution,* Baker Books, 1983, page 58.

2 Is There Scientific Support for the Theory of Evolution?

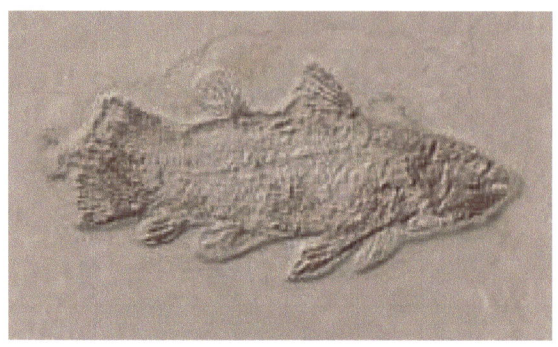

A Coelacanth fossil

Miss Courtenay-Latimer with her find, courtesy of www.goosen.org/index.html

Another coelacanth was not found until 1952. They have subsequently been shown to be living in plentiful numbers in the waters around South Africa and Indonesia.

The Australian Museum Fish Site makes the following statement:

Coelacanths are known from the fossil record dating back over 360 million years, with a peak in abundance about 240 million years ago. Before 1938 they were believed to have become extinct approximately 80 million years ago, when they disappeared from the fossil record.

Coelacanths today

A few of the many examples of living fossils.[81]

A present day Nautilus compared with one '167 million' years old.

A fossil herring, 65 plus 'million' years old is similar to a living one.

 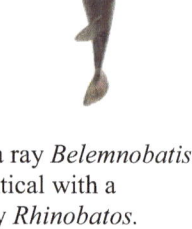

A fossil of a dinosaur-era ray *Belemnobatis sismondae* is almost identical with a modern Shovelnosed Ray *Rhinobatos. productus*

---

[81] The photos of fossils: Nautilus and Starfish are compliments of fossilmuseum.net and the Herring, Ginkgo, Horseshoe Crab and Nematonutus are compliments of fossilmuseum.com.

2 Is There Scientific Support for the Theory of Evolution?

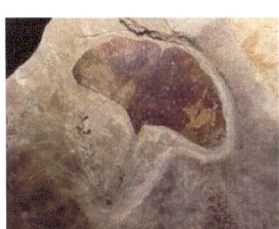

Note the similarity between the '170-million'-year-old fossil *Ginkgo* sp. and the leaves of the living plant.

A '445-million'-year-old Horseshoe crab is no different to specimens alive today. It possessed the same complex features and equipment as do present day ones.

Nematonutus, a Cretaceous period ('146-65 million' years ago) fossil fish is very similar to an Orange Roughy.

A '490 million' year old starfish is very similar to a living one.

In August 1994, David Noble, New South Wales' Parks and Wild Life Project Officer, noticed while bushwalking, a group of tall trees unlike anything he had seen previously. After several months of investigation, it was found that they were a completely new genus and that they are related to a group of pines only known in the fossil record. They were called Wollemi Pines, since they were found in the Wollemi National Park.

The ABC science show *Catalyst* asked the question: *How has it managed to survive through 200 million years of shifting continents and changing climates*? How indeed?

A compilation of living fossils taken from Wikipedia is shown below.[82]

Bacteria
Stromatolite, a layered structure created as sediment is trapped by shallow-water, oxygen-creating, blue-green bacteria

Plants
Amborellaceae – a plant from New Caledonia, possibly closest to base of the flowering plants *Araucaria araucana* – the Monkey Puzzle tree
Cycads
Ginkgo tree (Ginkgoaceae)

---

[82] Source: wikipedia.org/wiki/living_fossil, retrieved January 7, 2011.

2 Is There Scientific Support for the Theory of Evolution?

Horsetails – *Equisetum* (Equisetaceae)
Metasequoia – Dawn Redwood (Cupressaceae
Sciadopitys tree (Sciadopityaceae)
Liquidambar – tree (Altingiaceae)
Whisk ferns – *Psilotum* (Psilotaceae)
Welwitschia (Welwitschiaceae)
Wollemia tree (*Araucariaceae*)

Fungi
Neolecta

Animals
   Vertebrates
   Mammals
- Aardvark (*Orycteropus afer*)
- Cypriot mouse (*Mus cypriacus*)
- Red Panda (*Ailurus fulgens*)
- Koala (*Phascolarctos cinereus*)
- Laotian Rock Rat (*Laonastes aenigmamus*)
- Volcano rabbit (*Romerolagus diazi*)
- Amami rabbit (*Pentalagus furnessi*)
- Iriomote cat (*Prionailurus iriomotensis*)
- Monito del Monte (*Dromiciops gliroides*)
- monotremes (the platypus and echidna)
- Mountain Beaver (*Aplodontia rufa*)
- Okapi (*Okapia johnstoni*)
- Opossums
- Przewalski's Horse (*Equus ferus przewalskii*, *Equus przewalskii* or *Equus caballus przewalskii* classification is debated)
- Elephant shrews

   Birds
- Acanthisittidae (New Zealand "wrens") – 2 living species
- Hoatzin (*Ophisthocomus hoazin*) – One living species
- Broad-billed Sapayoa (*Sapayoa aenigma*) – One living species
- Bearded Reedling (*Panurus biarmicus*) – One living species
- Coliiformes (mousebirds) – 6 living species in 2 genera
- Magpie Goose (*Anseranas semipalmata*) – One living species

Reptiles
- Pig-nosed turtle
- Snapping Turtle (*Chelydra serpentina*)
- Alligator Snapping Turtle (*Macrochelys temminckii*)
- Crocodilia (crocodiles, gavials and alligators)
- Tuatara (*Sphenodon punctatus* and *Sphenodon guntheri*)
- Flying Dragon (*Draco* sp.)

Amphibians
- Purple frog (*Nasikabatrachus sahyadrensis*)
- Giant salamanders (*Cryptobranchus*, and *Andrias*)

Lampreys
- Northern Brook Lamprey (*Ichthyomyzon fossor*)

Bony fish
- Arowana and Arapaima (*Osteoglossidae*)

Bowfin (*Amia calva*)
Coelacanth (the lobed-finned *L menadoensis* and *L chalumnae*)
Queensland lungfish (*Neoceratodus fosteri*)
Sturgeons and Paddlefish (Acipenseriformes)
Bichir (*Polypteridae*) Family
Hagfish (*Myxinidae*) Family

Sharks

Frilled shark (*Chlamydoselachus anguineus*)
Goblin Shark (*Mitsukurina owstoni*)
Elephant shark (*Callorhinchus milii*)

Invertebrates
Insects

Mantophasmatodea (gladiators; a few living species)
Mymarommatid wasps (10 living species in genus *Palaeomymar*)
Nevrorthidae (3 species-poor genera)
Notiothauma reedi (a scorpionfly relative)
Orussidae (parasitic wood wasps; about 70 living species in 16 genera)
Peloridiidae (peloridiid bugs; fewer than 30 living species in 13 genera)
Sikhotealinia zhiltzovae (a jurodid beetle)
Syntexis libocedrii (Anaxyelidae cedar wood wasp)

Crustaceans

glypheoid lobsters (2 living species)
Stomatopods (mantis shrimp)
Triops cancriformis (also known as tadpole shrimp)

Molluscs

Nautilina (e.g. *Nautilus pompilius*)
Neopilina galateae, a Monoplacophoran
Ennucula superba - Nut clam
Vampyroteuthis infernalis - Vampire Squid

Other invertebrates

crinoids
Horseshoe crabs (only 4 living species of the class Xiphosura)
Lingula anatina (an inarticulate brachiopod)
Liphistiidae (trapdoor spiders)
onychophorans
Valdiviathyris quenstedti (a craniforman brachiopod).

We do not see any credible transitional forms, yet if evolution were true, we would expect there to be hundreds of such life forms. The fossil record does show, however, that the whole range of animal phyla and all of the major plant divisions which are living today were also alive at the time of the dinosaurs. This was affirmed by a thirty-year study by Dr Carl Werner who, with his wife, visited sixty museums and numerous fossil digs throughout the world documenting the evidence and recording interviews with the scientists involved. His report is the subject of his book: *Living Fossils Evolution: The Grand Experiment, Volume 2*, New Leaf Press, 2008 (see also the page opposite). After such a thorough study, he concluded that:

The fossil evidence does not support changes of one species into another.

2 Is There Scientific Support for the Theory of Evolution?

All of these life forms, or very similar species, were present with the dinosaurs.

Source: C. Werner, *Living Fossils Evolution: The Grand Experiment, Volume 2*, New Leaf Press, 2008

2 Is There Scientific Support for the Theory of Evolution?

The First and Second Laws of Thermodynamics and Information

The First Law

The first and second laws of thermodynamics are two of the most basic laws of nature. They have been used, refined and confirmed repeatedly by experimentation since the mid nineteenth century.

The first Law states in its original form that matter cannot be created or destroyed. However, this was amended to include energy after the discovery of thermonuclear reactions, of which the sun and all suns are a good example. For here, energy is produced by the fusion of two hydrogen atoms to form one helium atom. The actual process involves nuclei and other elements, but this is the overall effect. It can be written as follows:

$$\text{Hydrogen} + \text{Hydrogen} \rightarrow \text{Helium} + \text{Energy}.$$

The total amount of mass and energy on the left hand side of the equation equals the total amount of mass and energy on the right hand side. So the First Law means that the total amount of energy plus mass in the universe is constant.

The Bible is in beautiful agreement with this First Law when it states that at the end of the sixth day, God finished His work of creation.[83]

The Second Law

The Second Law of Thermodynamics states that any natural process (for isolated systems, which the Universe is by definition) will proceed to greater entropy, which has to do with disorder or randomness. That is, entropy must increase. Although it is not easy to see at first, the Second Law means that when they are brought together, hot objects will cool and cold objects will warm until they are at the same temperature. When this is applied to the whole universe, the result is that order will go to disorder, the cosmos will go to chaos and the total amount of usable energy in the universe will decrease, eventually to nothing. Since the universe as a whole is running down, it must have commenced in a 'wound up' state. How did it come into existence 'wound up'? A Creator 'outside' of the universe is a logical answer.

An example of the application of the Second Law is the geothermal generation of electricity by the pumping of water down holes which penetrate parts of the earth's surface that are very hot. In the process, the water is converted into steam, and this drives a turbine, which in turn generates electricity. Electricity can only be generated for as long as the source of heat, usually hot rocks, remains hot, for as the process proceeds, the rocks cool as their heat is extracted.

We see applications of the Second Law all of the time. Machines stop working as they age and they disintegrate. This applies to everything, including us. This is a relentless tendency in all systems. With either intelligence, or the right sort of programmed machinery operating in an open system, things can go in the opposite direction without violating this law, such as when a machine is repaired or manufactured. However, big – bang – to – you evolution demands **the exact opposite to what we observe and to what the Second Law requires.** Such a grand sweep

---

[83] Genesis 2:1-3.

requires a chaos-producing explosion to have become the hugely ordered universe of today. Evolutionists claim of course, that natural selection plus mutation provides a mechanism which has lifted single-celled organisms to higher states of complexity, without violating the Second Law. However, we will see that this mechanism is not adequate (pages 46 – 48). And in any case, until there is the 'first living cell'—a machine of staggering complexity (able to make copies of itself), natural selection cannot operate. The relentless tendency to disorder that gives us the Second Law stands as an impenetrable barrier to the idea that disordered molecules have by themselves given rise to the staggering complexity of a reproducing living thing. The evolution of this first living cell requires disordered molecules to have combined to form larger and more ordered ones. For example, the molecules of life; amino acids, are meant to have combined in a very precise way to form proteins and similarly, nucleotides to have formed DNA. However, in real chemistry, the overwhelming tendency is for natural processes to do the opposite, for complex molecules to degrade into simpler ones.

Sir Arthur Eddington summed up the situation succinctly in his book, *The Nature of the Physical World,* with this statement:

But if your theory is found to be against the second law of thermodynamics I give you no hope; there is nothing for it but to collapse in deepest humiliation.[84]

We have seen that when we look at the universe as a whole, the notion that chaos has morphed into today's highly ordered cosmos all by itself, would indeed violate this law.

The Biological Age of Fossils

Also in compliance with this second law is the fact that if a mixture of amino acids were left alone, they would not join together in a precisely ordered way to produce a protein. Nor would a mixture of ribose, bases and phosphate form itself into the tremendously complex and ordered DNA molecule. On the contrary, when proteins, DNA, RNA, carbohydrates, fatty acids or any other biological molecules are left, they simply degrade. Environmental factors such as humidity, temperature, light, pH, microbial activity, etc, affect the rate of degradation. Using the decomposition of buried bodies as a guide, it has been found that biological specimens may last hundreds or even thousands of years under ideal conditions, at the absolute maximum.

Imagine the surprise of paleontologist Dr Mary Schweitzer of Montana State University Laboratory when she cut the thighbone of a '68-million-year-old' Tyrannosaurus rex in half and discovered:

1. That it had not fossilized.
2. That it had a distinctly cadaverous odor.

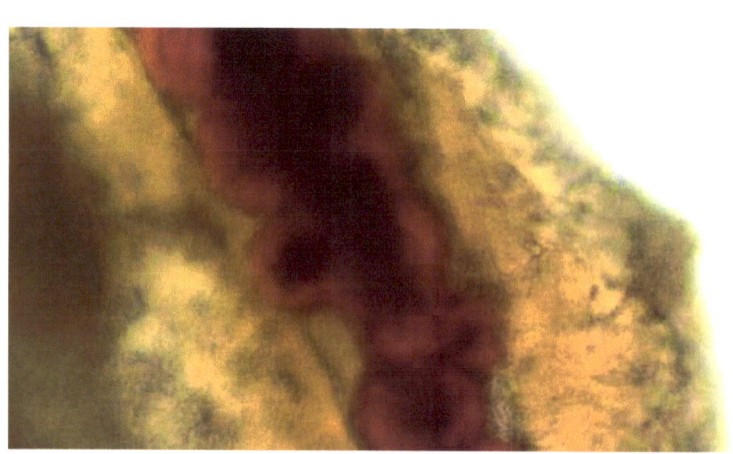

---

[84] A. Eddington, *The Nature of the Physical World,* Macmillan, New York, 1930, page 74.

2 Is There Scientific Support for the Theory of Evolution?

3. That soft tissue was present.

When she placed some of this soft tissue under a microscope, she could see still intact blood vessels, which contained red blood cells showing cell nuclei, as in the previous photo.

The pictures to the right show T. rex's soft tissue as still being flexible and resilient.

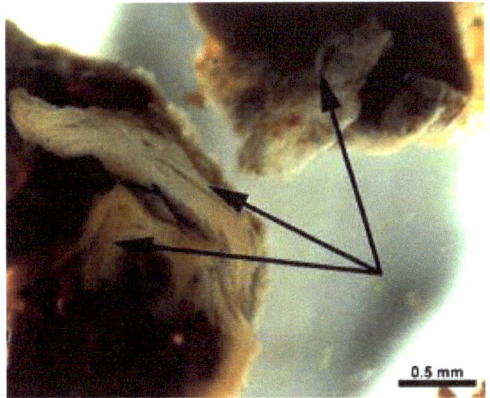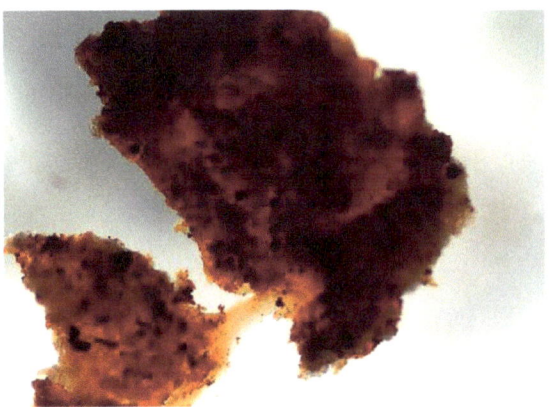

The discovery was reported widely.[85] An item in US science magazine *Discover* was published under the heading *Schweitzer's Dangerous Discovery*. The finding is only dangerous if you subscribe to the Theory of Evolution![86]

A follow-up report revealed that collagen had been extracted and that its constituent amino acids sequenced.[87]

Then came a further announcement by Schweitzer and others[88] in the prestigious journal *Science*[89] of substantial additional evidence to bolster her previous findings. The specimen on this occasion was a piece of fossil hadrosaur (duckbilled dinosaur—*Brachylophosaurus canadensis*) bone regarded by evolutionary assumptions as being 80 million years old.

In short, the researchers found evidence of: *the same fibrous matrix, transparent, flexible vessels, and preserved microstructures she had seen in the T. rex sample*. Only this time they went to exceptional lengths to silence critics.

Extraordinary measures were taken to keep the sample away from contamination until it reached the lab. They

---

[85] M. Schweitzer and T. Staedter "The Real Jurassic Park", *Earth*, June 1997, pages 55–57; Schweitzer, M. H., Wittmeyer, J. L., Horner, J. R. and Toporski, J. K., *Soft-tissue vessels and cellular preservation in Tyrannosaurus rex*, *Science*, 2005, (307), pages 1952-1955; B .Yeoman, *Discover,* 2006, vol. 27 No 4, pages 37–41; *New Scientist*, March 24, 2005.

[86] Other references to this discovery are: *Creation*, 1993, 16(1), 9; 1997, 19(4), 42; 2005, 27(4), 7.

[87] *The Weekend Australian,* April, 2007, pages 14-15.

[88] The following report is provided by Dr Carl Wieland of Creation Ministries International; source: creation.com/dinosaur-soft-tissue-and-protein-even-more-confirmation, retrieved September 8, 2009.

[89] M. H. Schweitzer *et al.*, Biomolecular characterization and protein sequences of the Campanian hardrosaur *B.canadensis*, *Science,* 324 (5927): 626-631, 1 May 2009.

used an even more sophisticated and a newer mass spectrometer, and sent the samples to two other laboratories for confirmation. They reported finding not just collagen, but evidence of two additional proteins; elastin and laminin. They also found structures uncannily resembling the cells found in both blood and bone, as well as cellular basement membrane matrix. And there were, once again, hints of hemoglobin, gleaned from applying hemoglobin-specific antibodies to the structures and seeing if the antibodies would bind to them.[90]

There were eight collagen proteins discovered in the hadrosaur fossil alone, which revealed twice as many amino acids as the previous tyrannosaur specimen. These were compared with sequences from animals living today, as well as from mastodon fossils and Schweitzer's *T. rex* sequences. The hadrosaur and tyrannosaur collagens were closer to each other than the others, and each was closer to chickens and ostriches than to crocodilians, for instance—results which also confirmed her previous identification of *T. rex* collagen.[91]

As Schweitzer says:

These data not only build upon what we got from the T. rex, they take the research even further.

'Still juicy after 10 million years' is the heading of an article which appeared in *New Scientist*.[92] The article reported that Maria McNamara of University College, Dublin, Ireland, had found the first unfossilised bone marrow in frogs that lived 10 million years ago. The article went on to assert that the discovery shows that decay-prone tissue can survive for an astonishingly long time, even in small amphibians' bones. The article stated:

McNamara was studying frog fossils from Spanish sulphur mines when she noticed bone marrow in a bone that had split. Curious, she examined other fossils and found preserved marrow in 10 percent of the adult frogs. Electron microscopy verified that the original structure of the bone marrow was preserved, as well as giant cells called osteoclasts found at the boundary between bone and marrow.

The fossil marrow consists of organic material. Tests for amino acids, proteins and tantalisingly, DNA, are in progress.[93]

380 million years old

Australian researchers were 'astounded' to recover well-preserved blood vessels, nerve cells and muscle tissue from a fossilised armor-plated fish (*Eastmanosteus calliaspis*) dated at '380 million' years old. The reports noted that rapid burial was a factor in its preservation. As well, the fish's muscles were:

Very much like our red muscles that we use for our most active pursuits such as running...[94]

300-million-year-old fish brain preserved as a fossil

---

[90] *New Scientist*, January 22, 2011, pages 42-45.
[91] C. Wieland, creation.com/dinosaur-soft-tissue-and-protein-even-more-confirmation, retrieved April 6, 2011.
[92] *New Scientist*, 5 August 2006, page 17.
[93] *Geology*, vol 34, p. 641; *New Scientist*, January 22, 2011, pages 42-45.
[94] *Creation*, June–August, 2007, **29** (3), page 10 citing; *Biological Letters*, April 22, 2007, **3** (2), 197–200; *The Western Australian*, February 14, 2007.

2   Is There Scientific Support for the Theory of Evolution?

Under the heading: *First fossil brain is a fishy discovery*, New Scientist reported that:

The first fossil brain ever discovered is that of a 300-million-year-old fish. Alan Pradel of the French Natural History Museum and his team took X-rays of four iniopterygian fish fossils from the Carboniferous period—Pradel was stunned to realize that the faint object 'like a ghost' inside one skull meant that the brain itself had been preserved.[95]

There have been other reports of unfossilised dinosaur bones.[96]

Scott R Woodward's paper, *DNA Sequence from Cretaceous Period Bone Fragment* states that:

Under physiological conditions, it would be extremely rare to find preserved DNA that was tens of thousands of years old.[97]

Bacteria alive and well after "millions" of years

It requires an even greater step of faith to believe that complete entities, such as bacteria, can be isolated after millions of years with all of their biochemical and biological parts functioning well such that they can resume living. But this is what is being claimed.

1. Bacteria frozen in Antarctic ice 'dated' to 8 million years old have been revived in the laboratory.[98]

2. In a paper titled *Microorganisms isolated from amber*, C. l. Greenbatt and co-workers reported to have resuscitated bacteria encapsulated in amber which was claimed to be 120 million years old.[99]

3. Bacteria have been isolated from salt taken from a mine 600 m below the surface in Mexico. The salt supposedly dates from 250 million years ago.[100]

Rock salt crystals

Because of the large number of biomolecules being found in fossils supposedly millions of years old, some scientists have conducted experiments with the aim of estimating the maximum time under the most ideal conditions in which a biomolecule can remain intact. One such group published their results[101] and arrived at maximum survival times for DNA of 125,000 years (0° C), 17,500 years (10° C) and 2,500 years (20° C). Since these are maximum survival times under the most ideal

---

[95] *New Scientist*, March 7, 2009, page 14.

[96] K. Davies, Journal of *Palaeontology*, 1992, 61 (1), pages 198–200; *Geological Society of America Proceedings* abstract, 1992, 17, page 548; V. Morell, "30-Million-Year-Old DNA Boosts an Emerging Field," *Science*, 1992, 257, 1862; R. J .Cano et al, "Amplification and Sequencing of DNA from a 120–135 million Year Old Weevil," *Nature*, 1993, 363, 536–538; G. O. Poiner Jr., "Recovery of Antediluvian DNA," *Nature*, 1993, 365, page 700.

[97] *Science*, 1994, 266, page 1229.

[98] *Creation*, 2008, **30** (3), page 12.

[99] *Microbial Ecology*, 1999, **38**, pages 58–68, cited in *Creation*, 2008, **30** (3), page1.

[100] *Nature*, 2000, 407 (6,806), 897–900, cited in *Creation*, 2008, **30** (3), page 12.

[101] C. Nielsen-Marsh, *The Biochemist*, June 2002, page 12.

conditions, they represent an enormous conundrum for evolutionists, as the fossilised creatures could have only lived thousands rather than millions of years ago.

Further evidence comes from a study of the degradation of DNA from 158 radio carbon dated bones of the extinct New Zealand Moa and assuming an effective burial temperature of 13.1^0 C. This study gave a half-life for DNA of 521 years. So in ten half lives: 5,210 years, there would be no measurable DNA present.[102]

Genes

Genes contain the information and instructions for building the species, and are another major problem for evolutionists. Evolution requires an enormous increase in genetic information as a single cell species, for example a bacterium, evolves into a human being. A bacterium only has about 500,000 nucleotides comprising its DNA (nucleotides in DNA pair off and are known as 'base pairs,' or 'letters' when the analogy with the alphabet is used) and lacks the DNA instructions to make all of the parts which comprise a human being, for example, eyes, ears, lungs, heart, brain etc; hence evolutionists must posit the addition of about three billion 'letters' of DNA instructions to change a microbe into a man (human beings have in excess of three billion nucleotides in their DNA). Proponents say this occurs through the processes of mutations and natural selection. However, both can be shown to bring about a reduction in genetic information rather than an addition to it.

Although this book aims to be as non-technical as possible, it is sometimes necessary to go into some depth in order to explain, even in a superficial way, the workings of living entities. This is the case with the present section on genes. What is presented is nonetheless a simplified overview, since the working of the genetic code is extremely complex and is not fully known—and quite possibly may never be completely understood.

The components of genes are the same for all living species. This does not necessarily mean that all life evolved from one basic entity, but rather, it can suggest the existence of a common Designer.

If all life were not of the same genetic makeup, then life would not be able to continue. For example, the grass that cows eat contains the very chemicals the cows need for their sustenance.

Genes consist of very long strings of nucleotides called deoxyribonucleic acid, abbreviated as DNA.

What is DNA?

The nucleotides themselves consist of three components; a sugar called deoxyribose, a phosphate molecule through which the nucleotides are joined, and a nitrogen-containing compound called a base. There are four different types of bases in genes and these give rise to four different nucleotides. The bases are called; adenine, guanine, cytosine and thymine, abbreviated to A G T and C. These long chains of nucleotides are not straight or in random coils but they exist in a double helical spiral like a length of twisted railway line, with the two chains held to each other by

---

[102] Allentoft et al, *Proceedings of the Royal Society B Biological Sciences* doi: 10.1098/rspb.2012.1745.

2 Is There Scientific Support for the Theory of Evolution?

weak bonding, known as hydrogen bonds, between the adjacent bases, as shown in the schematic on the next page. However, bonding only takes place through certain pairs of bases; A only bonds to T and G only to C.

The human genome contains in excess of 3 billion nucleotides. The order in which the nucleotides are joined together is of critical importance, because this order contains the information necessary to construct and to run the species whether it is a microbe, mango, mouse or man. Every chemical in a living organism is either made directly from this information, as in the case of proteins and enzymes, or indirectly, through a bewildering array of biochemicals which themselves have been made from this information. Groups of these double helixes are packed extremely tightly into bundles known as chromosomes. The nucleus of every cell, except for reproduction cells, contains a complete set of chromosomes (see the diagram below). During sexual reproduction one set of chromosomes is passed on to the progeny from each parent. Only species with the same number of chromosomes can produce viable offspring. We have 46 chromosomes, that is, 23 pairs, with one set of 23 coming from each parent; all apes (orangutan, gorilla, and chimpanzee), have 24 pairs of chromosomes.

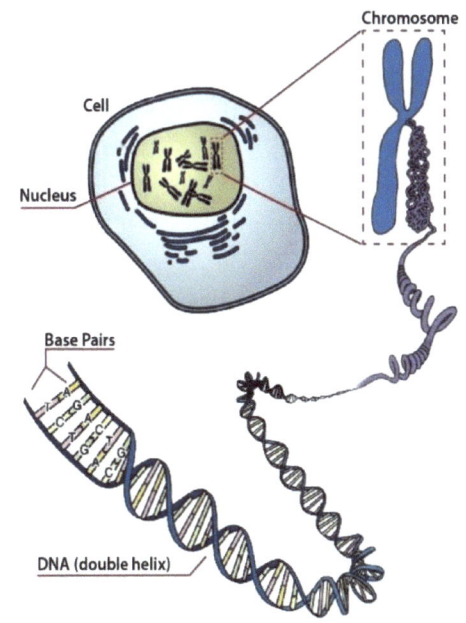

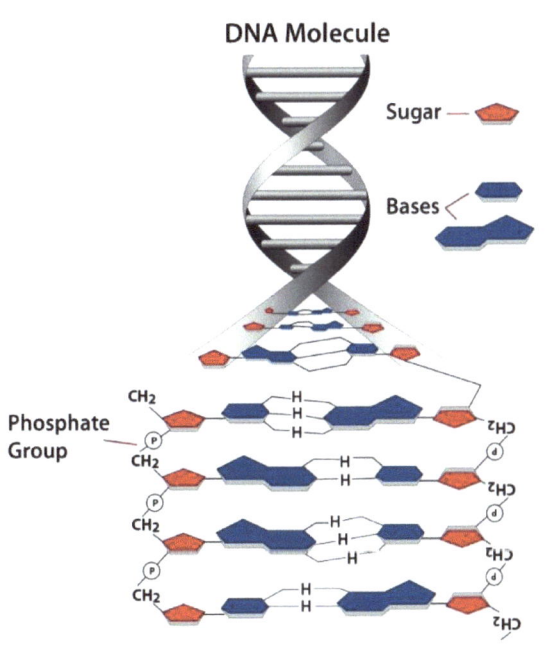

The information contained in the DNA in the cells of the human body can produce at least 100,000 different types of proteins, all with a unique function. As a cell divides, there are chemicals that not only check to see that the DNA has been duplicated exactly, but there are also chemicals that correct any duplicating errors caused by mutations. All have been manufactured in accordance with the information in the DNA. By way of explaining this information, consider the way letters of the alphabet can be arranged:

Disorder: AHDJIK BRY FHMSZXXONEM TYGFN

Order: ABCD ABCD ABCD ABCD ABCD ABCD

Information: KEEP OFF THE GRASS

2 Is There Scientific Support for the Theory of Evolution?

Not only is information contained in the DNA of the cells of living entities, so are the mechanisms for reading and using this information. The statement, "KEEP OFF THE GRASS," is only of value if it can be seen, read and understood. An almost incomprehensible array of chemicals and processes are present in cells that enable the information to be used. To propose that this all came about by the chance joining together of chemicals is ludicrous. Information cannot arise by chance; it has to have been present from the start.

Even atheist apologist Professor Richard Dawkins had to admit:

There is enough information capacity in a single human cell to store the Encyclopaedia Britannica, all 30 volumes of it, three or four times over.[103]

Philosopher Antony Flew explained the reason for his conversion to theism, after 50 years of atheism, as the fact that the investigation of DNA:

… has shown, by the most unbelievable complexity of the arrangements which are needed to produce life, that intelligence must have been involved.[104]

Even the greatest technological achievements of mankind do not begin to approach the sheer brilliance found in Creation:

In 2007, all the general computers in the world could together perform 6.4×10^{18} instructions per second. That roughly equals the number of nerve impulses produced by one human brain each second.[105]

Mutations

Mutations are an alteration of the DNA (genetic code) and can be caused by ionising radiation, ultraviolet radiation and some chemicals. As well, they are caused by mistakes in the genetic copying process. Each living cell has intricate molecular machinery designed for accurately copying DNA as the cell divides. But as in other copying processes, mistakes do occur, although not very often. Once in every 10,000–100,000 copies, a gene will contain a mistake. The cell has machinery for correcting these mistakes, but some mutations still slip through.

What kinds of changes are produced by mutations? Most have no effect at all, or produce so small a change that they have no appreciable effect on the creature. But some mutations produce significant deleterious effects, such as Sickle Cell Anemia (see page 25); Type 1 Hemochromatosis (see page 25), which is a disruption of a person's iron regulating system; and Factor V Leiden, which reduces the body's ability to dissolve blood clots. There are 50,000 known human disorders produced by gene mutations.[106] However, in some very rare cases, a mutation can be of an advantage to a species. For example, suppose beetles inhabit a windswept island and they are being

---

[103] R. Dawkins, *The Blind Watchmaker*, W W Norton, New York, 1996, page 115.

[104] A. Flew with R. A. Varghese, *There is a God, How the world's most notorious atheist changed his mind*, Harper One, 2007, page 75.

[105] *New Scientist*, February 19, 2011, page 5.

[106] Chris Tyler-Smith et al, *American Journal of Human Genetics*, doi.org/jxq cited in *New Scientist*, December 15, 2012, page 19.

2 Is There Scientific Support for the Theory of Evolution?

blown into the sea when they fly; a mutation that prevented them from flying could possibly be an advantage to them. But this is a loss of function rather than an addition and evolution requires additions.

In an effort to explain how new genetic information can arise in a species, evolutionists point to mutations. Mutations have been shown to cause fruit flies to develop an extra set of wings, or to grow legs where antenna should be. In the case of an extra set of wings or legs, these are non-functioning because the muscles and nerves that are required for them to work are not present. Consequently, they are a burden to the species and would be eliminated very quickly by natural selection.

Approximately 3,000 mutations have been identified in fruit flies (*Drosophila melanogaster*), all of these mutations are harmful or neutral, and none of them has produced a better or more successful fruit fly as required by Darwinian evolution. Evolutionists are unable to point to one case where a mutation has added a new structure or even a new biological pathway. Yet the whole theory hangs on this very point.

The fruit fly right has legs where antenna should be.

Dr H. J. Muller, who won the Nobel Prize for his extensive work on mutations caused by radiation, and an evolutionist himself, said that:

Most mutations are bad. Good ones are so rare we can consider them all bad.[107]

Dr Ian Macreadie is Principal Research Scientist at the Biomolecular Research Institute of Australia's CSIRO. He has won some of his nation's leading awards for research in his field. Dr Macreadie, who claims no official CSIRO endorsement for his views on origins, says:

All you see in the lab is either gene duplication, reshuffling of existing genes with a loss of information that might help a bug to survive; e.g., by not binding to an antibiotic as effectively. But you never see any new information arising within a cell. Evolution would argue for things improving, whereas I see everything falling to pieces. Genes, being corrupted, mutations [mistakes as DNA is copied for each generation] causing an increasing community burden of inherited diseases. All things were designed well initially.[108]

For a thorough dissertation on the impossibility of mutations adding information to the genome such that microbes are able to turn into men, the reader is directed to John C Lennox's book, *God's Undertaker. Has Science Buried God?*[109] Dr Lennox has impeccable qualifications to discuss the subject. He holds multiple higher degrees, including an MA, PhD and DSc; he is a Reader in Mathematics at the University of Oxford, and a fellow in Mathematics and the Philosophy of Science at Green College. As well, he is a Bible believing Christian.

---

[107] *Time: The Weekly Newsmagazine*, November 11, 1946, page 96.
[108] *Some Modern-day Scientists Who Oppose Evolution and Millions of Years*, a leaflet produced by Creation Ministries International (creation.com).
[109] J. C. Lennox, *God's Undertaker. Has Science Buried God?*, Wilkinson House, England, 2007.

2   Is There Scientific Support for the Theory of Evolution?

Evolutionists claim that there are other mechanisms that increase the amount of DNA in an organism. These include duplication, polyploidy and insertion. But this does not help explain evolution, because an increase in DNA does not necessarily increase the amount of functional genetic information that is required to turn legs into wings and scales into feathers. In fact, duplication of a single chromosome is normally harmful, as in Down's syndrome. Insertions are very efficient ways of completely destroying the functionality of existing genes. Biophysicist Dr Lee Spetner, in his book: *Not By Chance*,[110] analyses examples of mutational changes that evolutionists have claimed represent increases in information and shows that they are actually examples of loss of information.[111]

Natural Selection

We observe natural selection operating all of the time. It is completely analogous to the process that breeders use, whether they breed plants, birds or animals. But natural selection can only select from what is already present in living organisms. It can never introduce new information into a species to change it from, say, a lizard into a bird. Darwin's finches, with their different-sized beaks giving some birds a selective advantage, do not constitute an example of molecules-to-man evolution, but merely an example of adaptation to a changing environment. They were finches then and they are finches now and there is no evidence that new information has been added to the gene pool, whether by mutations or anything else.

Consider the hypothetical example of two genes in a dog; one coding for long hair and the other coding for short hair. As a consequence, there would be a mixture of long and short-haired dogs. Suppose a cold snap came about and all of the short-haired dogs died due to lack of thermal insulation. In this case the environment has selected for long-haired dogs. Once all of the short-haired dogs have died, the gene for short hair is lost and so this natural selection process has resulted in the loss of genetic information. The Theory of Evolution requires the opposite.

A real-life example of selection, this time by breeders rather than the forces of nature, is the range of colors that breeders have been able to produce in budgerigars by breeding from the native green bird. With each breeding step, there has been a loss of genetic information, such that it is not possible to breed from, say, a grey bird back to the original green and repeat the breeding program and produce other colors again.

Another example is the Peppered Moth (*Biston betularia*). As its environment changed from light colored bark on trees to dark bark during England's Industrial Revolution and then back to light as antipollution laws took hold, so did the relative populations of the dark and light-colored varieties, presumably as dark moths on light trees were more visible to predatory birds and vice versa. Again, this is not an example of evolution but rather changes within the populations of the two types of Peppered Moth brought about by environmental selection from what was present already. No new genetic information was added to the species.

---

[110] L. Spetner, *Not By Chance,* The Judica Press, New York, 1997.
[111] For a full discussion on this topic, see J. Sarfati, *Refuting Evolution 2,* Master Books, 2002, pages 104–108.

2   Is There Scientific Support for the Theory of Evolution?

Fact and theory become confused when evolutionists conflate the phenomenon of natural selection with the hypothesis of evolution. Despite the implicit assumption behind phrases like 'observing evolution happening,' an examination of the facts will more than likely reveal that what is being observed is natural selection through mutations and the associated loss of genetic diversity. A very common example of this is bacteria acquiring resistance to antibiotics. As Dr Macreadie points out on the previous page, this can occur when, for example, bacteria loses a site that the antibiotic can attach itself to, thereby making it resistant to that particular antibiotic,[112] or species developing resistance to pesticides.[113]

Conclusion

The evidence presented demonstrates that the Theory of Evolution lacks scientific support.

It is preposterous to believe that everything came from nothing; that the elegant laws of physics, chemistry, nuclear reactions and planetary motion, as well as symmetry, order and harmony, sprang from chaos; and that life came from a mixture of chemicals, which eventually spawned intelligence, logic, self-consciousness and morality. On the contrary, design is evident everywhere—from the blood clotting 'cascade' involving more than 100 mutually dependent steps employing a range of components, some of which are generated by bacteria residing in the human gut, which enables human life to exist (see also page 107); to the amazing symbiotic relationship between bees and flowers; to the awe-inspiring symmetry, harmony and precision of the motion of the heavenly bodies. To witness such design and then to deny a Designer defies logic.

The following statement appeared in *New Scientist:*[114]

There is design in nature, and we should take that word away from the Intelligent Design movement.

This statement was made by the biologist and key proponent of evolution, Kenneth Miller, in a talk titled: *Communicating Science in a Religious America*. It is an amazing admission, given that in order for there to be design there must have been a Designer.

Even the pro-evolution magazine, *National Geographic*, in an article proclaiming the virtues of the theory, made this amazing admission:

...the fossil record is like a film of evolution from which 999 of every 1,000 frames have been lost on the cutting room floor.[115]

If 99.9 percent of the evidence that supports the theory is missing, why has the theory not been discarded? Because belief in the Theory of Evolution is a faith position which supports a particular worldview.

---

[112] For a thorough explanation of this topic, the reader is directed to a paper by Dr Jerry Bergman at creation.com/does-the-aquisition-of-antibiotic-and-pesticide-resistance-prove-evidence-for-evolution.
[113] David Catchpoole, *Creation*, 2011, **33** (3), pages 38-39.
[114] *New Scientist*, 23 February, 2008, page 8.
[115] *National Geographic*, November, 2004, page 25.

2 Is There Scientific Support for the Theory of Evolution?

Professor Graeme Clark, who developed the Bionic Ear, which has enabled thousands of previously deaf people to hear, spoke of the complexity of the human brain in the first of his Boyer lectures:[116]

It has been calculated that there are 100 billion nerve cells in the adult human brain. Each brain cell is connected to between 10 and 10,000 other brain cells, so therefore there are about 100 million million connections in the brain. So there are an amazing number of possibilities in the brain for sensing and processing information.

He poses the question and then answers it:

Could the physical universe, which physicists now show had only the remotest chance of producing carbon-based life, have evolved into human consciousness by mindless chance? I think not. The human brain is so sophisticated a mechanism that scientists have still not been able to design engineering systems that can match its crucial functions. For me that means a supernatural entity, namely God was responsible, rather than saying it assembled itself by mindless chance. In any case a human being would have to know everything to actually know there is no God.

It is not surprising then, that Dr Michael Denton, Senior Research Fellow in the Department of Biochemistry at the University of Otago, New Zealand, wrote the book: *Evolution: A Theory in Crisis*[117]. Denton states that he is not a Christian, but when he examined the evidence in his own field of biochemistry, he found overwhelming evidence for design. He went so far as to write that the world itself is anthropocentric, meaning that it was designed for man, who was to live in it.

In his book, *Darwinism: The Refutation of a Myth*, the Swedish scientist Soren Lovtrup has this to say on the subject:

I suppose that nobody will deny that it is a great misfortune if an entire branch of science becomes addicted to a false theory. But this is what has happened in biology: for a long time now people discuss evolutionary problems in a peculiar 'Darwinian' vocabulary—'adaptation,' 'selection pressure,' 'Natural selection,' etc—thereby believing that they contribute to the explanation of natural events. They do not... I believe that one day the Darwinian myth will be ranked the greatest deceit in the history of science.[118]

When Michael Behe, Professor of Biochemistry at Lehigh University in Pennsylvania, looked at the evidence, everything he could see supported design. In fact he coined the name Intelligent Design and wrote the book *Darwin's Black Box: The Biochemical Challenge to Evolution*.[119]

The 'gene gun' approach to the genetic engineering of plants has had a major impact on agriculture worldwide. Its co-inventor, Dr John Sanford of Cornell University, was an evolutionist but became

---

[116] *The Weekend Australian*, November, pages 10–11, 2007.

[117] M. Denton, *Evolution: A Theory in Crisis,* Adler and Adler 1986.

[118] S. Lovtrup, *Darwinism: The Refutation of a Myth,* Croom Helm, New York, 1987, page 422.

[119] For a thorough technical treatise on *Irreducible Complexity*, the basic argument for *Intelligent Design*, the reader is directed to Dr Alex Williams' article: Life's Irreducible Structure – Part 1: Autopoiesis, *Journal of Creation*, August 2007, **21**(2), pages 109-115.

2   Is There Scientific Support for the Theory of Evolution?

a creationist when he examined the evidence in his field for himself. In fact, his book *Genetic Entropy and the Mystery of the Genome* is a methodical demolition of Darwinism. He comments:

My recent book resulted from many years of intense study. This involved a complete re-evaluation of everything I thought I knew about evolutionary theory. It systematically examines the problems underlying classic neo-Darwin theory. The bottom line is that Darwinian Theory fails on every level.[120]

Professor Richard Smalley won the Nobel Prize in Chemistry in 1996 for his discovery of a new form of carbon which he called buckminsterfullerene—nicknamed buckyballs because they are a similar shape to soccer balls only on the nanometer scale. His discovery is credited with starting the explosion in nanotechnology. Up until only a few years before his death in 2005, he was a strong advocate for evolution, until he was challenged to investigate the science behind it. This caused him to conclude, "This is bad science." As a result of his scientific investigation, coupled with his study of the Bible, he became a Bible-believing creationist and an outspoken anti-Darwinist.[121]

Research scientist Dr John Ashton wrote:

At university several years ago, I heard a research scientist state that he did not believe that any scientist with a PhD would advocate a literal interpretation of the six days of creation.

Dr Ashton then set about disproving this assertion and edited the book, *In Six Days, Why 50 Scientists Choose to Believe in Creation.*[122] In its preface he remarks on the scientists who explain the reasons for their belief:

All contributors have an earned doctorate from a state-recognised university in Australia, the United States, the United Kingdom, Canada, or Germany. They include university professors and researchers, geologists, zoologists, biologists, botanists, chemists, mathematicians, medical researchers and engineers.

Space and a publishing deadline prevented him from including contributions from many other scientists.

A man who looked at the evolution/creation debate from a totally different angle is Phillip Johnson, Professor of Law at the University of California, Berkeley. He concluded that the reason why so many academics are atheists is because their primary commitment is to the philosophy of naturalism. If the facts contradict materialistic conclusions, then the facts are either explained away, ignored, or dismissed as just plain wrong. Therefore, evolutionists like Richard Dawkins can say things like:

Biology is the study of complicated things that give the appearance of having been designed for a purpose.[123]

---

[120] *Creation*, September–November, 2008, **30** (4), pages 45–47.
[121] *Creation*, 2011, **33** (2), page 42.
[122] J. F. Ashton, *In Six Days, Why 50 Scientists Choose to Believe in Creation*, Master Books, 2001.

2. Is There Scientific Support for the Theory of Evolution?

Johnson exposes the self-perpetuating nature of the prevailing academic worldview with this statement:

Modernist discourse accordingly incorporates semantic devices—such as the labeling of theism as religion and naturalism as science—that work to prevent a dangerous debate over fundamental assumptions from breaking out in the open. As the preceding chapter showed, however, these devices become transparent under the close inspection that an open debate tends to encourage. The best defense for modernist naturalism is to make sure the debate does not occur.[124]

Professor Johnson has written four books on the subject, *Darwin on Trial*, *Reason in the Balance*, *Defeating Darwinism by Opening Minds* and *Objections Sustained*.

In a blaze of publicity, the 2010 Global Atheist Convention—named: *The Rise of Atheism,* was held in Melbourne on Sunday March 14. Some of the atheist's world most vocal big hitters, such as Richard Dawkins, Peter Singer, A. C. Grayling and the vitriolic anti-Christian blogger P. Z. Myers, were present. They proclaimed the atheist's mantra that evolution is science and is fact, and that only religious fanatics deny this clear teaching of science. Strangely, when challenged to a public debate by Creation Ministries International, they refused. CMI went to extraordinary lengths to accommodate them, right there in the city where they were gathered. It is perplexing that they refused this opportunity to expose these Christian zealots for the 'false science' they peddle.

Creation Ministries International did not waste their time with requesting a public debate with members of the 2012 Global Atheist Convention. These people can only operate when they have a compliant and uncritical media. They shy away from any real opposition.

The real reason people believe in evolution

George Wald, a 1967 Nobel Prize winner and an evolutionist, states:

When it comes to the origin of life there are only two possibilities–creation or spontaneous generation. There is no third way. Spontaneous generation was disproved one hundred years ago, but that leads us to only one other conclusion, that of supernatural creation. We cannot accept that on philosophical grounds; therefore, we choose to believe the impossible: that life arose spontaneously by chance![125]

Questions evolutionists to answer

- How can you harmonise the Big Bang idea that chaos produced the order of the cosmos, with the second law of thermodynamics which states that for the universe as a whole, order must degenerate to chaos?
- Since the Theory of Evolution is based on the twin concepts of natural selection and variation through mutations, and natural selection has been shown to reduce variability rather than increase it, where does one see amidist the thousands of mutations happening

---

[123] R. Dawkins, *The Blind Watchmaker,* W W Norton, 1996, page 1.

[124] P. E. Johnson, *Reason in the Balance: The Case Against Naturalism in Science, Law and Education,* Downers Grove, IL: InterVarsity Press, 1995, page 45.

[125] G. Wald, The Origin of Life, *Scientific American,* 191:48, May 1954.

2 Is There Scientific Support for the Theory of Evolution?

continually, even a dozen or so examples of a genetic mutation or any other process that can be demonstrated to have added useful information (specified complexity) to the genome?[126]
- Can you propose any mechanism whereby chemicals can order themselves into a living entity?
- How do you explain the conundrum of oxygen having to be absent from the early earth because it would destroy some of the chemicals of life (chemicals within cells are protected), yet without oxygen in the form of ozone to absorb harmful ultraviolet radiation, all life would be destroyed?
- Please explain in evolutionary terms, the process of metamorphosis whereby a caterpillar constructs a cocoon around itself and sometime later emerges as a butterfly or moth.

The implications of the Theory of Evolution do not end with the dispute about science. It has a much more sinister side. The logical conclusion, to which it leads, is a society without any moral basis. For if we came from a series of chance chemical reactions in some 'primordial soup' and we got to where we are by 'survival of the fittest' then who is to say what is right and what is wrong? Stealing, adultery, abortion, murder, homosexuality; are these wrong? Without God it is simply the views of one person against another's. The Bible documents a similar, God-rejecting society in the historical book of Judges:

In those days there was no king in Israel, but every man did that which was right in his own eyes.[127]

Unfortunately the Theory of Evolution is doing its part in accelerating the demise of the moral foundations of our society.

The idea that everything came from nothing is preposterous.

Chemical evolution is impossible.

Evidence of design is overwhelming.

The Theory of Evolution is not supported by science. It is a religion which its adherents believe by faith.

---

[126] Readers are invited to visit the YouTube website and watch Professor Richard Dawkins squirm for an embarrassingly long time, even asking for the cameras to be turned off, and still remain unable to answer the above question. www.youtube.com/watch?v=zaKryi3605g.
[127] Judges 17:6.

Chapter 3

Is There Any Scientific Support for Biblical Creation?

The biblical story of creation is often criticised, with many people, including liberal Christians, insisting that it is not meant to be taken literally, but must be allegorised.

Before addressing biblical creation, a brief examination of how other religions explain our existence is presented so that their account of creation can be compared with that of the Bible.

The Hindu texts known as the Upanishads describe the creation of the world as the breaking of a cosmic egg.

The Aztecs of Mexico believed that the present world was the fifth that the gods had created. It was fated to end in universal destruction by earthquakes. The four previous worlds had been destroyed by a great flood, the falling of the sky, a firestorm, and a windstorm.

The Maya believed that the gods made three unsuccessful attempts to create human beings before achieving a satisfactory result. Their first creations–animals, people made of mud, and wooden people–disappointed them in various ways, and they abandoned or destroyed them. Finally, the gods made people of maize (corn) who were perfect, so perfect that their creators clouded their vision to prevent them from seeing too far.

A Japanese tradition, preserved in a volume of mythological history called the *Kojiki*, says that before creation, there was an oily sea. Gods came into being in the High Plains of Heaven. After seven generations of deities, there came the first human ancestors, whose task was to make solid land. They stirred the sea with a jeweled spear. Drops that fell from the spear formed the islands of Japan.

A Chinese creation story tells how Pan Gu was hatched from a cosmic egg. One part of the eggshell formed the heavens; the other part became the earth. For 18,000 years, Pan Gu stood between them, keeping them apart by growing ever taller. Finally he became weary, lay down, and died. From his eyes came the sun and moon, from his hair the stars, from his breath the wind, and from his body the earth.

A Norse creation story tells how the giant Ymir took shape in the huge icy emptiness called Ginnungagap. Ymir's great cow licked the ice, creating the first gods, including Odin. The gods killed Ymir and divided his body into a series of worlds on three levels: Asgard, the realm of gods; Midgard, the realm of people, giants, dwarfs, and elves; and Niflheim, the realm of the dead. The gods created the first man and woman from an ash and an elm tree.

According to **Polynesian** tradition, a creator god named Tangaloa sent a bird messenger over an endless primal sea. At last Tangaloa threw a rock into the sea so the tired bird would have a place

3   Is There Scientific Support for Biblical Creation?

to land. Then the god created all the islands in the same way. The bird made the first people by giving arms, legs, hearts and souls to maggots.

It is easy to see that these creation stories were devised by man. Now let's compare them with the biblical account of creation.

Biblical Creation

The biblical account of creation appears in the first chapter of the book of Genesis. The narrative is detailed and the act of creation is attributed to God in its entirety. It was accomplished in six days. It was orderly and highly structured, with each day having its own start and finish. That is: morning and evening. Each day was completed before the next act of creation was started. It is a logical sequence of events with the pinnacle of creation being man—the only being created in the image of God.

What does Genesis tell about creation that can be examined?

1. God spoke everything into existence out of nothing.
2. God created every living thing complete and fully functioning, with trees bearing fruit, animals able to procreate and Adam and Eve as adults of childbearing age.
3. Every creature was to reproduce after its kind. And they were to be to be fruitful and to multiply.
4. Adam and Eve, unlike the rest of creation, were created in the image of God.
5. After six days, all creation was complete and finished.

Each of these propositions is discussed below.

1. God Spoke Everything into Existence out of Nothing

(a) Cosmological Argument (The First Cause Argument)

The Cosmological argument is a powerful philosophical tool, which is based on a universal law, applicable in all science and human experience. It leads to the conclusion that there must have been a Creator.

The argument goes like this: in our everyday experiences we observe and know that nothing happens by itself, but rather that everything that happens has a cause. Something cannot come from nothing. For example, suppose you were with a friend and you heard a loud bang, and you said to your friend, "What was that?" and he said, "Nothing, just a bang," you would know that his answer could not be right, because there cannot be a bang without something causing it. Every effect must have a cause.

The universe consists of a series of events stretched across time in a long causal chain. Each one of these events is the *cause* of the event that comes after it, and the *effect* of the event that comes before it; the world as it is came from the world as it was which came from the world as it was before.

If we trace this series of events back in time, we find two possibilities: either we eventually reach the first event in the series, the cause at the beginning of the universe that set everything going,

3   Is There Scientific Support for Biblical Creation?

or there is no first event in the series and the past stretches back into infinity.

Since it is not possible to come back from infinity, because infinity never ends, or for that matter to go forward to infinity, then the second argument must be ruled out.

If the law of cause and effect applies, as it does, it must apply to the whole universe and to every part of it. The entity that brought about that first cause by the process of creation must be independent (or outside) of creation and also outside of time. This Creator must be living, eternal, omnipotent, omniscient, omnipresent, conscious and moral,[128] and creation must have been volitional. Thus, the basic premise of biblical theology: *In the beginning God created the heaven and the earth* is in complete harmony with the argument presented.[129]

The most common objection to the argument of a creator God is, "Who created God in the first place?" The response is: the universe had a beginning and the First Cause argument applies. God did not have a beginning as He is outside of time. In fact, time started at the instant of creation, so the First Cause argument does not apply to God.

(b) The Trinity of Creation

The apostle Paul states that God's eternal power and Godhead are clearly evident in creation; to such an extent that mankind is without excuse for not believing.[130] The Godhead is the trinity of God the Father, God the Son and God the Holy Spirit that is, three in one. Consequently, we would expect to see the number three appearing many times in creation since Paul, writing under the influence of the Holy Spirit, asserted that the Godhead is clearly seen in creation.

It is significant then, that His created universe actually consists of three parts, with each of its distinct components of time, space and matter comprising and pervading the whole universe. And each of these components consist of thee parts. Time has past, present and future. Space has the three dimensions of length, breadth and width; and matter can exist in three forms—solid, liquid and gas. As well, the basic unit of matter, the atom, is composed of three main parts—protons, neutrons and electrons. The whole electromagnetic spectrum (gamma rays, x-rays, ultraviolet, visible light, infra red, microwaves and radio waves) is comprised of three components—electric fields, magnetic fields, and motion. Clearly, God has left His signature on His creation.

(c) God Spoke Everything into Existence

The abundance and diversity of life: We see around us an enormous array of life with its myriad of forms—animals, birds, insects, aquatic species, microbial species and plant life—all in great abundance, even to the extent that life is present in the most unlikely places.

Life below the sea: God said: *Let the waters abound with an abundance of living creatures.*[131]

---

[128] Since the concepts of morality and righteousness, although abstract, are nonetheless real, they must be part of the First Cause.
[129] H. M. Morris, *The Biblical Basis for Modern Science,* Baker Book House, 1984, page 33.
[130] Romans 20:1.
[131] Genesis 1:20.

3 Is There Scientific Support for Biblical Creation?

This is certainly the case. It is interesting that some aquatic creatures live on deep-sea hydrothermal vents some 8 to 10 kilometers below the sea surface. These are characterised by pitch darkness, poison gas, heavy metals, extreme acidity, enormous pressure, and water at times frigid and at other times searing in temperature. The vents are formed when water heated as high as 400°C by the earth's magma billows from a sea-floor chimney and comes in contact with the surrounding water at 2–5°C. The iron sulphide from the earth's interior precipitates, giving the vent its color and lending the name of 'black smoker'. If there is a harsher place to live than on a hydrothermal vent, it hasn't been found yet. Yet surprisingly, some 300 different species of marine creatures live there.

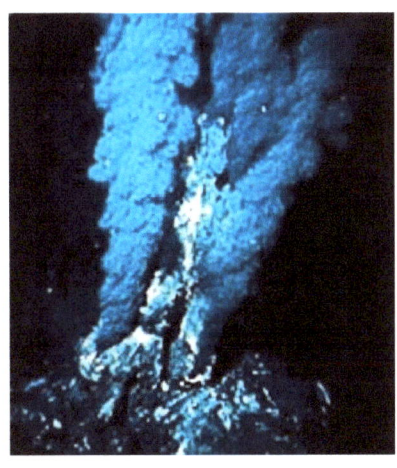

A Hydrothermal Vent

Many have wondered why God would be bothered to create such a large range of species, some with their own unique metabolism, even way down at the bottom of the ocean. Or why would God create the great vastness of the universe when only an infinitesimal part can be viewed from earth? Part of the answer is found in Genesis chapter 1. God spoke everything into existence, and thereby He demonstrated His omnipotence. He didn't have to make anything, He simply spoke and it came into being. It was no harder for God to say, "Let there be some aquatic species" than it was for Him to say, "Let the waters abound with an abundance of living creatures." Thus, His statement was fulfilled in every detail. The other part of the answer is that God created for His pleasure.[132]

(d) Our World is Designed to Support Human Life (Anthropocentric)

Not only did God create life, He designed the earth to support it. The word used to describe the fact that the earth was designed to support human life is 'anthropocentric'. The sphere on which we live is absolutely unique in the whole known cosmos. Some of the many characteristics of the earth that enable it to support human life are as follows:

1. Life is only possible because the earth is exactly the right distance from the sun, giving us a temperature range mainly between 0°C and 40°C. If we were five percent closer to the sun, the oceans would boil; five percent further away and all of the oceans would freeze.

2. The earth's orbit around the sun is nearly a perfect circle. If it were more elliptical, it would be too hot in the summer and too cold in the winter.

3. If the earth's rotation about its axis was slower, the days would be unbearably hot and the nights unbearably cold. If the rotation was faster, the wind would blow so strongly that people would not be able to stand up.

4. The earth has a very unusually large moon and its gravitational pull causes the tides, which, in turn, cleanse the ocean's shores and put oxygen back into the water by moving it—thereby enabling it to support aquatic life.

---

[132] Colossians 1:16; Isaiah 43:7; Revelation 4:11.

5. The huge planet Jupiter, with its strong gravity, is in just the right position to pull many comets and meteors into it, averting them from crashing into the earth and killing much of its life.

6. The earth is tilted on its axis of rotation at an angle of 23.5 degrees. This is important because the greater proportion of land mass is located in the northern hemisphere. Land absorbs more of the sun's heat than the sea, so the earth is much warmer when the northern hemisphere is pointing towards the sun and this happens to be when the earth is farthest from the sun. This fact gives rise to the seasons and moderates the seasonal temperatures.

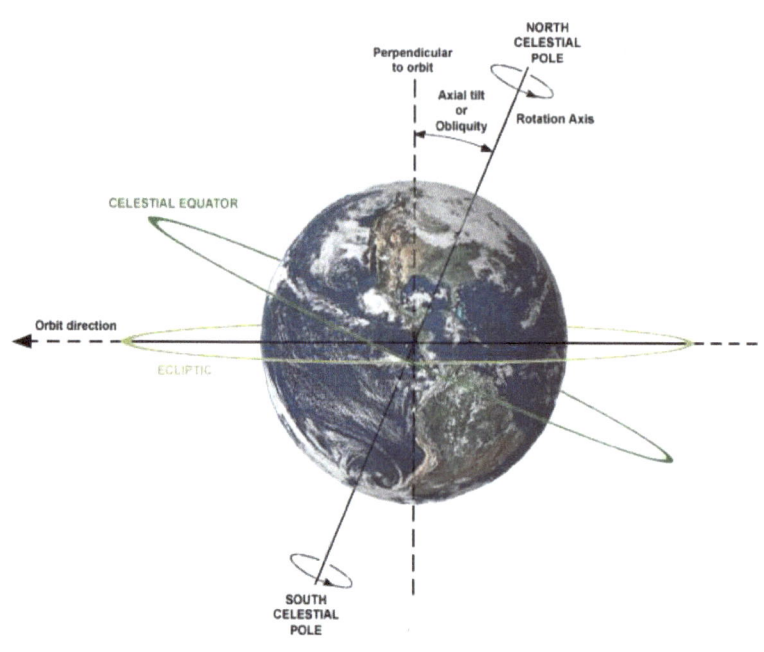

7. The earth's unusually thin atmosphere is compatible with life. For example, our near neighbor, Venus, is smaller and yet it has an atmosphere 80 times that of the earth. As a result, its runaway greenhouse effect has produced searing temperatures.

8. The earth has a very large and heavy magnetic core, giving it the highest density of any of the planets in the solar system. Our iron and nickel core produces a large magnetic field which protects us from lethal solar wind. Without such a huge magnetic field, life would not be able to exist.

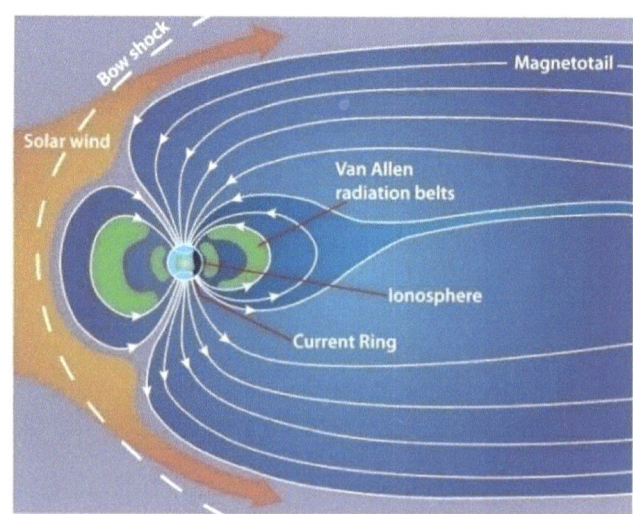

9. The earth's gravity is at just the right strength to enable its inhabitants to be able to move easily.

10. As the earth spins on its own axis, it has a tendency to wobble, owing to varying pulls from other bodies such as the sun. The unseen force of our unusually large moon's gravity gently damps the wobble, preventing

rotational instabilities which would have caused dramatic changes in earth's climatic zones over time, thereby making it inhospitable to life.[133]

11. Our solar system is in just the right position in our galaxy (a spiral galaxy called the Milky Way), in what has become known as the Galactic Habitable Zone (GHZ). Too far from the galactic center and all of the elements necessary for life would not be present; too close to the center or on one of the galaxy's spiral arms, and x-ray and gamma radiation from neutron stars would destroy life, and the gravitational pull of nearby stars would affect the motion of the planets in our solar system. Our solar system sits at a comfortable halfway from the galactic center and between two of its spiral arms.[134]

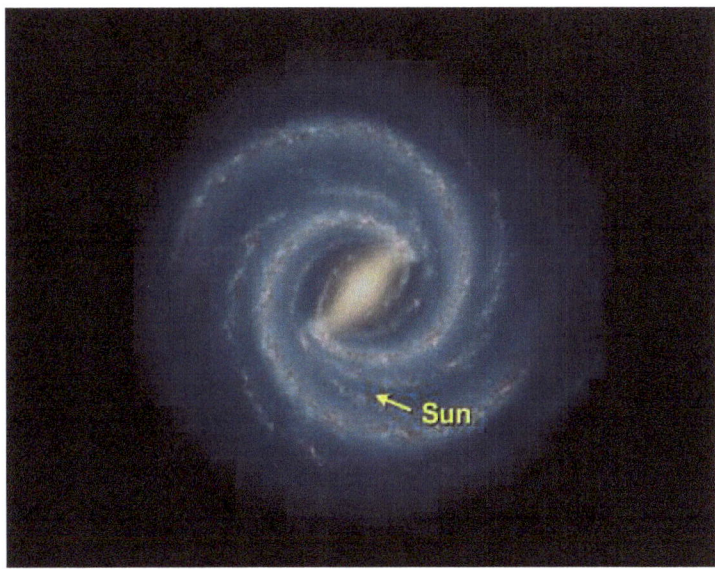

An artist's impression of our galaxy

12. The physical constants of the Universe are amazingly finely tuned. The constants of the laws of physics, such as the speed of light; weak nuclear forces; the ratio of neutron mass to proton mass; the gravitational constant and thirty other physical constants are finely tuned to a very precise degree—such that if they were altered even slightly, the universe would either be prevented from existing, would not have matter, or would be unsuitable for any form of life.[135]

13. The one substance without which life would be impossible is liquid water; our world has it in abundance. That is why people at NASA are desperately trying to find liquid water on some other heavenly body. If and when they do, they hope against hope that they will find some form of life, because they believe that life arose from a bunch of chemicals that organized themselves into self-replicating organisms. What is driving this multi-million dollar search? Simply this: if they can find life, that will support the argument that evolution is true and that there is no God; as a consequence, they will not be responsible to their Creator for how they have lived.

Let us examine some of the unique properties of water.

---

[133] *New Scientist*, January 31, 2009, page 31.
[134] P. D. Ward and D. Brownlee, *Rare Earth*, Copernicus, Springer-Verlag, New York, 2000.
[135] *New Scientist*, July 23, 2011, page 35.

Wonderful Water

Water has many unusual properties and is necessary for the existence of life. Like all liquids, water contracts and becomes denser as it cools; but amazingly, this process reverses when water reaches 4°C. On further cooling, water begins to expand and becomes less dense and lighter, giving rise to the phenomenon that it freezes from the top down, while all other liquids, which become denser as they cool, freeze from the bottom up. It is this property of water that causes bottles to break if they are filled with water and placed in a freezer; it causes icebergs to float, and it is why the sea and even lakes do not freeze completely. This  property allows marine life to live. In fact, ice has such good  insulating properties that even with the air temperature as low as minus 50°C, the ice layer can be as little as one meter thick and the water below it will remain liquid. In addition, water is the only liquid that exists on earth in all of its three forms; solid, liquid and gas.

Water has other exceptional properties that enable life to exist. One of its amazing physical properties is surface tension. That is, water sticks to itself very strongly, more strongly in fact than any other common liquid. This high surface tension can be demonstrated by very carefully placing a needle onto the surface of water contained in a cup, for example. The needle will float, but as soon as one drop of a surfactant (such as a detergent) is added, the surface tension will be broken and the needle will sink immediately.

When this property is expressed in another form, known as capillary action, it enables plants to transport water from their roots up to their leaves. As the water is transported, it carries with it nutrients and this highlights another unique feature of water; its great solvent capacity; greater than any other liquid, in fact. Without this property, life would not be able to exist.

Another distinctive property of water that enables capillary action to proceed is its very low viscosity.

These properties combine to allow water to carry nutrients through very small tubes called capillaries. This same process of carrying nutrients to extremities operates in all forms of life. In animals and people, the process keeps our extremities flushed with oxygen by nutrient-carrying blood.

3 Is There Scientific Support for Biblical Creation?

Water has the amazing characteristic of being able to absorb a lot of heat. This property is known as heat capacity, and it enables the earth's vast amount of water (70 percent of the earth's surface is covered by water) to moderate its temperature. By contrast, the moon has no air or water and as a consequence it has an average maximum daytime temperature of 107^0C and an average minimum night temperature of minus180^0C; conditions under which life could not exist.

Not only does water have a great capacity to absorb heat, it also gives off a lot of heat when it evaporates. This is known as the latent heat of vaporization and it enables us to keep our body temperature at 37^0C when we exercise, because the hotter we get the more we perspire, and the more we perspire, the more water is evaporated from our bodies and the more we cool.

There is no other liquid like water with respect to its compatibility with life—and our earth has it in abundance.

It is possible to see in all of these amazing facts that the earth was designed to support life. This is a confirmation of God's word to His prophet Isaiah:

For thus says the LORD, Who created the heavens, Who is God, Who formed the earth and made it, Who has established it, Who did not create it in vain, Who formed it to be inhabited: "I am the LORD, and there is no other."[136]

An interesting statistic

The sun's diameter is close to 400 times that of the moon and the distance between the earth and the sun is close to 400 times the distance between the earth and the moon. This means that when we experience a solar eclipse, the moon fits exactly over the sun. This may not be more than a coincidence. However, it does allow us to observe the sun's chromosphere when its enormous output of light is blocked and this aids our investigation of heavenly bodies.

A total solar eclipse

(e) How Long Ago?

If we add up the life spans of the people mentioned in the Old Testament from Adam to Christ, as did the seventeenth century Anglican; Bishop Ussher,[137] and take the Bible at face value, then we can deduce that God created mankind about six thousand years ago. If we allow for the genealogy of the Old Testament to be incomplete; as we might glean by comparing the genealogies of Luke 3:31 with Genesis 10:24 and 11:12, where Luke records Cain and between Arphaxad and Salah while Genesis doesn't; and Matthew 1:8 records that Jehoram begat Uzziah, whereas 1 Chronicles states that the genealogy went from Jehoram through Joash and Amaziah to Uzziah—we can extend that date by about 1,000 years at the maximum. But it is generally claimed that the alleged Big Bang occurred 13.5 billion years ago and that the earth came into existence 4.5 billion years ago. And a long age presumption is required for the theory of evolution to have any credibility at all.

---

[136] Isaiah 45:18.
[137] *Creation*, 1998, 20, pages 42-43.

3 Is There Scientific Support for Biblical Creation?

Mitochondrial Eve

The DNA in the mitochondrial part of our cells is passed on to us exclusively from our mother and it is identical to hers except for a few mutational changes. Recent studies have suggested that all women originated from a single woman, estimated to have lived some 150,000 years ago—In fact evolutionists call her 'Mitochondrial Eve'. This story was carried in newspapers around the world. What was not nearly so well publicised was the fact that the scientists who carried out the work had miscalculated the rate of mutations—the rate was later shown to be much faster than previously thought and the revised date for 'Mitochondrial Eve' is now 6,000 to 6,500 years ago.[138] Interestingly, there is a parallel case with males. All males inherit their Y chromosome from their fathers and studies have shown that all men come from a single man who existed at about the same time as Mitochondrial Eve; he is known as Y-Chromosome Adam.[139]

Using mitochondrial DNA studies, Dr Robert W Carter makes an interesting case that there are three basic mitochondrial lineages across the world and that these can be related to the three wives of Noah's sons who were aboard the ark.[140]

Radiometric dating

Radioactive elements are ubiquitous in the soil, water and air. Each radioactive element has its own rate of decay, which has been established in laboratories. The element that decays is called the parent and the element into which it breaks down is called the daughter. Radiometric dating does not measure dates but rather it measures the ratio of parent to daughter elements. Then, knowing the rate of decay, it is possible to infer the time the process has taken. However, there are three major and unprovable assumptions involved with this method:

1. The initial amount of the daughter element is assumed to be zero.

2. The rate of decay is assumed to have been constant for the period of time calculated which in most cases is in the order of thousands; although evolutionists would claim millions of years.

3. It is assumed that the system has remained closed. That is, no parent or daughter elements have entered or left the system during the calculated period.

Because of these assumptions involved in radiometric dating, it is inherently unreliable.

There are many examples, some of which are listed below, where radiometric dating has given the wrong dates for specimens of known historical age.[141]

---

[138] L. Loewe and S. Scherer, Mitochondrial Eve: the plot thickens, *Trends in Ecology and Evolution* 12, 1997, pages 422–423; A. Gibbons, Calibrating the mitochondrial clock, *Science*, 1998, 279(5347), pages 28–29.
[139] R. L. Dorit, H. Akashi and W. Gilbert, Absence of Polymorphism at the ZFY Locus on the Human Y-Chromosome, *Science,* 26 May 1995, 268, 5214, pages 1183–85; perspective in the same issue by S. Pääbo, cited in J. Sarfati, *Refuting Evolution,* Creation Book Distributors, 2002, page 89.
[140] Source: creation.com.noah-and-genetics, published May 11, 2010.
[141] Note: the last three examples involve sea creatures, and their incorrect dates are partly or wholly, due to the 'Reservoir Effect.' But this simply explains why the C-14 results are wrong. In fact, all radiometric dates which are

3 Is There Scientific Support for Biblical Creation?

- Rock from the lava dome at Mt St Helens, which was formed in 1986, was dated by the potassium-argon method as being 0.35 ± 0.05 million years old.[142]

- Rock from lava flows from Mt Ngauruhoe in New Zealand, which occurred in 1945, 1954 and 1975, was dated at 0.27 to 3.5 million years.[143]

- Wood buried in a basaltic lava flow was variously dated by carbon-14 to be 45,000 years old and by K-Ar to be 45 million years old.[144]

- Hawaiian lava flows from eruptions in 1800 and 1801 gave the following dates by the potassium/argon method: 1.41 and 1.60 million years[145] and up to 3 billion years.[146]

- Carbon-14 has a half-life of 5,730 years and consequently, after 57,300 years, that is, 10 half-lives, if no more C-14 is added to the system which is the case with dead plants and animals there would be virtually no C-14 remaining. Radiometric dating laboratories require a sample containing no C-14, for use as a blank. Such a sample cannot be found. Even in coal or diamonds, which are meant to be millions of years old, there are measurable amounts of C-14.[147]

- Fossil wood found in Upper Permian rock that is supposedly 250 million years old still contained C-14.[148]

- A dinosaur bone, supposedly 140 million years old, was sent to the University of Arizona for dating by the carbon-14 method. The tests were carried out on two samples and gave dates of 9,890 years and 16,120 years.[149]

- Shells from living molluscs were carbon-14 dated to 23,000 years.[150]

- A freshly killed seal was carbon-14 dated to 1,300 years.[151]

---

wrong have valid explanations, most of which are due to the flawed assumptions behind the method, as explained above. The existence of valid explanations does not change the fact that the method gives wrong answers.

[142] J. Sarfati, *Refuting Evolution,* Creation Book Distributors, 2002, page 111.
[143] *ibid.*
[144] A. Snelling, *Creation*, 1997, **20** (1), pages 24–27.
[145] S. Austin, *Creation Ex Nihilo Technical Journal*, 1996, **10** (3), 335–343; G. B. Darymple, *Earth and Planetary Sciences Letters*, 1969, **6**, pages 47–55.
[146] J. C. Funkhouser and J. J. Naughton, *Journal of Geophysical Research*, 1968, 73, pages 4601–4607.
[147] J. Sarfati, *Creation*, 2006, **28** (4), 26-27). See also page 71.
[148] A. Snelling, Stumping Old Age Dogma, *Creation*, 1998, **20** (4), pages 48–50; creation.com/stumping-old-age-dogma.
[149] Source: angelfire.com/mi/dinosaurs/carbondating.html, retrieved October 28, 2008.
[150] *Science,* 1963, **141**, pages 634–637.
[151] *Antarctic Journal*, 1971, **6**, page 211.

3 Is There Scientific Support for Biblical Creation?

- Shells from living snails were carbon-14 dated to 27,000 years.[152]

William Stanfield, Professor of Biological Sciences at California Polytechnic State University, an evolutionist and anti-creationist, concedes in his book:

It is obvious that radiometric techniques may not be the absolute dating methods they are claimed to be. Age estimates on a given geological stratum by different radiometric methods are quite often different, sometimes by hundreds of millions of years. There is no absolutely reliable long-term radiological clock.[153]

Ice Core Dating

The process of dating ice begins by extracting a cylindrical sample, obtained by boring very deep into the ice. The layers in the cross-section of ice are then counted. This process is similar to tree ring dating, with each ring or layer assumed to represent one year. The layering of ice is brought about by seasonal snow falls, different crystal sizes of the ice, dust and acids from volcanic eruptions, etc. The measurement of layers is performed not only by observation, but also by measuring acid content and the relative amounts of the isotopes of oxygen 16 and 18. For the most recent 500 years, the layering is quite distinct, but in older samples, the weight of ice compresses the layers and causes them to intermingle and become less distinct. Consequently, attempts to count layers formed more than 500 years ago become vastly less accurate.[154]

The joint European Ice Core Project (GRIP) of 1990–1992 took a 3,000-metre core, in segments, from the Greenland ice sheet. A report claims that layers equivalent to 110,000 years of ice history have been counted.[155]

On July 15, 1942, six P38 Lightning fighter planes and two B52 Flying Fortress bombers were forced to land on a large glacier in Greenland. Nine days later all crew were safely rescued by dogsled from their abandoned planes (see photo). The war ended and as the years went by, warplanes became rare and increased in value significantly. As a consequence, efforts were made to locate the planes. This proved successful in 1988, with the help of a sophisticated form of radar and an Icelandic geophysicist.

---

[152] *Science*, 1984, **224**, pages 58–61.
[153] W. Stanfield, *Science of Evolution,* MacMillan, 1977, pages 80–84.
[154] M. Oard, *Technical Journal*, 2001, **15** (3), pages 39–42.
[155] Meese at al, *Journal of Geophysical Research* 1997, **102** (C12), 26,411–26,423; cited by Michael Oard, *Technical Journal*, 2001, **125**(3), pages 39–42.

3 Is There Scientific Support for Biblical Creation?

Instead of dusting a meter or so of snow off the planes, refueling, and flying them back to the US, the team was amazed to find that they were buried 75 meters below the surface of the glacier. After much effort using specially developed ice-melting equipment, they finally reached the planes. The pressure of the ice had crushed the B52s beyond repair; however they managed to salvage one of the P38s.

A P38 seventy five meters below thesurface

Seventy five meters of ice had accumulated over the planes in 50 years. The planes could not have melted the ice underneath them causing them to sink through the snow. If they had sunk, they would have gone down nose first.[156]

By applying the ratio of 75 meters in 50 years, the 3,000 meters GRIP core gives a period of time of 2,000 years rather than the speculative 110,000 years stated earlier. Regardless of how convinced the scientists are regarding their dating method, nothing can beat a real situation to reveal the truth.

More Evidence for a Young Earth[157]

Dr Russell Humphreys was awarded his PhD in physics from Louisiana State University in 1972. He worked for the General Electric Company and then for Sandia National Laboratories in nuclear physics, geophysics, pulsed-powered research and theoretical atomic physics. He was the co-inventor of special laser triggered 'Rimfire' high-voltage switches. Dr Humphreys has published 20 papers in scientific journals, holds US patents and has received special awards for his scientific work. He was working for Creation Ministries International, but is now in semi-retirement. Below is his evidence:

Overview

Here are sixteen natural phenomena that conflict with the evolutionary idea that the universe is billions of years old. The numbers listed below in **bold print** (usually in the millions of years) are often **maximum possible** ages set by each process, using the evolutionist's own assumptions, not the actual ages. The numbers in *italics* are the age*s required by evolutionary theory* for each item. The point is that the maximum possible ages are always much less than the required evolutionary ages, while the biblical age (6,000 years) always fits comfortably within the maximum possible ages. Thus, the following items are evidence against the evolutionary time

---

[156] *Creation Magazine*, 2003, **26** (1), pages 20–21; 1997, **19** (4), page 29; 1997, **19**(3), pages 10–14.

[157] The following items of evidence for a young earth are taken from Dr Russell Humphreys' booklet, *Evidence for a Young World,* 2008. Permission to use this information has kindly been given by Creation Ministries International (creation.com).

scale and for the biblical time scale. Much more young-world evidence exists, but I have chosen these items for brevity and simplicity. Some of the items on this list can be reconciled with the old-age view only by making a series of improbable and unproven assumptions; others can fit in only with a recent creation.

1. Galaxies wind themselves up too fast

Whirlpool Galaxy (image courtesy of NASA)

The stars of our own galaxy, the Milky Way, rotate about the galactic center at different speeds, the inner ones rotating faster than the outer ones. The observed rotation speeds are so fast that if our galaxy was more than **a few hundred million years** old, it would be a featureless disc of stars instead of its present spiral shape.[158] Yet our galaxy is supposed to be at least *10 billion years* old. Evolutionists call this 'the winding-up dilemma,' which they have known about for fifty years. They have devised many theories to try to explain it, each one failing after a brief period of popularity. The same "winding-up" dilemma also applies to other galaxies. For the last few decades the favored attempt to resolve the puzzle has been a complex theory called 'density waves.'[149] The theory has conceptual problems, has to be arbitrarily and very finely tuned, and has been called into serious question by the Hubble Space Telescope's discovery of very detailed spiral structure in the central hub of the "Whirlpool" galaxy M51.[159]

2. Comets disintegrate too quickly

According to evolutionary theory, comets are supposed to be the same age as the solar system, *about five billion years*. Yet each time a comet, which is a "dirty iceberg", orbits close to the sun, it loses so much of its material that it could not survive much longer than about **100,000 years**. Many comets have typical ages of less than **10,000 years**.[160] Evolutionists explain this discrepancy for 'ong period' comets by postulating a spherical 'Oort cloud' well beyond the orbit of Pluto. This was supposed to resupply comets to the inner solar system when a passing star's gravity disturbed the cloud. However, there are many problems, including: (a) No

Comet Tempel 1, courtesy of NASA

---

[158] Scheffler, H. and Elsasser, H., *Physics of the Galaxy and Interstellar Matter*, Springer-Verlag, 1987, Berlin, pages 352–353, 401–413.

[159] D. Zaritsky, H-W. Rix, and M. Rieke, Inner spiral structure of the galaxy M51, *Nature,* **364**:313–315, July 22, 1993.

[160] Sarfati, J., Comets: Portents of doom or indicators of youth? *Creation* **25** (3):36–40, 2003; (creation.com/comets).

observational support;[161] (b) Collisions would have destroyed most comets, leaving a combined mass of comets of only about one Earth, or at most 3.5 Earths with some doubtful assumptions;[162,163] (c) The 'fading problem', whereby the models predict about 100 times more of these comets than are actually observed. So evolutionary astronomers postulate an 'arbitrary fading function',[164] so that the comets must disrupt before we get a chance to see them.[165] It seems desperate to propose an unobservable source to keep comets supplied for the alleged billions of years, then make excuses for why this hypothetical source doesn't feed in comets nearly as fast as it should.

More recently, a 'Kuiper Belt' beyond Neptune was postulated to resupply short-period comets. However, only about a thousand have been discovered, which is far short of the billions that would be needed to maintain the supply of comets.

Furthermore, the Kuiper Belt Objects (KBOs) discovered so far are much larger than comets. While the diameter of the nucleus of a typical comet is around 10 kilometers, the recently discovered KBOs are estimated to have diameters above 100 kilometers. For example, Quaoar has a diameter of 1,300 kilometers, and Sedna may be even larger, and even the former ninth planet Pluto (1,200-kilometer diameter) is sometimes regarded as a KBO. Note that a KBO with a diameter only ten times that of a comet has about 1,000 times the mass. So, in fact, there has been no discovery of actual *comets* in the region of the hypothetical Kuiper Belt, thus it is so far a non-answer.[166]

3. Not enough mud on the sea floor

Each year, water and winds erode about 20 billion tons of dirt and rock from the continents and deposit it in the ocean.[167] This material accumulates as loose sediment on the hard basaltic (lava-formed) rock of the ocean floor. The average depth of all the sediment in the whole ocean is less than 400 meters.[168] The main way known to remove the sediment from the ocean floor

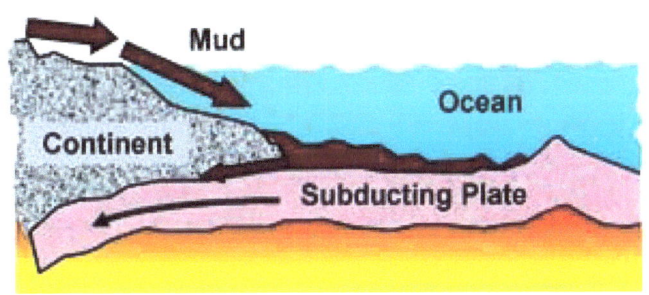

Rivers and dust storms dump mud into the sea much faster than plate tectonic subduction can remove it

---

[161] Sagon, C. and Druyan, A., *Comets*, Michael Joseph, London, p. 175, 1985.

[162] Stern, S. A. and Weissman, P. R., Rapid collisional evolution of comets during the formation of the Oort cloud, *Nature*, **409**(6820): 589–591, 2001.

[163] Faulkner, D., More problems for the 'Oort comet cloud', *J. Creation* (TJ) **15**(2):11, 2001; (creation.com/oort).

[164] Bailey, M. E., Where have all the comets gone? *Science*, **296**(5576):2251–2253, 2002, Perspective on Levison, Ref. 8.

[165] Levison, H. F. *et al.*, The mass disruption of Oort Cloud comets, *Science*, **296**(5576):2212–2215, 2002.

[166] Newton, R., The short-period comets 'problem' (for evolutionists): Have recent 'Kuiper Belt' discoveries solved the evolutionary/long-age dilemma? *J. Creation* (TJ) **16**(2):15–17, 2002.

[167] Milliman, John D. and James P. M. Syvitski, Geomorphic/tectonic control of sediment discharge to the ocean: the importance of small mountainous rivers, *The Journal of Geology*, vol. 100, pp. 525–544, 1992.

[168] Hay, W. W., *et al.*, Mass/age distribution and composition of sediments on the ocean floor and the global rate of sediment subduction, *Journal of Geophysical Research*, **93**(B12):14,933–14,940. 10 December 1988.

is by plate tectonic subduction. That is, sea floor slides slowly (a few centimeters per year) beneath the continents, taking some sediment with it. According to secular scientific literature, that process presently removes only 1 billion tons per year.[159] As far as anyone knows, the other 19 billion tons per year simply accumulate. At that rate, erosion would deposit the present mass of sediment in less than **12 million years**. Yet according to evolutionary theory, erosion and plate subduction have been going on as long as the oceans have existed, an alleged *three billion years*. If that were so, the rates above imply that the oceans would be massively choked with sediment dozens of kilometers deep. An alternative (creationist) explanation is that erosion from the waters of the Genesis flood running off the continents deposited the present amount of sediment within a short time about 5,000 years ago.

4. Not enough sodium in the sea

Every year, rivers[169] and other sources dump over 450 million tons of sodium into the ocean. Only 27 percent of this sodium manages to get back out of the sea each year.[170, 171] As far as anyone knows, the remainder simply accumulates in the ocean. If the sea had no sodium to start with, it would have accumulated its present amount in less than 42 million years at today's input and output rates.[162] This is much less than the evolutionary age of the ocean, *3 billion years*. The usual reply to this discrepancy is that past sodium inputs must have been less and outputs greater. However, calculations that are as generous as possible to evolutionary scenarios still give a maximum age of only **62 million years**.[162]

5. Many strata are too tightly bent

In many mountainous areas, strata thousands of feet thick are bent and folded into hairpin shapes. The conventional geologic time scale says these formations were deeply buried and solidified for *hundreds of millions of years* before they were bent. Yet the folding occurred without cracking, with radii so small that the entire formation had to be still wet and unsolidified when the bending occurred. This implies that the folding occurred **less than thousands of years** after deposition.[172]

---

[169] Meybeck, M., Concentrations des eaux fluviales en elements majeurs et apports en solution aux oceans, *Revue de Géologie Dynamique et de Géographie Physique* **21**(3):215, 1979.

[170] Sayles, F. L. and P. C. Mangelsdorf, Cation-exchange characteristics of Amazon River suspended sediment and its reaction with seawater, *Geochimica et Cosmochimica Acta* **43**:767–779, 1979.

[171] Austin, S. A. and. Humphreys, D. R., The sea's missing salt: a dilemma for evolutionists, *Proceedings of the Second International Conference on Creationism*, vol. II, Creation Science Fellowship (1991), Pittsburgh, PA, pp. 17–33, order from: icc03.org/proceedings.htm.

[172] Austin, S. A. and Morris, J. D., Tight folds and clastic dikes as evidence for rapid deposition and deformation of two very thick stratigraphic sequences, *Proceedings of the First International Conference on Creationism*, vol. II, Creation Science Fellowship (1986), Pittsburgh, PA, pp. 3–15, out of print, contact: icc03.org/proceedings.htm for help in locating copies.

3 Is There Scientific Support for Biblical Creation?

6. The earth's magnetic field is decaying too fast

The total energy stored in the earth's magnetic field ('dipole' and 'non-dipole') is decreasing with a half-life of 1,465 (± 165) years.[173] Evolutionary theories explaining this rapid decrease, as well as how the earth could have maintained its magnetic field for *billions of years*, are very complex and inadequate. A much better creationist theory exists. It is straightforward, based on sound physics, and explains many features of the field: its creation, rapid reversals during the Genesis flood, surface intensity decreases and increases until the time of Christ, and a steady decay since then.[174] This theory matches paleomagnetic, historic, and present data, most startlingly with evidence for rapid changes.[162] The main result is that the field's total energy (not surface intensity) has always decayed at least as fast as the present. At that rate the field could not be more than **20,000 years** old, but evolutionists say that the magnetic field is as old as their age for the earth (*4.7 billion years*).[175]

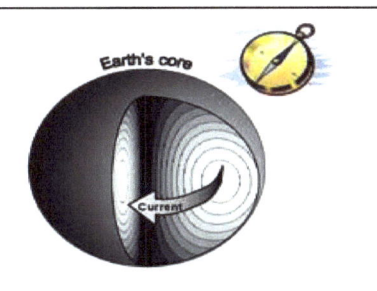

Electrical resistance in the earth's core wears down the electrical current, which produces the earth's magnetic field. That causes the field to lose energy rapidly.

7. Injected sandstone shortens geological 'ages'

Strong geological evidence[176] exists that the Cambrian Sawatch sandstone (formed an alleged 500 million years ago) of the Ute Pass fault, west of Colorado Springs, was still unsolidified when it was extruded up to the surface during the uplift of the Rocky Mountains (allegedly 70 million years ago). The hardened formations are called 'clastic dykes' or 'rockwalls', and are formed as a soft, plastic, slurry of particles is squeezed up through the overlying material. It is inconceivable that the sandstone would not solidify during the supposed *430 million years* it was underground. Instead, it is likely that the two geological events were **less than hundreds of years** apart, thus greatly shortening the geologic time scale.

8. Fossil radioactivity shortens geological 'ages' to a few years

Radiohalos are rings of color formed around microscopic bits of radioactive minerals in rock crystals. They are fossil evidence of radioactive decay.[177] 'Squashed' Polonium-210 radiohalos indicate that Jurassic, Triassic and

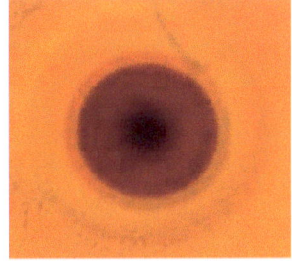

Radio halo (photocourtesy of Mark Armitage)

---

[173] Humphreys, D. R., The earth's magnetic field is still losing energy, *Creation Research Society Quarterly*, **39**(1):3–13, June 2002. creationresearch.org/crsq/articles/39/39_1/GeoMag.htm.

[174] Humphreys, D. R., Reversals of the earth's magnetic field during the Genesis flood, *Proceedings of the First International Conference on Creationism*, vol. II, Creation Science Fellowship, 1986, Pittsburgh, PA, pp. 113–126, out of print but contact: icc03.org/proceedings.htm for help in locating copies.

[175] Humphreys, D. R., Physical mechanism for reversals of the earth's magnetic field during the flood, *Proceedings of the Second International Conference on Creationism*, vol. II, Creation Science Fellowship, 1991, Pittsburgh, PA, pages 129–142, order from: icc03.org/proceedings.htm.

[176] Austin and Morris, ref. 18. pages 11–18.

[177] Gentry, R. V., Radioactive halos, *Annual Review of Nuclear Science* **23**:347–362, 1973.

Eocene formations in the Colorado plateau were deposited within months of one another, not *hundreds of millions of years* apart as required by the conventional time scale.[178] 'Orphan' Polonium-218 radiohalos, having no evidence of their mother elements, imply **accelerated nuclear decay** and very rapid formation of associated minerals.[179, 180]

Of course, if nuclear decay had been accelerated in the past that falsifies a key assumption of radiometric dating, that is, that the decay rate has been constant.

9. Helium in zircons has not had time to diffuse

The RATE (Radioisotopes and the Age of the Earth) project measured the amount of helium in zircons ($ZrSiO_4$ crystals) in graphite.[181, 182] The results show two things:

1. There must have been 1.5 billion years of decay *at current decay rates*.

2. Large amounts (up to 58 percent) of the helium are still there.

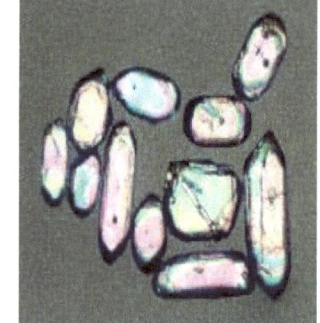

Zircon crystals (Photo by R V Gentry)

Helium comprises small, hard, slippery atoms that diffuse readily; that is why helium balloons quickly deflate. The new RATE experiments (confirmed by published data from other laboratories) show that helium diffuses so rapidly out of zircon that it should have all but disappeared after about 100,000 years. In fact, **the rate of helium leakage dates 'billion-year-old' zircons at 5680 ± 2,000 years.** Therefore, the decay that produced the helium must have occurred within that timeframe. But then how could so much helium have been produced and accumulated in so little time? The best answer seems to be an *episode of accelerated nuclear decay*, during Creation week or the Flood year, or more likely both.

10. Not enough Stone Age skeletons

Evolutionary anthropologists now say that the "stone age" lasted for at least *100,000 years*, during which time the world population of Neanderthal and Cro-Magnon men was roughly constant, between 1 and 10 million. All that time they were burying their dead, often with

---

[178] Gentry, R. V. *et al.*, Radiohalos in coalified wood: new evidence relating to time of uranium introduction and coalification, *Science* **194**:315–318, 1976; Taylor, S., McIntosh, A. and Walker, T., The collapse of 'geological time' : tiny halos in coalified wood tell a story that demolishes 'long ages', *Creation* **23**(4):30–34, 2001; (creationontheweb.com/radiohalo).

[179] Gentry, R. V., Radiohalos in a radiochronological and cosmological perspective, *Science***184**:62–66, 5 April 1974.

[180] Gentry, R. V., *Creation's Tiny Mystery*, Earth Science Associates, Knoxville, TN, 1986. Snelling, A. A. and Armitage, M. H., Radiohalos – a tale of three granitic plutons, *Proc. Fifth Int. Conf. On Creationism*, **22**: 243–267, 2003; Snelling, A., Radiohalos – significant and exciting research results, ICR *Impact***353**, 2002; icr.org/article/301, 11 April 2008.

[181] Humphreys, R., Nuclear decay: evidence for a young world, *Impact***352** 2002; icr.org/article/302, 11 April 2008.

[182] Humphreys, D. R., Austin, S. A., Baumgardner, J. R. and Snelling, A. A., Helium diffusion rates support accelerated nuclear decay; in: ed. Ivey, R. L., Jr., *Fifth Int. Conf. On Creationism,* pp. 175–196, 2003; icr.org/research/icc03/pdf/Helium_ICC_7-22-03. pdf, 11 April 2008.

artifacts. By that scenario, they would have buried at least 4 billion bodies.[183] If the evolutionary time scale is correct, buried bones should be able to last for much longer than 100,000 years, so many of the supposed 4 billion stone age skeletons should still be around (and certainly the buried artifacts). Yet only a few thousand have been found. This implies that the Stone Age was much shorter than evolutionists think, perhaps only **a few hundred years** in many areas.

11. History is too short

According to evolutionists, Stone Age man existed for *100,000 years* before beginning to make written records about **4,000 to 5,000 years** ago. Prehistoric man built megalithic monuments, made beautiful cave paintings, and kept records of lunar phases.[184] Why would he wait a thousand centuries before using the same skills to record history? The biblical time scale is much more plausible.[185]

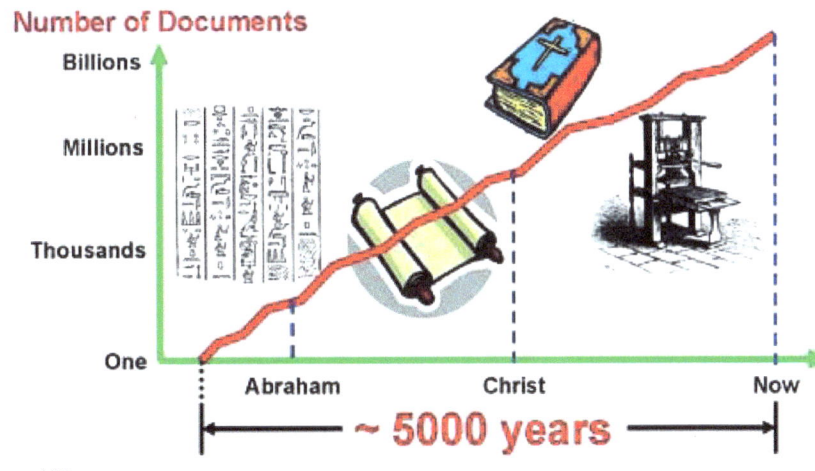

12. Agriculture is too recent

The usual evolutionary picture has mankind existing as hunters and gatherers for *100,000 years* during the Stone Age before discovering agriculture less than 10,000 years ago.[174] Yet the archaeological evidence shows that Stone Age men were as intelligent as we are. It is very improbable that none of the 4 billion people mentioned in item 10 should discover that plants grow from seeds. It is more likely that men were without agriculture for **less than a few hundred years** after the Flood, if at all.[176]

13. Ubiquitous carbon-14

Carbon-14 or radiocarbon (^{14}C) is used in a well-known dating method. Many have the impression that it "proves" millions of years, but this is impossible because it decays so fast. Its half-life ($t_{1/2}$) is only 5,730 years, that is, every 5,730 years; it has decayed to only half its initial amount. After two half lives, only a quarter is left; after three half lives, only an eighth; after 10 half lives, less than a thousandth is left.[186] In

---

[183] Deevey, E. S., The human population, *Scientific American*, **203**:194–204, 1960.

[184] Dritt, J. O., Man's earliest beginnings: discrepancies in the evolutionary timetable, *Proc. Second Int. Conf. On Creationism* **1**:73–78, 1990.

[185] Marshack, A., Exploring the mind of Ice Age man, *National Geographic* **147**:64–89, January 1975.

[186] The time t since radioactive decay commenced can be given by $N/N_0 = e^{-\lambda t}$, where N is the number of atoms measured in the present; N_0 is the initial number; λ, the decay constant, which is related to the half life $t_{1/2}$ by $\lambda = $ **ln2/$t_{1/2}$**. See also Sarfati, J., *Refuting Compromise*, ch. 12, Creation Book Publishers, 2004.

fact, a lump of ^{14}C as massive as the earth would have completely decayed in less than a million years.[187] So if samples were over a million years old, there should be no radiocarbon left.

The RATE research group[188] investigated ^{14}C in a number of samples of coal and diamond. A secular radiocarbon lab measured their ^{14}C content.[189] There should be no ^{14}C at all if the coal and diamonds really were hundreds of millions of years old as claimed, yet there was over 10 times the limit for detection. Thus they had radiocarbon 'ages' far less than a million years (indeed, **less than 100,000 years**). Evolutionists date diamonds at *over a billion years* old. Rather than constituting proof of billions of years, radiocarbon is powerful evidence against them!

14. Dinosaur blood vessels, cells and preserved heme

Dr Mary Schweitzer analysed T. rex bones under a microscope and described:

"Tiny round objects, translucent red with a dark center."

Then a colleague took one look at them and shouted:

"You've got red blood cells. You've got red blood cells!"[190]

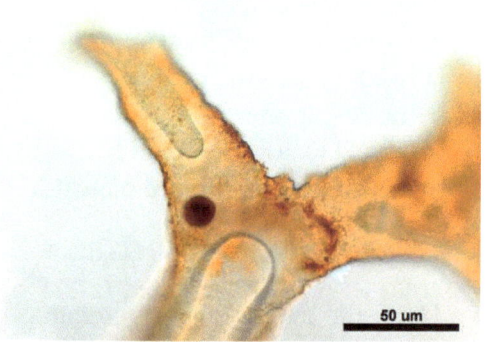

A T. rex red blood cell in vascular tissue

She even showed that there was enough of the hemoglobin fragments to produce an immune reaction in rats, and that the hemoglobin had the correct spectra.[191] Later, after dissolving the bone matrix, she discovered soft, fibrous tissue remaining, including blood vessels containing blood cells.

She first said to the lab technician:

"The bones are, after all, 65 million years old. How could blood cells survive that long?"[192]

Later she said:

---

[187] The earth's mass is 6×10^{27} g; equivalent to 4.3×10^{26} moles of ^{14}C. Each mole contains Avogadro's number ($N_A = 6.02 \times 10^{23}$) of atoms. It takes only 167 halvings to get down to a single atom ($\log_2(4.3 \times 10^{26}$ mol $\times 6.022 \times 10^{23}$ mol$^{-1}) = \log_{10}(2.58 \times 10^{50}) / \log_{10} 2$), and 167 half lives is well under a million years.
[188] Vardiman, L., Snelling, A. and Chaffin, E., *Radioisotopes and the age of the earth*, Vol. II, ch. 8, Institute for Creation Research, El Cajon, CA, 2005.
[189] Baumgardner J., ^{14}C evidence for a recent global flood and a young earth; in Ref. 31, ch. 8.
[190] Schweitzer, M. and Staedter, T., The real Jurassic Park, *Earth*, pp. 55–57, 1997.
[191] Schweitzer, M. *et al*, Heme compounds in dinosaur trabecular bone, PNAS **94**:6291–6296, 1997; pnas.org/cgi/reprint/94/12/6291, 11 April 2008.
[192] Schweitzer, M., Montana State University Museum of the Rockies; cited on p. 160 of Morell, V., Dino DNA: The hunt and hype, *Science* **261**(5118):160–162, 1993.

3. Is There Scientific Support for Biblical Creation?

"If you take a blood sample, and you stick it on a shelf, you have nothing recognisable in about a week. So why would there be anything left in a dinosaur?"

It is more scientific to go with the *observed* dinosaur blood and tissue and *observed* rates of decay, which suggest an age of **thousands of years** at the most, rather than the unobserved *millions of years* as Schweitzer does.[193]

15. DNA decays too fast

Natural radioactivity, mutations and decay degrade DNA and other biological material rapidly. Measurements of the mutation rate of mitochondrial DNA recently forced researchers to revise the age of "mitochondrial Eve" from a theorised *200,000 years* down to possibly as low as **6,000 years**.[194] DNA experts insist that DNA cannot exist in natural environments for longer than 10,000 years, yet intact strands of DNA appear to have been recovered from fossils allegedly much older, such as Neanderthal bones, insects in amber, and even from dinosaur fossils.[195] Bacteria allegedly *250 million years* old apparently have been revived with no DNA damage.[196]

16. Too few supernova remnants

According to astronomical observations, galaxies like our own experience about one supernova (an exploding star) every 25 years. The gas and dust remnants from such explosions (like the Crab Nebula) expand outward rapidly and should remain visible for over a million years. Yet the nearby parts of our galaxy in which we could observe such gas and dust shells contain only about 200 supernova remnants. That number is consistent with only about **7,000 years** worth of supernovas, *not millions of years.*[197]

Crab Nebula, Courtesy of NASA

---

[193] Catchpoole, D. and Sarfati, J., 'Schwietzer's Dangerous Discovery', (creationontheweb.com/schweit), 2006.

[194] Loewe, L. and Scherer, S., Mitochondrial Eve: The Plot Thickens, *Trends in Ecology and Evolution*, **12**(11):422–423, 1997: Gibbons, A., Calibrating the Mitochondrial Clock, *Science* **279**(5347):28–29, 1998; Wieland, C., A Shrinking Date for 'Eve', *J Creation* **12**(1):1–3, 1998; (creation.com/eve).

[195] Cherfas, J., Ancient DNA: still busy after death, *Science* **253**:1354–1356 (20 September 1991). Cano, R. J., H. N. Poinar, N. J. Pieniazek, A. Acra, and G. O. Poinar, Jr. Amplification and sequencing of DNA from a 120–135-million-year-old weevil, *Nature* **363**:536–8 (10 June 1993). Krings, M., A. Stone, R. W. Schmitz, H. Krainitzki, M. Stoneking, and S. Pääbo, Neandertal DNA sequences and the origin of modern humans, *Cell* **90**:19–30, Jul 11, 1997. Lindahl, T, Unlocking nature's ancient secrets, *Nature* **413**:358–359, 27 September 2001.

[196] Vreeland, R. H.,W. D. Rosenzweig, and D. W. Powers, Isolation of a 250 million-year-old halotolerant bacterium from a primary salt crystal, *Nature* **407**:897–900, 2000; (creationontheweb.com/saltysaga).

[197] Davies, K., Distribution of supernova remnants in the galaxy, *Proceedings of the Third International Conference on Creationism*, vol. II, Creation Science Fellowship (1994), Pittsburgh, PA, pp. 175–184, order from icc03.org/proceedings.htm.

Dr Humphreys confined himself to just sixteen measurable parameters and his work is included here because it is well researched and comprehensively referenced. However, there are many more examples.

Other parameters[198] include the rate at which the moon is receding from the earth, the presence of pressure in oil wells, the rate at which the sun is shrinking, the rate of accumulation of salts in the Dead Sea, the rate at which Niagara Falls is receding, rapid mountain uplift, the amount of helium and lead in zircons, Saturn's rings, Mercury's density and magnetic field and recently, active geysers that have been discovered on Enceladus, one of Saturn's moons.[199] Liquid water is consistent with a young Universe.[200] Dr Don Batten of Creation Ministries International cites 101evidences for a young earth.[201]

2. God Created Every Living Thing Complete and Functioning

The fact that God created every living thing complete and fully functioning enables all life to carry out His command to *be fruitful and multiply*.[202]

If the above statement concerning God doing the creating is true, then we should be able to see some evidence of design in what He has made. In fact, we see features of design around us all the time. Imagine, for example, if I told you that as I walked past a junkyard one day, there was an enormous explosion that threw bits of molten metal, plastic, leather and an assortment of other material into the air. And as I looked, I saw a watch condensing out of the plasma that the explosion created. When I picked it up, I found that it was not only running, but that it was also set to the right time. Anyone hearing me would rightly conclude that my story was too preposterous to believe. Yet this is what evolutionists maintain, only to a vastly more fanciful extent. The fact remains that the hallmarks of design are patently obvious, even to a casual observer.

Evidence of Design

There are numerous examples of design evident in all forms of life, such that the creature, body part or function could not possibly have come about by a series of small incremental changes. This is called 'irreducible complexity'.

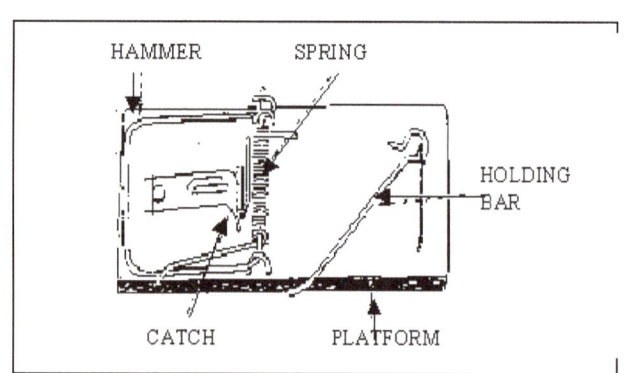

A good illustration of irreducible complexity is the mousetrap. It consists of five pieces; platform, hammer, spring, catch and holding

---

[198] For even more information on a young earth, the reader is directed to: creation.com/search and insert 'young earth'.
[199] *New Scientist*, August 23, 2008, page 7.
[200] *Creation*, 2008, **31** (1), page 8.
[201] Don Batten, 101 Evidences for a Young Age of the Earth and the Universe, creation.com/age-of-the-earth, June 4, 2009.
[202] Genesis 1:22.

3 Is There Scientific Support for Biblical Creation?

bar. Each piece is essential for the whole to function. Without any of these pieces the trap would not work. All must be present at the same time. It could not have evolved.

There are many examples of design in biological systems that incorporate irreducible complexity. That is, a function cannot be reduced further and still work. All components must be present at the same time. Three examples have been selected for closer analysis.

1. The Bombardier Beetle.

This tiny beetle defends itself from attacking predators by firing an explosive mixture at 100° C into the face of its attacker. This defence mechanism is brought about by the beetle storing a mixture of hydrogen peroxide and hydroquinone in a pouch in its rear end. There is also an inhibitor to stop the two chemicals from reacting with each other. At the moment of danger, the creature sends the mixture into a reaction chamber where not only is the inhibitor removed, but simultaneously two catalysts are added and the oxygen, which is released from the hydrogen peroxide, reacts explosively with the hydroquinone. The hot mixture is then fired under pressure out of twin tubes extending from the beetle's rear.

Common sense tells us that, this little insect cannon, which can fire four or five bombs in succession, could not have evolved piece by piece. Explosive chemicals, inhibitor, enzymes, glands, combustion tubes, sensory communications, muscles to direct the combustion tubes and reflex nervous systems—all had to work perfectly the very first time, or all hopes for the existence of the beetle and its children would have exploded.

2. The Angler Fish.

This is an ugly looking fish with the female of the species having a long filament protruding from the middle of its head with a fleshy growth (esca) on the end—hence the name. When an inquisitive fish approaches the fleshy growth, it is immediately seized by the creature as its enormous jaws are triggered in automatic reflex by contact with its tentacle. Both jaws are equipped with rows of long pointed teeth facing inwards so a fish may move into the mouth relatively unimpeded. However, the return journey is a lot more difficult. Anglerfish are found throughout the world's oceans. Some of the more than 200 species grow to one meter (three feet), while most are about 300 mm (one foot) in length.

The deep-sea variety has a population of light-emitting bacteria (*Photobacterium luciferum*) colonising the esca. The bacteria give the esca a soft glow in the darkness of the deep ocean and the fish wiggles this 'lure' to attract curious prey. Reproduction for these fish in the total absence of light could be quite difficult and the way that it happens is most unusual. At birth, males are equipped with extremely well developed olfactory organs that can detect faint scents in the water. When the male anglerfish is mature, its digestive system degenerates, making it incapable of feeding independently, which necessitates it quickly finding a female anglerfish. When he finds a female by following the scent (pheromone) she gives off, he bites into her skin and simultaneously releases an enzyme that digests the skin of his mouth and her body, thereby fusing the pair down to the blood-vessel level. The male, which is considerably smaller that the female, then decomposes into nothing more than a pair of gonads (testes), which remain appended to the side of the female. When her eggs are ready to be fertilised, the testes release sperm in response to hormones in the female's bloodstream. This extreme sexual dimorphism ensures that when the female is ready to spawn, sperm is readily available.[203]

Male anglerfish attached to a female

This form of propagation is very difficult, or more to the point, impossible, to explain from an evolutionary viewpoint, which holds that mutations,[204] which are corruptions of the DNA (genes), bring about every function and characteristic an animal has by a series of small changes. Each change has to be beneficial to the creature or else it would be eliminated by natural selection. How, then, could a progression of changes turn off the male's digestive system such that he has to, in total darkness, find and then sink his teeth into a female? And then, for an enzyme to be released that is specifically designed to dissolve her skin and the flesh of his mouth, so that their blood systems join? And then, for the rest of the male's body to rot away leaving only its testes, which do not rot, but remain ready to receive a hormone from the female, and once received, release the sperm contained in them, to fertilise her eggs? The obvious conclusion is that the whole system was designed by a Master Designer.

3. The Human Eye

The human eye is extremely complicated—a perfect and interrelated system of about 40 individual subsystems, including the retina, pupil, iris, cornea, lens and optic nerve. For instance, the retina has approximately 137 million special cells that respond to light and send messages to the brain. About 130 million of these cells look like rods and handle the black and white vision. The other seven million are cone-shaped and allow us to see in color. The retina cells receive

---

[203] Source: wikipedia.org/wiki/Anglerfish, retrieved 8 April, 2011.
[204] See page 46.

3 Is There Scientific Support for Biblical Creation?

light impressions, which are converted to electric pulses and sent to the brain via the optic nerve. A special section of the brain, called the visual cortex transforms the pulses to color, contrast, depth, etc., which allows us to see 'pictures' of our world in three dimensions. Amazingly, the eye, the optic nerve and the brain's visual cortex are totally separate and distinct subsystems. Yet, together they capture, deliver and interpret up to 1.5 million pulse messages every millisecond (one thousandth of a second)!

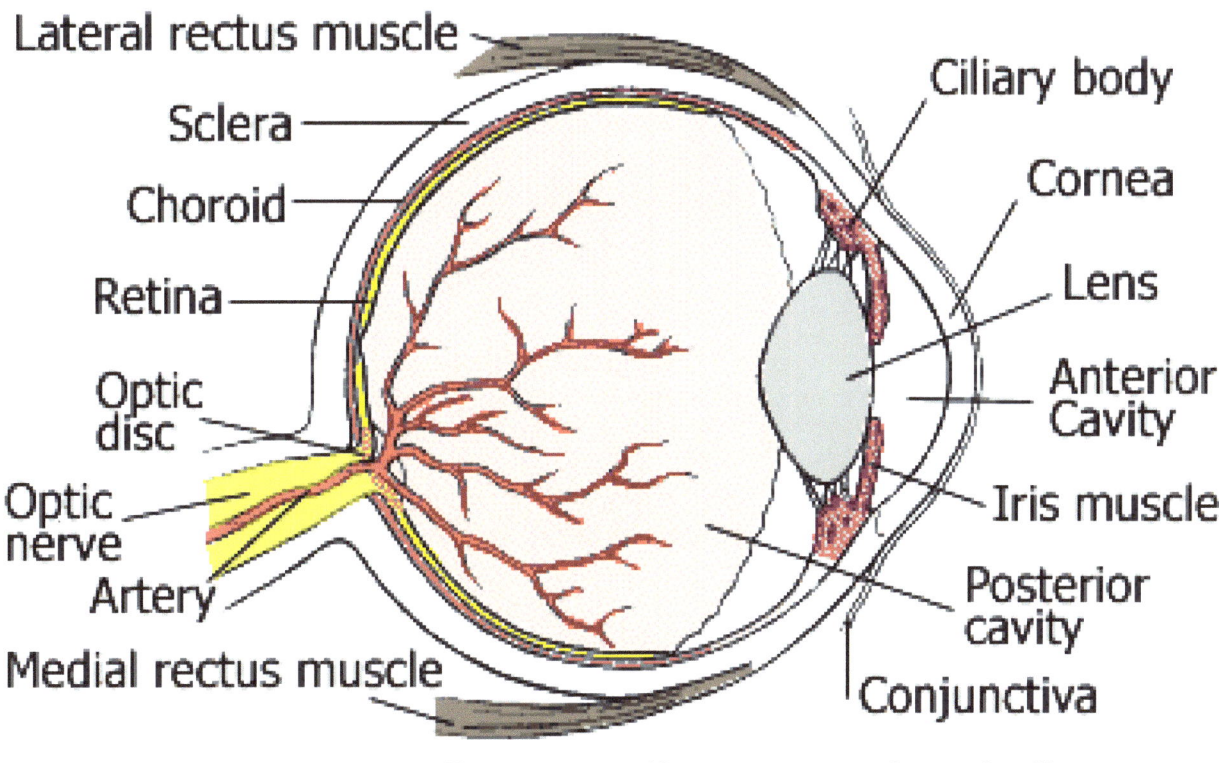

Transverse (horizontal) section of eyeball

Another aspect of the eye, (one that Darwin would not have known about), which adds to its almost incomprehensible complexity, is a group of tiny eye movements. There are three nearly imperceptible motions of the eye referred to as 'tremors', 'drifts' and 'saccades'. Tremors continuously and rapidly wobble the eyeball about its center in a circular fashion. The diameter of the circle around which the eye moves is a minute one thousandth of a millimeter (0.00004 inch). The wobble this movement produces happens 30 to 70 times per second, which on average results in one million circular motions every 5½ hours. Without such eye tremors, vision would not be clear.

When focused on a target, the eye drifts relatively slowly and smoothly away until it reaches an angle equal to about 12 times the size of a tremor, at which time it suddenly jerks back to its original position. This quick jerking back is by way of a saccade. There can be several saccades every second. These three imperceptible eye movements prevent the light-sensing cells in the retina from becoming 'stabilised'; a condition that would prevent them from sending updated information to the brain. A lack of fresh information would cause the image the brain perceives to become a uniform grey.[205]

Militant atheist Professor Richard Dawkins claims that the 'fact' that our eyes are wired backwards disproves the idea that the eye is an example of good design.[206] This assertion is based on the fact that the nerves which carry information from the retina to the brain actually go across the retina, thereby obscuring some of the incoming light and creating a blind spot when they go back through it to the brain. However, *the idea that the eye is wired backward comes from a lack of knowledge of eye function and anatomy*, says ophthalmologist Dr George Marshall. In fact, the eye would not function if this forest of connecting bundles of nerves came from the back of the retina.[207] Recently, in a major blow to the proponents of 'backward wiring', Israeli scientists have shown that this structure of the vertebrate eye actually improves vision because the nerve net contains cells (Müller cells) which act as optical fibers that help filter and focus light, making images clearer and keeping the colors sharp.[208] Kate McAlpine, author of the *New Scientist* article, states:

It looks wrong, but the strange, 'backwards' structure of the vertebrate retina actually improves vision.

So the eye is an excellent example of design, after all.

To suppose that the eye with all its inimitable contrivances for adjusting the focus to different distances, for admitting different amounts of light, for the correction of spherical and chromatic aberration, could have formed by natural selection seems, I freely confess, absurd in the highest degree.[209]

Darwin posed this statement rhetorically and then attempted to explain how the eye could have evolved through natural selection. But as explained on page 48, natural selection can only select from what is present already; it cannot create a new biological pathway, a new system of enzymes, or new genes, it can only concentrate traits that are present in the living species. Darwin's original statement was true then as it is now.

If it could be demonstrated that any complex organ existed which could not possibly have been formed by numerous, successive, slight modifications, my theory would absolutely break down. But I can find no such case.[210]

Darwin may not have, or did not want to, but many other people have. Dr Jonathan Sarfati discusses many more amazing examples of irreducible complexity in his book *By Design*, under the subheading: Evidence for nature's Intelligent Designer—the God of the Bible.[211]

---

[205] T. Wagner, *Creation*, September 1994, **16** (4), pages 10-13.
[206] R. Dawkins, *The Blind Watchmaker*, Norton and Company, 1986, pages 93-94.
[207] J. Sarfati, *Fibre optics in eye demolish atheistic 'bad design' argument*, creation.com, 2007.
[208] *New Scientist*, May 8, 2010, page 12.
[209] C. Darwin, *The Origin of Species*, Senate, London, sixth edition, 1872, page. 143
[210] C. Darwin, *The Origin of Species*, New York University Press, sixth edition, 1988, page 154
[211] Available from Creation Ministries International (creation.com).

3. Every Creature Was Made to Reproduce After its Kind

This is so obvious that it hardly needs to be stated. We witness it all of the time. The seeds of a pumpkin will grow into a pumpkin; a rabbit gives birth to rabbits.

The cells which form a carrot or form the liver of a mouse consistently retain their respective tissue and organism identities after countless cycles of reproduction.[212]

Genetically inherited characteristics

The man who has became known as the 'Father of genetics' and who formulated the laws of heredity based on his work with plants is Augustinian priest Gregor Johann Mendel. He lived from 1822 to 1884, making him a contemporary of Charles Darwin. As will become clear, his discovery conflicted with Darwin's hypothesis and seems to have been shelved in the scientific rush to embrace evolution.

He was inspired by both his professors at university and his colleagues at the monastery to study variation in plants, and he conducted his study in the monastery's garden. Between 1856 and 1863 Mendel cultivated and tested some 29,000 pea plants.

Initially, Mendel wondered what color the flowers of a sweet pea would be if he crossed a pure red flowering pea with a pure white one. So he did and found that all of the progeny's flowers were red. Many people would have thought "well that's nice—if I cross red with white then red flowers are produced." But Mendel undertook an additional, crucial experiment which turned out to be very revealing. He crossed the red flowers that were produced from the first crossing with each other, and this time he produced a mixture of red and white flowers in the ratio of three red to one white.

He repeated the crossing experiment and looked at six other traits that can be easily recognized and they followed the same pattern.

This observation that there are traits that do not show up in offspring plants as intermediate forms was critically important. The leading theory in biology at the time was that inherited traits were acquired from generation to generation. Mendel picked common garden pea plants for the focus of his research. Garden peas can be grown easily in large numbers and their reproduction can be manipulated. Pea plants have both male and female reproductive organs. As a result, they can either self-pollinate or cross-pollinate with another plant. In his experiments, Mendel was able to selectively cross-pollinate purebred plants with particular traits and observe the outcome over many generations. The ratio of 3:1 occurs in later generations as well and is the key to understanding the basic mechanisms of inheritance.

He came to three important conclusions from these experiments:

---

[212] P. C. Hanawalt, Simple Inorganic Molecules to Complex Free-living Cell, *Molecules to Living Cells,* W H Freeman, San Francisco, 1980 , page 3.

- The inheritance of each trait is determined by 'units' or 'factors' (now called genes) that are passed on to descendants unchanged.

- An individual inherits one such unit from each parent for each trait.

- A trait may not show up in an individual but it can still be passed on to the next generation.[213]

Mendel published his groundbreaking discoveries in 1866 in the *Journal of the Brno Natural*

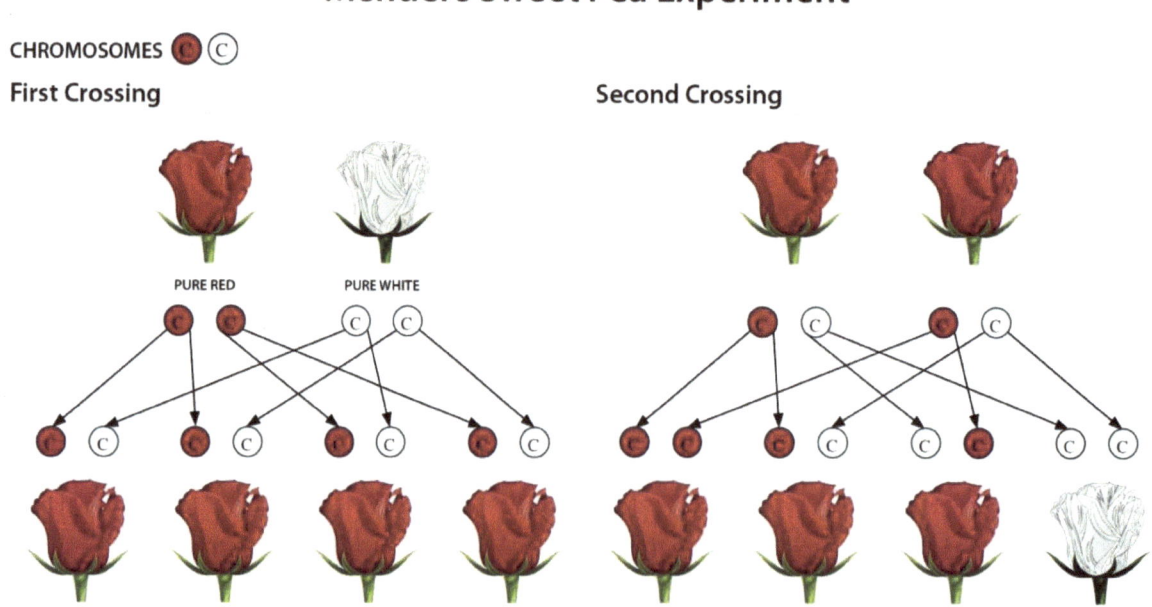

History Society. However, it was completely ignored by the scientific community and when Mendel died in 1884, he had no idea that his work would be rediscovered in 1900 and its importance understood.

Why was such an important discovery ignored? Darwin had published his *Origin of Species* in 1859 and this was embraced because it was consistent with the prevailing modernist mindset

---

[213] With all of the seven pea plant traits that Mendel examined, one form appeared dominant over the other. That is, one trait is dominant and the other recessive. So in his first pea experiment, the gene for red flowers is dominant over the gene for white flowers. Therefore, in the first crossing, each of the hybrids possessed one gene for red flowers and one gene for white flowers. With red being dominant over white, all hybrid plants had red flowers even though they possessed genes for both colors. The experiment is set out schematically above. Now when he crossed these plants, one plant will receive say a red flower gene from its first parent and a red flower gene from its second parent resulting in red flowers in the progeny. Another progeny will receive a red flower gene from its first parent and a white flower gene from its second parent. Result: red flowers. In another progeny, a plant will receive a white flower gene from its first parent and a red flower gene from its second parent. Result; red flowers. The final combination is for a plant to receive a white flower gene from its first parent and a white flower gene from its second parent. Result: white flowers. What actually happens is that each plant donates a complete set of chromosomes and the gene which gives the plant its color is on one of the chromosomes.

3 Is There Scientific Support for Biblical Creation?

which sought to explain the existence of life without God. Darwin's theory was based on species acquiring characteristics which were passed on to their progeny; whereas Mendel showed that species could only pass on characteristics that were already present in their genes. If there was not a gene for a particular trait, then that trait would not appear in the progeny and of course, it could not be passed on. Mendel demonstrated the veracity of his claims through experimentation, while Darwin's views were mere speculation. Darwin reasoned that prodeny could acquire characteristics through the environment which the creature experiences as it lives. Mutations which have been discussed on page 46 were proposed after Darwin, as a means for living entities to acquire new genetic information. However, it has been shown (pages 46 and 47) that mutations are not likely to produce new structures or even new biological pathways in creatures.

The Environment

This refers to all of the external factors which impact upon a creature during its lifetime. Using human beings as an example, suppose that a white skinned girl and a white skinned man lie in the sun for a long time because they want to have brown skin, and they stay that way for most of their life. If they were to conceive a child while they were brown, (hopefully they follows God's directive[214] and marry first) would their child have white or brown skin? The obvious answer is that their child will have white skin because that is what the child's parent's genes dictate, regardless of their environment. In another example; say a man lost one of his fingers through an accident with a power saw before marrying and having children; would his children be born with one finger missing? The answer again is clearly no, because his genes dictate that he has five fingers on each hand. Thus, it is not the environment that people experience which determines what their off-spring will be like, but rather, their genes and this fact is at odds with Darwinism.

Darwin's theory was eagerly embraced by an atheistic totalitarian regime of last century, which gave rise to a stark illustration of the impact of faulty science. Trofim Lysenko became director of the Institute of Genetics within the USSR's Academy of Sciences in 1934. He held to the Darwinian idea of 'acquired characteristics' and with the support of the Communist party, anyone who did not agree with Lysenko's theories was purged from office and many such people were imprisoned. As a consequence, advancement in genetics within the Soviet Union was severely retarded until 1964 when Mendelian genetics was re-instituted.

Charles Darwin based his ideas on the fallacy that environmentally-caused variations are passed on. He thus explained the origin of the giraffe's long neck:

Those individuals, who had some one part or several parts of their bodies rather more elongated than usual, would generally have survived. These will have intercrossed and left offspring, either inheriting the same bodily peculiarities, or with a tendency to vary again in the same manner; whilst the individuals, less favored in the same respects will have been the most liable to perish.... By this process long-continued, which exactly corresponds with what I have called

---

[214] Genesis 2:24, 4:1.

3 Is There Scientific Support for Biblical Creation?

*unconscious selection by man, combined no doubt in a most important manner with the **inherited effects of the increased use of parts**, it seems to me almost certain that an ordinary hoofed quadruped might be converted into a giraffe.*[215]

Darwin's view that giraffes evolved from some horse-like animal that continually stretched its neck to reach leaves on tall trees is false.

Giraffes are an excellent example of an animal possessing specific design features. For example, in order to get blood all the way up its neck to its head, the giraffe has one of the most powerful hearts in the animal kingdom, with double the normal blood pressure. But what happens when the animal lowers its head to drink? With its powerful heart not having to pump against gravity but rather having gravity on its side now, the rush of blood to the giraffe's brain would render it unconscious. Fortunately, the giraffe has at least three design features that make drinking quite easy. One is that they splay their front legs, thereby lowering their heart so that the difference between heart and head is not as great. Second, giraffes have a series of one-way check valves in their neck, which prevent a rush of blood when the head is lowered. And the third design feature of giraffes is the 'wonder net'; a spongy tissue filled with numerous small blood vessels located near the base of the brain. The arterial blood first flows through this net of vessels before it reaches the brain. So when the giraffe finishes its drink, it stands up, the check valves open, the effects of the wonder net and the various counter pressure mechanisms relax and all is well.

Even at the time of writing, evolutionists still cannot agree on a mechanism by which the giraffe evolved its long neck.[216]

In summary, Mendel showed through experimentation that offspring can only receive what is in their parents' genes. If the species does not possess the genes for feathers, the progeny will not have feathers. If the species does not have the genes for gills, the progeny will not have gills. Yet Darwin's theory requires that species gain traits from environmental effects and some other source of genetic novelty such as mutations in order to change into something else. Having said that, it needs to be made clear that there is a wide amount of genetic variation within species, as

---

[215] C. Darwin, *The Origin of Species,* Senate, London, sixth edition, 1872, page 177.
[216] Source: *New Scientist* web site; Zoologger: How did the giraffe get its long neck? By Michael Marshall, July 7, 2010.

evidenced by the great variety of dogs which originally came from the wolf type, but this occurs as the result of gene shuffling as species breed. Dogs have always been dogs and will remain dogs. There is a limit to how far these variations can go. For example, when breeders tried to increase the amount of sugar in sugar beet, they were able to increase it from 6 percent to 17 percent and no further, because at that point, they had concentrated all of the genes for sugar production into one species.

Thus Gregor Mendel showed that what the Bible stated is true, in that every creature was made to reproduce after its kind.

4. Adam and Eve Were Created in the Image of God

The first chapter of the book of Genesis tells us that man stands unique and is the pinnacle of God's creative work, for he was made in the image of God. Verses 26 and 27 state:

Then God said, "Let Us [The triune God; Father, Son and Holy Spirit] *make man in Our image, according to Our likeness; let them have dominion over the fish of the sea, over the birds of the air, and over the cattle, over all the earth and over every creeping thing that creeps on the earth." So God created man in His own image; in the image of God He created him; male and female He created them.*[217]

Michelangelo tried to capture the creation of Adam by God in his master painting. But of course, he falls a long way short, for it is not possible to paint something that is far beyond human comprehension. However, Michelangelo does convey something of the close and loving relationship God has with man. Yet evolutionists tell us that mankind was not created separate and unique, but rather, descended from primates.

So what evidence is there for this progression through a series of apemen? When the evidence is examined, we find that it derives mostly from the imagination and skill of the artist, and not from any archaeological evidence of the paleoanthropologist. All of the so-called 'Apemen' finds that has been made, regardless of all of the columns of newsprint published, fall loosely, into one of three categories: human beings, apes or fakes. Consider the following:

Neanderthals. Human-like bones were first found in a cave in the Neander Valley in Germany in 1856, hence the name. Later discoveries showed Neanderthals were big, strong, had large brains, and had distinct facial features that were characterised by a receding chin and forehead, and prominent brow ridges. They buried their dead and wore jewellery. In 1908 a Neanderthal-like skeleton was found in Poland wearing a suit of armor, it may have been that of a man who

---

[217] Genesis 1:26-27.

lived in the middle ages and possessed Neanderthal-like features which supports the next point.[218] Neanderthals were clearly human and their bone deformities may have been a result of severe rickets.

Scientists have been able to isolate mitochondrial DNA, sourced from Neanderthal bones that were found in a cave in Croatia, and use it to construct the Neanderthal genome. From this research they came to the following conclusions, as reported in *New Scientist*:

Extrapolating from the available sequences, the team estimate that Neanderthals and modern humans are almost as closely related as any two living humans: you might share 99.9 % of your DNA with a randomly selected human and 99.8 % with a Neanderthal.[219]

Recent research has shown that the human Y chromosome (which is possessed and passed on only by males) is significantly different from that of chimpanzees.[220]

Cro-Magnon Man. These skeletons were discovered in 1868 in the Cro-Magnon cave in the south of France. They were six feet tall, had large brains, and buried their dead with necklaces and tools. They believed in community support and took care of each other's injuries. They definitely human.[221]

Java Man. Found by Eugene Dubois in 1891, when one of his laborers found a skull cap along the Solo River, Java. A year later he found a femur 50 feet (26 meters) away from where the skull cap was found. Dispute still continues as to whether the two bones are from the same species. The femur is clearly human.

Piltdown Man. A skull was found in a mine in England in 1912. It fooled the scientific community for 50 years, until 1953, when Weiner and Oakley showed it to be a hoax. Someone had combined an ape jaw with a human skull, filed the teeth and stained them to give the appearance of a matching set.

Nebraska Man. In 1922 Dr Henry Osborn received a fossil human-like tooth that had been found in Nebraska. Evolutionists used the one tooth to build an entire species of primitive man, complete with illustrations of him and his family (see drawing). Further excavations revealed the tooth to belong to a pig.

This illustration appeared in the *Illustrated London News* in 1922

---

[218] Neanderthal in Armor, *Nature*, April 23, 1908, page 587.

[219] R. Green and S. Pääbo, *Science*, **328**, page 710; cited by Robert Adler, *New Scientist*, December 4, 2010, pages 32-36.

[220] J. F. Hughes *et al.*, Chimpanzee and human Y chromosome are remarkably divergent in structure and gene content, *Nature* 2010, 463, 536-539; cited by R. W. Carter at creation.com/chimp-y-chromosome.

[221] Source: Wikipedia.org/wiki/Cro-Magnon, retrieved November 1, 2008.

3 Is There Scientific Support for Biblical Creation?

Peking Man. A group of fossil specimens were found in 1923–27 during excavations at Zhoukoudian near Beijing. They mainly consisted of teeth and skull parts, which appeared to have been widened, as if to remove the brains. There were many animal bones present and others that were clearly human but no intermediate species. It was most likely a rubbish tip.

Australopithecus. According to evolutionists, the supposed ancestor to humans was a small, slenderly-built primate termed Australopithecus. There has been debate amongst them about this species, of which Lucy (A. afarensis) is a member. Anatomist Professor Charles Oxnard, after a detailed study, concluded that Australopithecines were not bipedal, but rather had a unique rolling form of locomotion, more like that of today's apes than of human beings.[222] Oxnard and his team (all evolutionists) concluded that this whole group was further removed from apes and human beings than the two were from each other, and were not anatomically intermediate. In short, they were a unique, extinct group of non-human primates that would have looked, if anything much more like apes than human beings, and had nothing to do with man's ancestry.

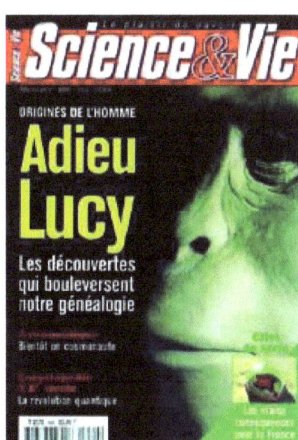

American anthropologist Holly Smith concluded, after completing a study of its teeth, that Australopithecus was an ape.[223] And finally, to conclude the matter, a French science journal,[224] under the headline 'Farewell Lucy' stated that Australopithecus could not be considered as the ancestor of man.

Hobbit. In a blaze of euphoria, *Nature* announced that *Homo floresiensis* was a new hominid species. These fossils of so-called apemen were only about 1 meter (3 feet) tall and had a relatively small brain; they were named 'Hobbit' after J. R. Tolkien's diminutive fictional character. They were found on the island of Palau about 1,600 km (1,000 ml) north of Indonesia. However, after the publicity subsided, it emerged that they may have been a pygmy race of humans:[225]

The skeleton is not a new species as claimed by these scientists, but simply a fossil of modern humans who lived 1,300–1,800 years ago.[226]

The plot thickened with this newspaper report:

"The Hobbit, the tiny human fossil found in a cave on an Indonesian island in 2003 and claimed as a new species, was a modern human, whose teeth had been worked on by a dentist, possibly in the 1930," according to a scientist whose new book is set to inflame debate, University of

---

[222] The place of Australopithecines in Human Evolution: Grounds for Doubt, *Nature*, **258**, page 389.
[223] *American Journal of Physical Anthropology*, 1994, **94**, pages 307–325.
[224] *Science et Vie*, February 1999.
[225] *Nature,* October 2004.
[226] Dr Teuku Jacob, *Jakarta Post*, November 8, 2004.

Adelaide Professor of Biological Anthropology and Comparative Anatomy Maciej Henneberg says in his new book.[227]

The weight of evidence is now strengthening the position that *Homo floresiensis* were pygmies—and pygmies were known to the area. Their relatively small brain is due to a pathological condition known as microcephaly in which the brain fails to grow. Such a condition has been found in other pygmies.[228]

Bernard Wood, Professor of Human Origins at George Washington University, and an evolutionist, wrote the following:

There is a popular image of human evolution that you'll find all over the place, from the backs of cereal packets to advertisements for expensive scientific equipment. On the left of the picture there's an ape—stocky, jutting jaw, hunched in the knuckle-walking position. On the right, a man—graceful, high forehead, striding purposefully into the future. Between the two is a succession of figures that become ever more like humans, as the shoulders start to pull back, the torso slims down, the arms retract, the legs extend, the cranium expands and the chin recedes. Our progress from ape to human looks so smooth, so tidy. It's such a beguiling image that even the experts are loath to let it go. But it is an illusion.[229]

Dr. Lyall Watson, anthropologist and evolutionist, made the following statement:

Modern apes, for instance, seem to have sprung out of nowhere. They have no yesterday, no fossil record. And the true origin of modern humans—of upright, naked, tool-making, big-brained beings—is, if we are to be honest with ourselves, an equally mysterious matter.[230]

And finally, a statement by anthropologist and atheist, Dr James Shreeve which he made in an article he wrote for *Discovery*:

Everybody knows fossils are fickle; bones will sing any song you want to hear.[231, 232]

What are the characteristics that set mankind apart from animals?

There are several characteristics that we human beings have that set us apart from the animals.[233] Our faculties are vastly superior to anything found in animals. They are not necessary for survival and reproduction and cannot be accounted for by evolution, but they are an integral part of our makeup, allowing us to have a relationship with God. Some are mentioned below.

---

[227] *The Australian,* April 19, 2008.
[228] Peter Line, *Journal of Creation*, 2006, **20** (3), pages 17-24.
[229] *New Scientist*, October 26, 2002.
[230] The Water People, *Science Digest*, vol. 90, May 1982, page 44.
[231] J. Shreeve, Argument Over Woman, *Discover*, 1990, **11** (2), page 58.
[232] For many more quotations from scientists working in the field on the total lack of hard evidence for monkeys-to-man evolution, the reader is directed to: creationwiki.org/Paleoanthrology_quotes, retrieved November 2, 2008.
[233] *New Scientist* produced a Special Issue covering eighteen pages on: What makes humans so special; *New Scientist*, March 16, 2013, pages 32-49.

3   Is There Scientific Support for Biblical Creation?

Creativity. No species of animal, including the apes, is able to create, understand and visualize as human beings do. The human hand, which largely allows mankind to create, is unique. It has been described as one of the most precise and wonderful mechanical devices in creation.

Self-awareness. The seventeenth century French philosopher René Descartes'[234] immortal phrase, *I think, therefore I am*, is the quintessential statement of our own self-awareness.

Consciousness. Human consciousness is a mystery that has evaded decades of intensive research by neurophysiologists. According to an article in *New Scientist*,[235] quoting from a book written by Nicholas Humphrey:

… worst, running the sort of super-heated consciousness humans possess is almost certainly costly in energy terms, thus raising questions of how it could have possibly evolved?

Expression. People have an amazing variety of ways of conveying information. Only mankind possesses the ability of speech. And only human beings have an array of about 40 facial muscles that can convey a multitude of emotions such as anger, empathy, sorrow, pride, love, relief, joy, jealousy, happiness, concern, hostility, shame, serenity, pain, tiredness, grief, suspicion, belief, unbelief, guilt, etc.

Language. The most obvious way in which mankind is set apart from animals is our ability to learn and use language. We can describe objects, situations and feelings, and we can discuss hypothetical matters, all because of the way our brains have been wired and our bodies constructed with tongue and voice box.

Mathematical Skills. Human beings have the ability to construct complex equations involving algebra, trigonometry and calculus to calculate velocity, thrust, acceleration, pressure, stress, strain, angles, angular momentum, work, forces etc.

Aesthetic Dimension. Human beings can assess the relative qualities of form, texture, color, order and design. For example, we can appreciate the intricate sewing on a wedding dress or the detail and skill imparted into a painting, or a finely crafted piece of furniture.

Abstract Thinking. After performing many experiments with chimpanzees, Dr Povinelli of the University of Louisiana made this statement:

Humans constantly invoke unobservable phenomena and variables to explain why certain things are happening. Chimps operate in a world of concrete, tangible things that can be seen. The content of their minds is about the observable world.[236]

Spirit and Soul. The spirit can be described as the set of characteristics that make up the advanced brain, including mind and emotion. Only birds and mammals exhibit these traits,

---

[234] 1596–1650.
[235] *New Scientist*, June 24, 2006, page 58.
[236] D. J. Povinelli, "Animal Self-Awareness: A Debate: Can Animals Empathise?" *Scientific American*, Nov. 1998.

which is why humans can form mutual relationships with birds and mammals. However, the soul is that unique part of humans that is able to love and experience God directly.

Moral Discernment. Genesis tells us that after they had sinned, Adam and Eve became like God in that they could distinguish between good and evil. After performing many experiments, Dr Jerome Kagan, in his book, *Three Seductive Ideas*, points out that:

Not even the cleverest ape could be conditioned to be angry upon seeing one animal steal food from another.

In addition, there are no animal models for human pride.

Keith Jensen and his team at Max Plank Institute for Evolutionary Anthropology in Leipzig, Germany, conducted experiments with chimpanzees in order to test their emotions. A *New Scientist* report on their research concluded that:

In showing that chimps lack spite, the team may have also inadvertently demonstrated that the possession of a set of connected emotions remains unique to humans. Many differences obviously remain between the species, Jensen observed:

Humans actually care about outcomes affecting others. The good side of that is altruism. Spite is the evil twin that can't be separated from it.[237]

Awareness of Mortality. Since Adam and Eve's rebellion against God, when death became a reality, humans—and only humans—know that we will die one day.

In conclusion, author and science writer Elaine Morgan, writing in reply to an article in *New Scientist* which concluded that humans are not so special, highlighted the "spectacular failure" and innate deception of Darwinian science:

But the battle can never be won by shutting our eyes to uncomfortable truths. The fact is with the most salient physiological features distinguishing humans from chimpanzees—habitual bipedalism, naked skin, a subcutaneous fat layer and so on—leading Darwinian scientists are, if anything, further away from any agreed explanation than they were a century ago. That is despite the fact that physiological differences are far more hard-edged and quantifiable than behavioral ones—and should be regarded as more reliable evidence. Something is clearly missing in their narrative.

The imminent bicentenary of Darwin's birth would be an excellent opportunity to confront this spectacular failure. Instead there is a tendency to sweep it under the carpet by refusing to talk about it. If Darwinian scientists are genuinely unaware of how many questions still remain unanswered, they are deceiving themselves. If they are aware of it, they are being disingenuous in glossing over these basic problems by distracting attention from them. In any case it is a deplorable situation and it is time somebody said so.[238]

---

[237] *New Scientist*, 21 July, 2007, page 16.
[238] *New Scientist*, June 21, 2008, Letters to the Editor.

3   Is There Scientific Support for Biblical Creation?

Again, the Bible stands true when it states that man is made in the image of God, and is therefore distinct from all the animals.

5. After Six Days, All Creation was Complete and Finished

The fact that God had finished His work of creation at the end of the sixth day is corroborated by one of the basic laws of science; the First Law of Thermodynamics,[239] whereby, simply put, 'matter cannot be created or destroyed.' This law stands, even though we know, thanks to Einstein's famous equation, $E=Mc^2$, that energy and matter are interchangeable. In other words, since God finished His work, no more creation has taken place. The only exceptions to this are when God Himself performed acts of creation on specific occasions as mentioned in the Bible.

So, the amount of energy/matter in the universe has remained and will remain constant since the time of creation. Interestingly, the Second Law of Thermodynamics[240] states that the natural tendency of a system is to an increase in entropy, that is, disorder. The whole universe is becoming more disordered. Another way of putting it, is that the energy useful for work is continually decreasing in the universe as a whole. In fact, Paul states in the book of Romans:

The creation itself also will be delivered from the bondage of corruption ... For we know that the whole creation groans and labors with birth pangs together until now.[241]

Similarly, Psalm 102 records:

In the beginning you laid the foundations of the earth, and the heavens are the work of your hands. They will perish, but you will remain; they will all wear out like a garment. Like clothing you will change them and they will be discarded. But you will remain the same and your years will never end.[242]

These Bible verses are consistent with the empirical evidence of what is actually happening. And of course, since the universe is running down, it must have come into existence already 'wound up' which is in keeping with the biblical position of it having been created that way.

Conclusion

The Bible's account of creation is in harmony with modern science.

The Apostle Paul's comment is fitting:

What may be known of God is manifest in them, for God has shown it to them. For since the creation of the world His invisible attributes are clearly seen, being understood by the things that are made, even His eternal power and Godhead, so that they are without excuse.[243]

---

[239] See page 41.
[240] See page 41
[241] Romans 8:21–22
[242] Psalm 102:25–27 (*Revised Standard Version*)
[243] Romans 1:19–20

Chapter 4

Can the Bible Withstand Scientific Scrutiny?

There are two pervasive misconceptions about the Bible. The one held by skeptics is that the Bible is an antiquated book, which is full of fables, stories, scientific fallacies and mistakes. The other view, which is mainly held by liberal theologians, is that the Bible is a religious book and as such, must be interpreted spiritually and allegorically and is not to be taken literally.

In fact, the Bible is self-authenticating,[244] divinely inspired and true throughout, whether it is dealing with history, science or medicine. And as we shall see, it can be relied upon totally.

The veracity of the Bible will be examined under the following five topics.

1. **Noah's Flood**
2. **The Universe and the Earth**
3. **Science**
4. **Medicine**
5. **Archaeology**

1. Noah's Flood

There is no event in the Bible that has caused as much controversy and endured as much attack as God's judgment on sinful mankind by way of Noah's flood. This treatment of Noah's flood is not meant to be comprehensive, but rather aims to demonstrate the plausibility of the episode and the evidence for its historicity.

Disbelief in the flood has become so entrenched that even some Christians don't believe it, even though the Bible states it plainly and Jesus affirmed it. The Lord's words are recorded in the book of Luke:

Just as it was in the days of Noah, so also will it be in the days of the Son of Man. People were eating; drinking, marrying and being given in marriage, up to the day that Noah entered the ark. Then the flood came, and destroyed them all.[245]

Almost all civilisations have a flood story as a legend or folklore in their culture. Evolutionary geologist Robert Schoch wrote:

Noah is but one tale in a worldwide collection of at least 500 flood myths, which are the most widespread of all ancient myths and therefore can be considered among the oldest.[246]

---

[244] 2 Timothy 3:16.
[245] Luke 17:26–27.
[246] R. M. Schoch, *Voyages of the Pyramid Builders,* Jeremy P Parcher/Putnam, New York, 2003, page 249.

4 Can the Bible Withstand Scientific Scrutiny?

Not only are flood stories ubiquitous amongst ancient civilizations, they are remarkably similar. James Perloff noted:

In 95 percent of more than 200 flood legends, the flood was worldwide; in 88 percent, a certain family was favored; in 70 percent, survival was by means of a boat; in 67 percent, animals were also saved; in 66 percent, the flood was due to the wickedness of man; in 66 percent, the survivors had been forewarned; in 57 percent, they ended up on a mountain; in 35 percent, birds were sent out from the boat; and in 9 percent, exactly eight people were spared.[247]

So much recorded history of a worldwide flood, originating from diverse civilizations, points to the conclusion that it actually happened.

One account which is similar to the Bible version is contained in the Epic of Gilgamesh, dating from the seventh century BC and found on the eleventh of twelve clay tablets during the excavation of Nineveh. Skeptics and some encyclopedias maintain that the Babylonian story is the original and the biblical account was based on it.

In comparing the two flood stories, the Genesis account is detailed (people on board, number of animals, the length of the time it rained, the dimensions of the ark and its construction, etc.), it is descriptive (fountains of the deep broke open, the whole world covered with water) and purposeful (divine judgment on a very wicked people). It makes more sense to believe that Genesis was the original, and the Gilgamesh Epic, which lacks the detail of the Genesis account, arose from and is a distortion of the original. For a thorough and well-referenced comparison of the two flood stories, the reader is directed to the work of Nozomi Osanai.[248]

What does the Bible say about Noah's Flood? (Genesis 6–8)

The book of Genesis states:

God saw that the wickedness of man was great in the earth, and that every imagination of the thoughts of his heart was only evil continually.[249]

It goes on to inform us that God said He would destroy man, but Noah found grace in the eyes of the Lord. So God told Noah to build a large boat and place selected animals in it, along with his wife, three sons and their wives, and that He would flood the entire earth.

Some people have suggested that the flood may have been only local. But the Bible makes it clear that it was global. If it was only a small regional flood, why would God have Noah build an ark? He simply could have walked away from the area of land that was to be flooded. Why place all of the animals, including birds, on it? If it was local, how could the waters rise 15 cubits[250] above the mountains?[251] And again, if it was local, God would have repeatedly broken His promise never to

---

[247] J. Perloff, *Tornado in a Junkyard: The Relentless Myth of Darwinism,* Refuge Books, 1999, page 45.
[248] Go to: creation.com/search and insert 'Nozomi Osanai.'
[249] Genesis 6:5.
[250] 8 meters (24 feet).
[251] Genesis 7:20.

send such a flood again.[252]

What would we expect to see today as the result of a worldwide flood?
- Most of the world would be covered by sedimentary layers, that is, rock laid down by water.
- Stratification or layering of the sedimentary rocks.
- Coal, oil and gas deposits as a result of vast floating mats of vegetation being buried.
- Evidence of rapid and jumbled burying of animals and vegetation and as a consequence, many well-preserved fossils.
- High mountains containing remnants of marine life.

Worldwide sedimentary layers

Sedimentary rock is formed by the laying down of sediments by moving fluids, such as water. These sediments are made up of pieces of rock or other material which existed somewhere else and were eroded or dissolved then redeposited in their present location. Seventy-five to eighty percent of the earth's land area is covered by sedimentary rock in a thin veneer over the earth's crust; the rest is volcanic igneous rock from volcanic eruptions.[253, 254]

In many places, the upper crust of the earth consists of a series of sedimentary layers built upon a basement of metamorphic rock. Their meeting is easily seen, for example, in the lower section of the Grand Canyon where the junction is called The Great Unconformity. Here, a sediment layer sits on a widespread, water-eroded surface. Similar examples can be seen on many continents. The water activity that produced the erosion of the metamorphic rock was a global phenomenon. Many sedimentary layers, which consist of limestone, sandstone and shale, cover much of the globe. One particularly obvious sedimentary layer is the coal-bearing Upper Carboniferous.

The Upper Carboniferous consists of large coal deposits derived from vegetation. It also contains the remnants of uprooted trees in a variety of positions. All of this is consistent with a large flood dump. As a noted geology professor observed:

The extensive coal and associated deposits of the Upper Carboniferous are almost incredibly widespread, from the American Midwest to the Donetz Basin in what was (until recently) the former Soviet Union.[255]

Other large layers include the chalk beds of southern England, the enormous sandstone layer containing the Australian Great Artesian Basin which runs continuously for thousands of kilometers, and the extensive coal beds of eastern Australia that contain millions of fossilised trees which give the appearance of having been dumped there. All the layers mentioned contain mixtures of land-based vegetation and marine fossils. It is difficult to account for the existence of such features other than by a worldwide flood.

---

[252] Genesis 9:11.

[253] Source: wikipedia.org/wiki/Sedimentary_rock, retrieved May 2, 2011.

[254] wiki.answers.com/Q/How_much_of_the_Earth's_surface_is_covered_by_sedimentary_rocks, retrieved May 2, 2011.

[255] D. Ager, *The New Catrophism: the importance of the rare event in geological history,* Cambridge University Press, 1995, page 46.

4 Can the Bible Withstand Scientific Scrutiny?

How do evolutionists account for these facts? They cannot dispute that the sedimentary rock was laid down by water and that it is widespread, but they maintain it was formed over millions of years by way of many localized floods, with each stratum of the sedimentary rock representing hundreds, thousands and even millions of years. They have great difficulty in explaining the vast sizes of the Carboniferous layers.

There are serious problems with the idea that layers of sediments were laid down over long periods of time, and these are discussed below.

Stratification

Stratification can happen quickly, as shown in this picture[256] of stratified material formed by the 1986 volcanic eruption of Mt St Helens in about one week.

The bending of strata

Some strata contain very sharp, almost hairpin bends, as shown in the accompanying photographs. Other strata have bends and folds so great that they can only be perceived from the air to obtain perspective as shown in the photograph below.

Evolutionary geologists are hard pushed to explain this phenomenon, as they assume formation took place over thousands and even millions of years as the strata were laid down one level at a time. They say high temperatures and pressures must have been involved. However, many of the strata contain fossils and shells, which negate the possibility of high temperatures.

Photo supplied courtesy NASA

A far more plausible explanation is that the folds occurred when the strata were laid down in a relatively short time—like, for example, one year, by way of a worldwide flood as described in the book of Genesis, chapters six to eight.

Such bending could only have occurred when the entire set of strata was still wet, soft and therefore supple; otherwise the layers would have cracked and even broken—and there is very little evidence of such cracking and breaking in the strata. The forces required to produce the type of bending seen in the second picture, which is seen in many repeated

Photo from: *Creation*, 2002, 25(1), 40-43.

---

[256] This imige is courtesy of Dr S. Austin.

instances that are widespread across the globe, must have been immense and would have involved the whole of the Earth's crust.

Such a cataclysmic event is consistent with the biblical account of Noah's flood as the Bible describes it:

-----all the fountains of the great deep broke up, and the windows of heaven were opened.[257]

At the conclusion of the event, the Bible states:

The fountains of the deep and the windows of heaven were stopped also, and the rain from heaven was restrained.[258]

Again, consistent with Scripture, there is no process operating now which could produce such dramatic changes to the earth's surface on a worldwide scale. What is seen today can be best explained by Noah's flood. No other explanation satisfactorily accounts for such bending and folding.

Stratified layers

There are many places around the world where rock layers are evident (known in evolutionary terms as 'the geological column')—none more so than the Grand Canyon (see photograph).

These layers provide a history of what has happened in the past. To evolutionary geologists, they represent millions of years, as each layer of a particular period forms on top of another layer with allegedly millions of years between them. However, there are some big problems with this assumption. First, since each rock layer has been assigned a particular age, normally by the fossils which the layer contains, there exists what are known as 'flat gaps' or 'paraconformities.' That is, each layer is claimed to be millions of years older than the one it lays directly over. Yet if there were millions of years between the formation of one layer and the next layer, then we would expect to see evidence of erosion on the surface of each layer, and to a very large extent, as wind, rain, floods and in some cases earthquakes and volcanic activity leave their mark. This is not what is observed. In fact, each layer is extremely flat, giving the appearance that they were laid down one after the other (as evidenced in the picture above of the Grand Canyon) and in accordance with what would be expected as the result of a global flood.

---

[257] Genesis 7:11.
[258] Genesis 8:2.

The photograph to the right makes this point very clear. The top layer is Coconino Sandstone and the bottom layer is Hermit Shale. There is meant to be a time gap of six million years between the two layers, but there is no evidence of erosion on the surface of the bottom layer as would be expected if it had been exposed to the elements for six million years. Instead, their junction is extremely flat.[259]

Polystrate Fossils

Another factor which stands in opposition to the idea of strata being laid down over great periods of time is the presence of polystrate fossils, which are fossils traversing many strata. As mentioned above, evolutionists believe that each stratum (or layer) of sedimentary rock represents thousands or even millions of years. But what has been found are trees, and in some cases animals, going through many strata. These have been documented for some time.

The image to the right is taken from an old print of two tree trunks that appear to be in a growing position at Nant Llech in the Valley, South Wales. Derek Ager, Emeritus Professor of Geology, University College of Swansea, stated that one estimate of the age of the strata these trees pass through is 100,000 years, which, he concludes, is ridiculous.

Tens of thousands of polystrate fossil trees have been found and they are scattered across the globe. Below are just four of the numerous examples. It is very clear that these trees transverse many strata.

---

[259] Millions of Years are Missing, *Creation*, 2009, 31 (2), pages 46-49.

4 Can the Bible Withstand Scientific Scrutiny?

Coal, oil and natural gas deposits

Coal is formed from massive mats of vegetation rotting over time. Oil and gas are by-products of this breakdown process. Since this procedure has never been observed, the details of the process remain the subject of speculation.

Those who reject the Bible claim that their formation took place over millions of years by way of trees falling into and rotting in large swampy areas. However, some of the trees that gave rise to coal can still be identified, and they are not species that grow in swamps.

For Bible believers, the process can be explained quite easily by Noah's flood, which would have resulted in giant masses of floating vegetation that became buried by the enormous amounts of silt and mud produced by this cataclysmic event.

Evolutionists counter with the fact that coal, oil and gas deposits are so vast that there is not enough vegetation on earth for them to have been formed at one time. However, they do not consider the possibility that pre-flood conditions were vastly different from those today. For example, there is much evidence from the coal seam vegetation of northern hemisphere deposits particularly, that they were derived from huge forests of vegetation designed to float. Such huge mats of forests floating on the shallower pre-flood seas, more than adequately answers the objection.[260]

Rapid burial

Rapid burial is one of the key preservation factors required for the formation of most fossils.[261]

Dramatic and undisputed examples of rapid burial include the marvelously detailed fossil of a mother ichthyosaur giving birth to her baby, and a fossilised fish eating another fish when they are suddenly frozen in time and fossilised.[262]

A logical explanation for the enormous quantity of rapidly buried preserved specimens is that they were covered by a massive wall of mud during a great upheaval such as Noah's flood.

---

[260] Creation.com/forests-that-grew-on-water.
[261] wikipedia.org/wiki/Fossil_collecting, retrieved April 9, 2011.
[262] These images are courtesy of the Institute for Creation Research (iooe.org/copyright).

4 Can the Bible Withstand Scientific Scrutiny?

Most Dinosaurs may have drowned

An article in *New Scientist* provides strong evidence that most dinosaurs drowned:

Recreating the spectacular pose many dinosaurs adopted in death might involve following the simplest injunction: just add water.

When paleontologists are lucky enough to find a complete dinosaur skeleton, there's a good chance it will be found with its head thrown backwards and its tail arched upwards—technically known as the opisthotonic death pose. No one is entirely sure why this posture is so common, but Alicia Cutler and colleagues from Brigham Young University in Provo, Utah, think it all comes down to a dip in the wet stuff.

Cutler placed plucked chickens on a bed of sand for three months to see if desiccation would lead to muscle contractions that pulled the neck upwards. The chickens decayed without contorting. When seven other chickens were placed into cool fresh water, however, their necks arched and their heads were thrown back within seconds, Cutler told the Society of Vertebrate Paleontology conference in Las Vegas, Nevada, earlier this month.[263]

The classic 'dead dino posture'—head thrown back, tail extended, with hind limbs bent—called *opisthotonus*, the result of muscle spasms caused by suffocation.

Fossil graveyards

If an animal dies today, it will not become a fossil. Within a very short time, carnivores will carry bits of its body away, birds of prey will be picking the bones clean, smaller scavengers such as rats, mice, beetles and ants will be taking what they can and, finally, micro-organisms will break down the remains. Thus, in a matter of months, the beast will have disappeared, with the possible exception of a few bones. The mere presence of fossils suggests that rapid burial has taken place.

Perhaps the most challenging fossil phenomena for evolutionists to explain are the massive graveyards of fossilised animal remains found throughout the world. For example:

---

[263] *New Scentist*, November 26, 2011, page 12

- **Agate Spring, Nebraska** is a fossil graveyard containing 9,000 animals buried in alluvial deposits. The remains of camels, three-toed horses, rhinoceroses, giant wild boars, birds, plants, trees, seashells and fish are all scrambled together.

- **Gobi Desert.** This area of Central Asia is one of the driest places on earth, yet it is a paradise for paleontologists. So far, 25 therapod dinosaurs and 200 skulls of mammals, along with other dinosaurs, lizards and small mammals have been unearthed, in an amazing state of preservation.

- **The Ashley Beds** is an area of phosphate bed comprising 100 square kilometers (40 square miles), located in South Carolina USA. It was first mentioned by Major Edward Willis in his book *Fossils and Phosphate Specimens*, 1881. It contains the remains of both land and sea animals—dinosaurs, plesiosaurs, whales, sharks, rhinoceroses, sheep, horses, mastodons, mammoths, porpoises, elephants, deer, pigs and dogs.[264]

- **Montceau-les Mines.** The mine is near Autun in France. The fossils are well preserved and in excellent condition. As well, they consist of a mixture of creatures. Some are saltwater dwellers, some are freshwater and some are land-based animals. For example, hundreds of thousands of marine creatures were buried with amphibians, reptiles and insects. Spiders, scorpions and millipedes were found as well. The find was reported in *Scientific American*[265] and the two paleontologists, Daniel Heyler and Cecile Poplin, were bewildered by the mixture and variety of animal fossils present.

Such large deposits of mixed animal and aquatic fossils spread throughout the world provide a clear demonstration of large scale violent and rapid burial. This is exactly what would be expected as the result of a worldwide flood.

Mountains Containing Remnants of Marine Creatures

The Bible states that all of the mountains were covered with water. This being the case, evidence may exist to support this fact. There is enough water in the oceans so that, if all the surface features of the earth were evened out, water would cover the earth to a depth of 2.7 kilometers.

Major mountain ranges are formed by the collision of continental shelves and many are still rising. For example, if Sir Edmond Hillary were to climb Mt Everest today, he would have to climb an extra meter and a half.

Interestingly, marine fossils are found at high altitudes, including Mt Everest and on all five continents.

There are many big ammonite fossils in the Muktinath area of the Kali Gandaki Valley, Nepal, at around the elevation of 4,000 meters above sea level. This is one of the proofs that the Himalayas were indeed once under water.

---

[264] genesispark.org/genpark/grave/grave.htm, retrieved April 9, 2011.
[265] *Scientific American,* September 1988, 256, pages. 70–76.

4 Can the Bible Withstand Scientific Scrutiny?

For many people who have faith in the Hindu religion, ammonite is one of the many forms of their Lord Vishnu (see page 5). They keep ammonite fossils in their worship room and worship them. The photograph left shows a Nepalese girl standing on a large ammonite fossil.

The Andes in South America have so many marine fossils that tour companies are now offering fossil hunting as part of their programs.

A photograph of a Nepalese girl standing on a large ammonite fossil

Questions Commonly Asked About the Flood

1. Was Noah's Ark big enough to hold all of the animals?

The Bible specifies the dimensions of Noah's Ark in cubits. A cubit is the distance from his elbow to the tips of a man's fingers, and this is between 450 and 550 mm (17½ and 21½ inches). Most scholars regard 460 mm (18 inches) as the length of a cubit. This being the case, the ark was 140 meters (450 feet) long, 23 meters (75 feet) wide and 14 meters (45 feet) high; and its displacement would have been more than 22,000 tonnes. It had 3 decks, a door in the side and it was sealed with pitch both inside and out. Its window consisted of a long continuous slot under the roof eaves, 460 mm (18 inches) high. It was a big boat!

The photograph shows Johan Huibers' replica of Noah's Ark, which he built to roughly one half of biblical dimensions. It resides in Schagen in the Netherlands, and it puts the size of the ark into perspective. It was a huge box with a volume of 40,000 cubic meters (1,396,000 cubic feet), which is enough room to carry 125,000 sheep. Various calculations have been made on how many animals Noah would have had on board, in accordance with God's instructions. One estimate from Dr Henry Morris is 35,000[266] while another study by John Woodmorappe[267] concluded only 2,000 animals would have been necessary. In any event, the ark could have carried 50,000 animals quite easily.[268]

---

[266] H. Morris, *The Biblical Basis for Modern Science,* Baker Book House, 1984, pages 291–293.

[267] J. Woodmorappe, *Noah's Ark: A Feasibility Study,* Inst for Creation Research, 1996.

[268] For a thorough analysis of this topic, the reader is directed to: christiananswers.net/q-eden/edn-c013.html, retrieved May 2, 2011.

4 Can the Bible Withstand Scientific Scrutiny?

2. **If the whole world was covered with water and all of the animals came out of the ark, how is it that we find kangaroos and koalas only in Australia and kiwis only in New Zealand?**[269]

There are severe practical limitations on our attempts to understand something that happened once, was not recorded in detail, and cannot be repeated, but we can make a few points.

When Krakatoa erupted in 1883, the island remnant remained lifeless for some years, but it was eventually colonised by a surprising variety of creatures, including and not only, insects and earthworms, birds, lizards, snakes and even a few mammals. This example demonstrates that animals can move freely between land masses.

Land bridges between continents did exist. They were possibly caused by an ice age, which creationists believe happened after the flood due to warm oceans and warmth from the sun being blocked by ash from volcanic activity.[270] Vast quantities of water would be locked up as ice, causing the sea levels to drop. Animals could have spread out in many directions. It is not necessary for two kangaroos to have hopped all the way from Mt Ararat to Australia just as two rabbits did not hop all around the whole continent of Australia after a small breeding colony was let loose in NSW about 150 years ago. Yet they are found in every corner of the vast continent. Once here, the animals could have become isolated in the post-ice-age period as sea levels rose.

The question which then arises is why don't we find fossils of, say, kangaroos in Asia or any other part of the world? Fossilisation is a rare event, requiring rapid burial to prevent scavenging and decomposition. Lions lived in Israel until recently. Yet no lion fossils have been found there. The millions of bison that roamed North America have left no fossils. So it is not surprising that no kangaroo fossils have been found.

There is a widespread, but mistaken, belief that marsupials are found only in Australia. However, living marsupial possums are found in North and South America. Similarly, monotremes were once thought to be unique to Australia. But the finding of a fossilised platypus tooth in South America stunned the scientific world.[271]

So it is possible that animals unique to Australia, or in fact any other island, could have come via now submerged land bridges, and that the animals that were not isolated died out, leaving no trace of their past presence.

Other Questions

There are other questions regarding the seeming impossibility of the whole story, such as: "How did the animals get to the ark?" or "What did they eat?" or "What about the carnivores eating some of the other animals?" and "How did the ark contain the huge dinosaurs?" Such questions cannot be answered with any precision. The fact is that the whole episode was a miracle of God. There is no doubt He would have chosen animals that possessed the greatest genetic diversity to mate. He

---

[269] Most of the following explanation is taken from Creation Answers Book; creation.com/images/pdfs/cabook/chapter17.pdf.
[270] Jonathan Sarfati, *Mammoth Riddle of the Ice Age*, 2,000, page 7, Available from Creation Ministries International; creation.com.
[271] *New Scientist*, 24 August, 1991, page 13.

4 Can the Bible Withstand Scientific Scrutiny?

would have brought them to the ark[272] and possibly placed them in some type of hibernation for the period. God would have chosen adolescent dinosaurs of the very large type. God did it all. But where science comes in is in answering the question "Is there any evidence that it actually took place at all?" This has been addressed and the answer is a resounding "yes".

2. The Universe and the Earth

The number of stars

Jeremiah, under the influence of the Holy Spirit, writes:

As the host of heaven cannot be numbered, nor the sand of the sea measured, so will I multiply the descendants of David My servant and the Levites who minister to Me.[273]

Jeremiah's words here echo the covenant promises to the patriarchs, including the fact that the stars are too numerous to be numbered.

The first person acknowledged to have counted the stars was Hipparchus in 190–120BC. After having made a study of the stars, he announced that there were 1,080 and 300 years later, Ptolemy put the number at 1,056. It is now generally accepted that without the aid of a telescope and on a very clear night, up to 4,000 stars can be seen. But back in 600 BC Jeremiah said the number of stars was countless. And even further back to about 1,500 BC we read a similar statement in Genesis 22:17. So, up until a few hundred years ago, it would have seemed that the Bible grossly exaggerated the number of stars in the sky. However, with the aid of powerful telescopes, it is estimated that there are 10 to the power 21 stars.[274] If it were possible to count 20 stars per second, it would take 100 million billion years to count to 10 to the power 21. And interestingly, this number is also an estimate of the number of grains of sand on the seashores. Of course, God, who has infinite knowledge, knows the number of stars. In fact, the Bible states in Psalm 14:

Stars at night

He counts the number of the stars; He calls them all by name.[275]

---

[272] Genesis 6:20
[273] Jeremiah 33:22.
[274] imagine.gsfc.nasa.gov/docs/ask_astro/answers/970115.html.
[275] Psalm 147:4.

4 Can the Bible Withstand Scientific Scrutiny?

The heavens declare God's glory

The psalmist tells us in 19:1 and 2:

The heavens declare the glory of God; the skies proclaim the work of his hands. Day after day they pour forth speech; and night after night they display knowledge.[276]

Here the psalmist is saying that the silent heavens are declaring the glory of their maker and their glory is a testament to the righteousness and faithfulness of the Lord who created them. Why does the Bible say it is the heavens that declare God's glory and not, say, the beauty of a flower as it opens, or the birth of a baby, which demonstrates the miracle of a new life?

Beside and below are a few images of the heavens taken from the Hubble telescope. They include images of supernova, that is, stars that have exploded a gas cloud and a galaxy.[277]

With the aid of a very modern telescope, it is easy to understand why the Psalmist states that it is the heavens that declare God's glory. Such beauty and symmetry on an incomprehensible scale so appropriately points to the Creator.

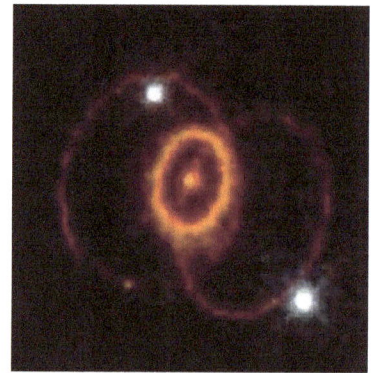

He stretches out the heavens

There are at least eleven references in the scriptures to the fact that God stretched or stretches (makes ongoing or makes continuous) the heavens.[278] Therefore, this is something to be believed.

Isaiah wrote in about 700 BC at a time when people thought that the stars were stuck on a canopy that covered the sky and the concepy of the depth of the cosmos was inconceivable. Yet the Bible states that the heavens are being stretched. As discussed, there is a general consensus among

---

[276] Psalm 19:1-2 (*New International Version*).
[277] Photographs are courtesy of NASA.
[278] Job 9:8; Psalm 104:2; Isaiah 40:22, 42:5, 44:24, 45:12, 48:13, 51:13; Jeremiah 10:12, 51:15; Zechariah 12:1.

4 Can the Bible Withstand Scientific Scrutiny?

contemporary cosmologists that the galaxies are not only moving apart but that their movement is accelerating.[279]

The earth is suspended in space

The ancient Greeks believed that the earth was held on the arms and shoulders of a giant named Atlas. A group of Hindus believed that it was supported on the backs of two huge elephants that stood on the shell of an enormous turtle that in turn was swimming in the cosmic sea. Other ancient peoples simply thought the earth was flat. But the Bible tells us that it is floating in space and nothing holds it up. Job wrote about 3,500 years ago:

Photo courtesy of NASA

He stretches out the north over empty space (תֹּהוּ, emptiness, vacuum); *He hangs* (תָּלָה, let down, dangle) *the earth on nothing*[280] (בְּלִימָה, nothingness, not—aught).[281]

The earth is round

In the year 1492 Christopher Columbus wanted to show that the world was round and that he could reach India by sailing west. He attempted to do just that, but ran into the continent of America or more accurately, the West Indies. Before this time, apart from a few exceptions, people thought the world was flat, to the extent that seamen would refuse to go on long sea voyages because of fear of sailing off the edge. In about 760 BC, however, the prophet Isaiah recorded this revealing insight into God's perspective of the Earth:

It is He who sits above the circle (חוּג, draw round, make circle)[270, 282] *of the earth, and its inhabitants are like grasshoppers.*[283]

As well, in about 1,000 BC David implies that the earth is round when he writes:

As far as the east is from the west, so far has He removed our transgressions from us?[284]

A similar thought is conveyed in Proverbs:

When he prepared the heavens, I was there; when he drew a compass upon the face of the deep.[285]

---

[279] *New Scientist,* May 19, 2007, page 44.
[280] Job 26:7.
[281] Hebrew meanings are taken from: Francis Brown, S.R. Driver and C. A. Briggs, *A Hebrew and English Lexicon*, Clarendon Press, Oxford, 1974.
[282] Roundness or sphericity taken from; *Strong's Hebrew and Greek Dictionaries as found in e-Sword, Rick Meyers, e-sword.net.*
[283] Isaiah 40:22.
[284] Psalms 103:12.
[285] Proverbs 8:27.

4. Can the Bible Withstand Scientific Scrutiny?

Here the word 'compass' can also be translated 'circle'.[286] That is, God contained the waters in a circle as evidenced by the view of a ship sailing away and as it does, its hull disappears first and the top of its mast last.

The earth is rotating

Luke depicts Christ's Second Coming as happening while some are asleep at night and others are working at daytime activities in the field—an indication of a rotating earth with day and night occurring in different places at the same time.[287]

3. Science

The area of science offers insight into whether the Bible is indeed divinely inspired or is simply an ancient book written by fallible men. Scientific knowledge has been growing exponentially, and so much more is known now than was known 2,000 to 3,500 years ago. If the Bible is divinely inspired, then statements that incorporate science will be correct. Below are some biblical texts that can be tested against what is now known to be true.

Time had a beginning

Both 2 Timothy 1:9 and Titus 1:2 tell us that Christ existed before time began. It is difficult for us to comprehend the absence of time. It was only Einstein's *General Theory of Relativity* that showed time to be a physical quantity like speed and gravity, for example, and that it can vary with either speed or gravity. Time dilation, that is, time slowing, has been observed experimentally when an object is travelling very fast; in fact, time stops at the speed of light. Time only came into being when the universe did. The verses tell us that Christ existed before the universe (creation) and consequently He existed before time.

Circulation of the atmosphere

Ecclesiastes 1:6 says:

The wind blows to the south, and turns to the north; round and round it goes, ever returning to its course.[288]

Here the Bible describes the circulation of the atmosphere, which was not contemplated at the time Solomon wrote these words, in approximately 1,000 BC.

Air has weight

Job 28:25 says:

To make the weight for the wind; and he apportions the waters by measure.

---

[286] *Strong's Hebrew and Greek Dictionaries as found in e-Sword*, Rick Meyers, www.e-sword.net.
[287] Luke 17:34–36.
[288] Ecclesiastes 1:6 (*New International Version*).

4. Can the Bible Withstand Scientific Scrutiny?

People at the time would have been familiar with water having weight and volume, but not the wind or air. In fact, we live under a lot of air, about 80 kilometers of it, all weighing down on us. We measure it as barometric pressure. Without that weight we would not be able to breathe. We simply open our lungs and they fill up with air.

Springs in the oceans

Job 38:16 states:

Have you entered the springs of the sea?

The idea of springs in the sea would have been quite foreign to Job and his friends, but as was shown in the previous chapter, the sea does indeed have springs. The image on page 59 depicts a hydrothermal vent issuing forth from a deep ocean trench. So springs in the sea floor certainly do exist.

The innumerable stars

Jeremiah 33:22 says:

As the hosts of heaven cannot be numbered, nor the sand of the sea measured.

Since the "hosts of heaven" is a biblical term for stars, Jeremiah is saying that they must be numbered in the billions, which has only been shown to be true relatively recently, in particular since the advent of the Hubble telescope. As mentioned earlier,[289] Hipparchus (190—120 BC) counted the stars and declared the total to be 1,080.

The Bible and entropy

Hebrews 1:10–11 states:

…You, Lord, in the beginning have laid the foundation of the earth; and the heavens are the works of your hands: They shall perish; but you remain; and they shall grow old as does a garment.

Who could have known 2,000 years ago that all of creation is wearing out? It is the case. The sun and other stars are burning away, the earth's rotation is slowing and its magnetic field is decreasing in strength. The second law of thermodynamics, which in effect states that the entire universe is becoming less ordered and degraded, was not discovered until comparatively recently. Yet the One who inspired the writer of Hebrews knew.

The exponential increase in knowledge and travel

In the twelfth chapter of his book, Daniel records his prophecies that concern the end times, and in verse four, he states:

…many shall run to and fro, and knowledge shall be increased.[290]

---

[289] See page 103.
[290] Daniel 12:4.

4 Can the Bible Withstand Scientific Scrutiny?

Taking this statement as it stands; we are continually amazed at the development of air travel. We can go from country to country in a matter of hours. In fact, we can traverse continents likewise. When we do, we find airports jammed with people doing the same thing. Similarly, knowledge has and is increasing exponentially, from communications to transport to medicine. It is happening at such a pace that we find it difficult to keep up with developments.

Paths in the sea

Psalm 8:8 mentions the *paths of the sea.* The sea seems to be just a huge mass of water, so how could it have paths? Man discovered the existence of ocean currents in the 1850s, but the Bible stated it 2,800 years ago. Matthew Maury is considered to be the father of oceanography. Apparently he was bedridden during a serious illness and asked one of his daughters to read a portion of the Bible. While listening, he noticed the expression 'the paths of the sea.' Upon his recovery, Maury took God at His word and went looking for these paths. His work on oceanography, which includes ocean currents, cut sailing times dramatically.

Each star is different

1 Corinthians 15:41 states:

There is one glory of the sun, and another glory of the moon, and another glory of the stars: for one star differs from another star in glory.

From earth the majority of stars look the same; only recently, with the aid of powerful telescopes, has it been revealed that every star is different.

The hydrologic cycle

The hydrologic cycle, which involves water evaporating from the sea, being transported over the land as clouds, and falling as rain, is mentioned in Amos,[291] Isaiah[292] and Psalms,[293] as well as in Job,[294] who wrote:

He draws up the drops of water, which distill as rain to the stream, the clouds pour down their moisture, and abundant showers fall on mankind.

And again in Ecclesiastes:

All the rivers run into the sea; yet the sea is not full; to the place from where the rivers come, there they return again.[295]

The Bible could not make this amazing cycle any clearer. Yet it was not fully comprehended until many hundreds of years after these texts were written.

---

[291] Amos 9:6.
[292] Isaiah 55:10.
[293] Psalm 135:7.
[294] Job 36:27–28 (*New International Version*).
[295] Ecclesiastes 1:7.

4 Can the Bible Withstand Scientific Scrutiny?

Clouds holding great amounts of water

The book of Job states:

He wraps up the waters in his clouds, yet the clouds do not burst under their weight.[296]

Here the emphasis is on how much water the clouds support. The clouds hold millions of tons of water and the consequences of this fact are seen in flooding rain that takes place from time to time. Again, the Bible is correct.

Agriculture

In the book of Leviticus at chapter 25, the Lord instructs Moses to tell the people to let the land rest every seven years. This seems to have two components to it—one agricultural and one spiritual. It is now well-established practice to allow land to rest periodically as continual planting and harvesting depletes the soil of its nutrients and allows for the build-up of viruses. Again we see the wisdom of the scriptures. It is interesting that God did not instruct his people to let one seventh of their land rest every year, but rather to let the whole land rest for one year. This is where the spiritual aspect comes in. The people had to trust God to provide for them during the year the land was to rest.

4. Medicine

As with science, so it is in the area of medicine; statements in the scriptures that relate to medicine can be analysed to assess whether or not they are consistent with modern medical knowledge.

Circumcision

Newborn babies have a heightened risk of hemorrhaging or continuous bleeding from a cut, especially if they are breastfed. The reason for this condition is that the infant's intestinal tract has not had time to develop a healthy population of bacteria. There are approximately 500 different species of bacteria that colonise the human gut. They perform a variety of functions which facilitate living, one of which is the production of vitamin K. Vitamin K is involved in the biosynthesis of a group of coagulation factors, which cause the blood to clot. An important one is factor 11, also called prothrombin. Interestingly, breast milk is very low in vitamin K, while cow's milk has about three times the amount. This condition is called hemorrhagic disease of the newborn, caused by vitamin K deficiency. The *Merck Manual of Diagnosis and Therapy,* which is the world's best selling medical textbook,[297] states that:

Worldwide, vitamin K deficiency can cause infant morbidity and mortality. Vitamin K deficiency causes hemorrhagic disease of the newborn, **which usually occurs 1 to 7 days postpartum**.[298]

---

[296] Job 26:8 (*New International Version*).
[297] wikipedia.org/wiki/Merck_Manual_of_Diagnosis_and_Therapy.
[298] *Merck Manual of Diagnosis and Therapy*, Merck Research Laboratories, 18th Edition, 2006, page 46; merckmanuals.com/professional/print/sec01/ch004/ch004m.html, retrieved June 17, 2011.

4 Can the Bible Withstand Scientific Scrutiny?

Circumcision is a very bloody procedure. And the Bible states that it is to be carried out on the **eighth day** after birth.[299] Again, the insight of the Bible is impeccable.

The reality of hemorrhagic disease is demonstrated by physician Dr Rex Russell, in his book *What the Bible Says About Healthy Living*. He writes:

My first surgical case was a newborn male who was scheduled to be circumcised. After finishing the operation, I carefully bandaged the wound. Four hours later, I checked the patient and discovered that the bandage was soaked with blood. We administered vitamin K to help clot the blood, but a slight bleeding persisted for several days before it completely stopped. A specialist checked the boy and found no evidence of hemophilia. No harm was done but the infant began life with an unnecessary risk.[300]

Only very recently, circumcision has been shown to protect men from both bacterial and viral infections. The procedure has worked wonders in Africa, reducing the infection rate of HIV by 60 percent, and New York is considering introducing a trial to promote circumcision among the city's men.[301] As well, circumcision has been shown to reduce the incidence of urinary tract infections among boys. Brian Morris, Professor of Molecular Medical Sciences at the University of Sydney, is reported as saying that circumcision significantly reduced the incidence of urinary tract infections and sexually transmitted disease:

Between 2 and 5 percent of uncircumcised boys will develop UTIs compared with 0.1 to 0.2 percent in boys who are circumcised.[302]

'Circumcision cuts cervical cancer rates' was the headline of a *New Scientist* article[303] that reported the results of a review of seven studies from five countries on a total of almost 2,000 couples.[304] Among the data supporting the headline was the fact that 20 percent of uncircumcised men and less than 6 percent of circumcised men carried the Human Papilloma Virus (HPV), which is known to cause cervical cancer in woman who has sexual intercourse with infected men. Another report[305] concluded that uncircumcised men are more than 20 times as likely to get cancer of this organ.

God's directives to His people are always for their benefit.

The chemical nature of flesh

It was not until the nineteenth century that chemists started to understand the molecular nature of all substances, including every part of us. But God said that He made Adam from the dust of the ground.[306] And He told Adam that he is going to return there.[307] All the chemical elements

---

[299] Genesis 17:12; Luke 1:59.
[300] R. Russell, *What the Bible Says About Healthy Living,* Candle Books, 1999, page 10.
[301] *New Scientist,* April 15, 2007.
[302] *The Weekend Australian,* August 25, 2007, page 3.
[303] *New Scientist* April 11, 2002.
[304] The study was published in the *New England Journal of Medicine,* 2002, 346, pages 1105–1112.
[305] *Journal of the American Academy of Dermatology*, 2006, 54 (3), page 369.
[306] Genesis 2:7.
[307] Genesis 3:19.

necessary to make a person are present in the earth; it is just a matter of joining them in the right way: a simple task for the Lord. The writer of Genesis would have had no understanding of biochemistry, and the text demonstrates, once again, that God inspired the Bible.

Adam's rib

It is interesting to notice that in order to fashion Eve, God put Adam into a deep sleep and removed one of his rib bones. From this, He formed Eve. The rib bone is the only bone in the human body that will grow again if it is removed. Surgeons often use a rib or part thereof if bone is required in another part of a person's body, and, providing the periosteum (outer membrane or sheath) is left intact, the rib will regrow most of the time.[308] This fact of the regrowth of ribs would have been completely unknown to ancient people.

Life is in the blood

Scripture declares that the blood is the source of life. Leviticus 17:11 says:

For the life of the flesh is in the blood.

Up until about the 1880s, sick people were often bled in an attempt to heal them and many died from the practice. It is now known that the blood is the source of life. We are composed of cells; muscle, skin, brain, nerve etc, and it is our blood that delivers to them, their life-sustaining oxygen and removes their waste product of carbon dioxide. It carries all of the body's regulating hormones, as well as essential vitamins and minerals. So if you lose your blood, you lose your life.

The uniqueness of Christ's blood

When Adam did what God said he was not to do and ate the fruit of the Tree of Knowledge of Good and Evil, his whole body, including his blood, became defiled and he died both spiritually and (eventually) physically. The process that led to death was instigated the moment he ate. God's punishment infected all of Adam and Eve's offspring and all succeeding generations. However, scripture speaks of Christ's blood as being different; it was His own,[309] precious,[310] justifying,[311] redeeming,[312] atoning,[313] purchasing,[314] etc. 5181

Christ was conceived uniquely by the Holy Spirit, and the human 'Seed' was incubated in a woman.[315] Admittedly, some of these statements are to be taken symbolically, but for the other statements to be true, Christ's pure blood as a fetus should not have mixed with His mother's blood which may have carried her sinful nature in some way. This is in fact what happened. The mother's

---

[308] Munro IR, Guyuron B (November 1981). "Split-Rib Cranioplasty". *Annals of Plastic Surgery* **7** (5): 341–346 (ncbi.nlm.nih.gov/pubmed/7332200); C. Wieland, creation.com/regenerating-ribs-adam-and-that-missing-rib.
[309] Acts 20:28.
[310] 1 Peter 1:19.
[311] Romans 5:9.
[312] Ephesians 1:7.
[313] Romans 3:25.
[314] Revelation 5:9.
[315] Matthew 1:18–23.

4 Can the Bible Withstand Scientific Scrutiny?

blood is never mixed with that of her fetus. The two vascular systems are completely separate, and even though nutrients and waste products freely transverse the placental membrane, the two bloods never mix. In fact, in many cases the mother and her fetus can have different blood groups, and the fact that the mother's antibodies do not attack the fetus as they would any other foreign tissue remains a mystery. Of course, as with many systems, they can break down when a small amount of the baby's blood leaks into the mother's circulatory system and if the mother's blood is Rh negative and her baby is Rh positive then the mother's antibodies attack the baby's blood. This is known as Rh Disease.

Even to the level of detail of an obscure point such as this, the Bible can be found to be reliable and consistent.

A prohibition against marrying within the family

When God had finished His work of creation, He pronounced it to be very good.[316] However, after Adam and Eve disobeyed God by eating the fruit from the Tree of Knowledge of Good and Evil,[317] sin entered the world and all creation was affected by it, right down to the molecular level. Mutations, which are faults or defects,[318] began to occur in strands of DNA in all forms of life.

Since we are *fearfully and wonderfully made*,[319] cells have mechanisms for repairing such faults, but some remain. These would build up very slowly at first, with the passing of generations. This accumulation of mutations may have been a causal factor in the reduction in life spans, particularly in the period after the flood. Sometime later, God gave the civil law through Moses. Part of this is a prohibition against sexual relations with close members of the family, for both moral and genetic reasons.[320]

When a child is conceived, one strand of the mother's DNA (which is bound up in packages called chromosomes)[321] combines with one strand of the father's DNA. Both strands contain mutations and at conception, as the two strands line up with one another, the function of the part containing the mutation is taken over by the corresponding part of the other parent's DNA and all is well. However, if the two strands contain similar mutations—as they would in the case where the parents were close relatives—when the two strands come together, the mutations line up and the mutation is expressed in the offspring.

As mutations accumulate, genetic disorders caused by intrafamily marrying are becoming common, not so much in western societies (presumably because their laws and practices were based on the Bible), but in groups who have not had the benefit of scripture. Howard Schneider writes in reference to Saudi Arabia's alarming increase in genetic disorders such as thalassemia, sickle cell anemia, hydrocephalus and diabetes due to intrafamily marriages:

---

[316] Genesis 1:31.
[317] Genesis 3:6.
[318] See page 47.
[319] Psalm 139:14.
[320] Leviticus 18:6-18; 20:17; Deuteronomy, 27:22.
[321] See page 44.

4 Can the Bible Withstand Scientific Scrutiny?

Nevertheless, even in a country hesitant to discuss its most intimate problems with the outside, a public dialog is developing.... Religious sheiks counsel young men to "choose a wife carefully" and with an eye towards health.[322]

A heading in the *Digital Journal*[323] was quite explicit: 'British Muslim Inbreeding Causing Genetic Disorders.'

Again we can see God's instructions to His people still apply today, even though they were given about 3,500 years ago.

A comparison of the Bible with Islamic writings

We have seen how the Bible can withstand close examination in the light of modern science, medicine and astronomy. By way of comparison, let us now apply the same close inspection to the Koran (Qur'an),[324] which was written no earlier than 600 AD and post-dates the Bible by several hundred to two thousand years.

The earth is flat

The Koran talks of the god of Islam, who has:

---made the earth for you like a carpet spread out.[325]

This certainly gives the impression of the earth being flat. And the Koran repeatedly refers to the earth as wide or spread out.[326] These statements hardly describe a sphere. Not only does the Koran imply that the earth is flat; it states it explicitly in a message to the unbelievers of Mecca:

Do they never reflect on the camels, and how they were created? The mountains, how they were set down? The earth, how it was made flat?[327]

Compare these statements with the Bible in Isaiah 40:22:

He sits above the circle of the earth

The sky is hard

He holds the sky from falling down upon the earth; this it shall not do except by his own leave. Compassionate is God, and merciful to mankind.[328]

In other words, the Koran asserts that the sky is hard and if it fell it would harm or kill the earth's inhabitants. Again, Koran 19:90 speaks of the fact that the heavens could crack. And finally:

---

[322] *Washington Post Foreign Service,* January 16, 2000, page A01.
[323] digitaljournal.com/article/250164, February 11, 2008.
[324] Quotations from the Koran have been taken from: *The Koran*, Trans. N. J. Dawood, Penguin Classics, 2004.
[325] Koran 20:53.
[326] Koran 13:3, 15:19, 50:7, 51:48, 55:10, 78:6, 79:30.
[327] Koran 88:20.
[328] Koran 22:65.

4 Can the Bible Withstand Scientific Scrutiny?

Are the disbelievers unaware that the heavens and the earth were but one solid mass which we tore asunder.[329]

The sun sets in a pool of black mud

He journeyed on a certain road until he reached the west and saw the sun setting in a pool of black mud.[330]

The assumption is that the sun is so small that it can set in a muddy pool on earth.

A fetus was made from a clot of blood

The germ [fetus] *we made a clot of blood, and the clot a lump of flesh. This we fashioned into bones then clothed the bone with flesh, thus bringing forth another creation.*[331]

Errors due to internal contradictions[332]

How many days for creation? Sura 7:54, 10:3, 11:7 and 25:59 clearly state that [the god of Islam] created the heavens and earth in six days. But in 41:9-12, the detailed description of the creation procedure add up to eight days.

What was created first, the heavens or the earth? First earth, then heavens.[333] Heaven, then after, the earth.[334]

Will all Muslims go to Hell? According to Sura 19:71, every Muslim will pass through Hell. Other passages state that those who die in Jihad, will go to Paradise immediately.[335]

Some miscellaneous errors

The Koran states that every ear of corn has 100 grains.[336] Clearly, this is not the case.

The Koran states that [the god of Islam] *has created all living things in pairs.*[337]

This is not true, because many plants and fungi reproduce asexually. However, to an ancient people this would seem correct; it is only with the advancement of science that the fallacy of the statement becomes evident.

The Koran tells of some men who slept in a cave for 309 years.[338] Under such conditions the men would have died after two or three weeks from dehydration and starvation.

---

[329] Koran 21:28.
[330] Koran 18:83-86.
[331] Koran 23:14.
[332] A small selection from the many listed at answering-islam.org/Quran/Contra.
[333] Koran 2:29.
[334] Koran 79:27-30.
[335] Koran 3:169, 157-158.
[336] Koran 2:261.
[337] Koran 43:12.

4 Can the Bible Withstand Scientific Scrutiny?

According to the Koran, mountains make decisions and possess fear:

We offered our trusts to the heavens, to the earth and to the mountains, but they refused the burden and were afraid to receive it.[339]

Not only did the clouds and earth talk but they decided whether they would come willingly or be forced to come. This statement ascribes a level of intelligence and independent agency to both the clouds and the earth:

Then turning to the sky, which was but a cloud of vapor, he said to it and the earth: "Come forward both, willing or perforce." "We will come willingly," they answered.[340]

According to the Koran, fiery comets chase evil spirits around the heavens:

We have decked the sky with constellations and made them lovely to behold. We have guarded them from every cursed devil. Eavesdroppers are pursued by fiery comets.[341]

There are many websites detailing errors in the Koran.[342] After listing ten areas of error, one of them sums it up like this:

The Holy Qur'an is full of inaccuracies, contradictions, inconsistencies, redundancies, no chronology or chapters, grammatical errors, etc.[343]

5. Archaeology

There exists a large body of archaeological evidence that confirms the authenticity of the people, places and events recorded in the Bible. Selected examples are given below. More can be found in many books; a particularly good one is Peter Masters' *Heritage of Evidence in the British Museum*.[344]

Old Testament

Samaria Ostracon

In 1910, G J Reisner discovered 63 potsherds containing inscriptions written in ink. These are called ostraca (plural) and ostracon (singular); an image of one is shown on the right. The inscriptions are in ancient Hebrew writing and are commercial records of the time.

Thirty of them identify the clan and district name of seven of the ten offspring of Manasseh that are recorded in Joshua 17:2–3.

---

[338] Koran 18:25.
[339] Koran 33:72.
[340] Koran 41:10-12.
[341] Koran 15:16-19.
[342] answering-islam.org/quran/contra; 1000mistakes.com; lightshinesindarkness.com/history_errors_koran; faithfreedom.org/Articles/SKM/contradictions.
[343] faithfreedom.org/articles/SKM/contadictions.htm, retrieved April 10, 2011.
[344] P. Masters, *Heritage of Evidence in the British Museum,* Stephens and George, 2004.

4 Can the Bible Withstand Scientific Scrutiny?

Amulet Scroll

The oldest passage of scripture currently known was found written on a tiny scrap of silver. It was rolled up and apparently worn around someone's neck, and was buried with the person. It was found by Dr Gabriel Barkay during the excavation of burial caves in the Shoulder of Hinnom area in 1979 and can be seen today in the Israel Museum in Jerusalem. It contains an inscription of the Aaronic Blessing of Numbers 6:24–26:

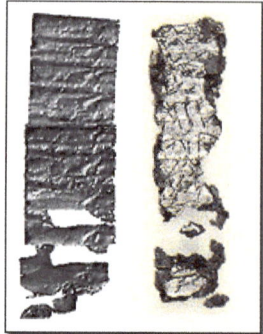

The LORD bless you, and keep you: The LORD make his face shine upon you, and be gracious to you: The LORD lift up his countenance upon you, and give you peace.

The Amulet Scroll

Pharaoh Shishak

The military campaign into Israel by Pharaoh Shishak, the first Egyptian king to be mentioned in the Bible,[345] was found recorded on the walls of the Temple of Amun in Thebes, Egypt.[346]

The Merneptah Stele

This stele dates to the reign of Pharaoh Merneptah (1236–1223 BC). It commemorates the victories of Egypt. However, the last paragraph contains a fascinating reference to Israel:

Canaan has been plundered in every evil way ... Israel is devastated having no seed.

This is the earliest documentation of Israel besides the Bible and the only known mention of Israel in Egyptian records. It resides in the Cairo Museum.

The Merneptah Stele

The House of David Inscription

In 1993, at the completion of a 25-year excavation of the archaeological site at Tel Dan in northern Israel, someone noticed lines of writing on a rock being highlighted by the afternoon sun. Upon closer examination, it was revealed to be a stele fragment mentioning King David's dynasty. It is the first mention of King David, and the earliest mention of a significant biblical figure, outside the Bible. The inscription is now in the Israel Museum in Jerusalem.

The House of David Inscription

---

[345] 1 Kings 14:25–26.
[346] K. A. Kitchen, Shishak's Military Campaign in Israel, Confirmed, *Biblical Archaeology Review*, May/June, 1989, pages 32–33.

4 Can the Bible Withstand Scientific Scrutiny?

The Fall of Samaria

The fall of Samaria[347] to Sargon II, king of Assyria, was found recorded on his palace walls, as was the defeat of Ashdod by Sargon II.[348, 349]

The Siege of Lachish

The siege of Lachish by Sennacherib[350] was found recorded on the Lachish reliefs.[351]

Hezekiah's Tunnel

The Bible states[352] that the Judean king Hezekiah commissioned a tunnel to be built to carry water from the Gihon Spring, which was outside the city wall, to within the city, in order to give Jerusalem an adequate water supply in the event of a siege from the threatening Assyrian army.

The tunnel was constructed between the period 727 BC and 698 BC and was discovered by Edward Robinson, an American Bible scholar, in 1838. It is still carrying water and people can walk along all of its 533 meters.

Hezekiah's Tunnel, courtesy BiblePlaces.com

Taylor Prism

As mentioned, King Hezekiah had his tunnel constructed in order to have a plentiful supply of water during a siege from the rampaging Assyrian army. The Assyrian king was Sennacherib and he laid siege to Jerusalem. Hezekiah prayed in the temple and in the morning, 185,000 men of the Assyrian army were dead.[353] Sennacherib consequently retreated to Nineveh. However, he did record his victories on stele.

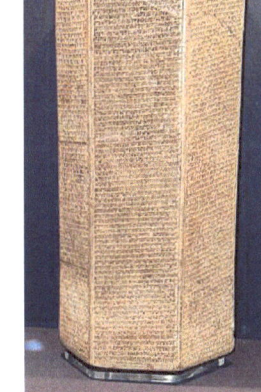

This stele has been named after Colonel Taylor, who discovered it in 1830, and it resides in the British Museum. It confirms the following points made in the Bible—Sennacherib did invade Judah; he conquered many cities and trapped Hezekiah in Jerusalem. In addition, the stele reveals that Hezekiah paid him tribute, but this happened before Sennacharib came to Jerusalem[354] and it seems likely that Sennacherib added this statement as a way of explaining why he did not lay waste to Jerusalem as he had done to 46 other cities. No mention is made of the capture of Jerusalem.

The Taylor Prism

---

[347] 2 Kings 17:3–6, 24; 18:9–11.
[348] Isaiah 20:1.
[349] Britannica Online, retrieved May 2, 2011.
[350] 2 Kings 18:13, 17.
[351] britishmuseum.org/explore/highlights/highlight_objects/me/s/panel,_palace_of_sennacherib-4.aspx.
[352] 2 Kings 20:20; 2 Chronicles 32:3–4.
[353] 2 Kings 19:35–36.
[354] 2 Kings 18:14-15.

The Assassination of Sennacherib

The assassination of Sennacherib by his own sons[355] was found recorded in the annals of his son Esarhaddon.[356]

Belshazzar

The existence of Belshazzar, king of Babylon, named in Daniel chapter 5, was doubted. The last king of Babylon was Nabonidus, according to recorded history. However, tablets were found showing that Belshazzar was Nabonidus' son who served as coregent in Babylon. This being the case, Belshazzar could only offer to make Daniel 'third highest ruler in the kingdom'[357] for reading the handwriting on the wall, the highest available position. Here we see the accurate nature of the biblical record, once again confirmed by the discoveries of archaeology.[358] The Nabonidus Chronicle resides in the British Museum.

Nabonidus Chronicle

The Moabite Stone

The Moabite Stone is an ancient slab of stone erected in 850 BC by King Mesha; it contains a long inscription commemorating a victory resulting from his revolt against King Ahab of Israel.[359] It was found at Dibon, Jordon, in 1886 by F. A. Klein, a German clergyman. Although it was broken when Klein tried to purchase it from the local Arabs, most of the fragments were recovered. The stone resides at the Louvre in France.

The Moabite Stone

Nebuchadnezzar II's Campaigns in the West

The tablet shown is one of a series that summarises the principal events of each year from 747 BC to at least 280 BC. Each entry is separated by a horizontal line and begins with a reference to the year of reign of the king in question.

The inscription states that after re-equipping his army, Nebuchadnezzar marched to Syria in 599 BC. He marched westwards again in December 598 BC, as Jehoiakim, the king of Judah, had ceased to pay tribute. Nebuchadnezzar's army besieged Jerusalem and captured it on 15/16th March 597 BC. The new king of Judah, Jehoiachin, was captured and carried off to Babylon. A series of expeditions to Syria brings this Chronicle to an end in

Cuneiform tablet with part of the Babylonian Chronicle (605–594 BC)

---

[355] 2 Kings 19:37.

[356] D. D. Luckenbill, *Ancient Records of Assyria and Babylonia* Vol. 2: *Historical Records of Assyria from Sargon to the End,* University of Chicago Press, 1927.

[357] Daniel 5:16.

[358] Homer Trecartin, Jr. 8 December 1996, Studies in Daniel, Professor Pastor Donn Leatherman, *The Relationship Between Nabonidus and Belshazzar*, biblestudymanuals.net/belshazzar.htm.

[359] 2 Kings 1:1; 3:4–27.

594 BC.[360] This Chronicle describes the events exactly as they are stated in the Bible.[361]

Nebuchadnezzar's Chief Official

While searching through Babylonian financial accounts in the British Museum's great Arched Room, visiting professor Michael Jursa came across a name he half remembered, Nabu-sharrussu-ukin, on a 2,600-year-old Assyrian cuneiform tablet. Professor Jursa, an Assyriologist, checked the Old Testament, and there in chapter 39 verse 3 of the Book of Jeremiah, he found, though spelt differently, the same name: Nebo-Sarsekim. He was, according to Jeremiah, Nebuchadnezzar's chief officer and he was present at the siege of Jerusalem. The tablet is dated to Nebuchadnezzar's tenth year, which was 595 BC, 12 years before Jerusalem was besieged. Dr Irving Finkel, a British Museum expert, commented:

This is a fantastic discovery, a world-class find. If Nebo-Sarsekim existed, which other lesser figures in the Old Testament existed? A throwaway detail in the Old Testament turns out to be accurate and true. I think that it means that the whole of the narrative (of Jeremiah) takes on a new kind of power.[362]

Cyrus the Great

The Cyrus Cylinder

Cyrus captured Babylon in 539 BC. But about 200 years before then, God foretold in the Book of Isaiah how He would raise up Cyrus and use him as His instrument.[363] Cyrus is also mentioned in Ezra 1:2–4 and in 2 Chronicles 36:22–23. The Cyrus Cylinder, which tells of Cyrus' exploits after he captured Babylon, was uncovered in 1879 and now resides in room 55 at the British Museum.

Cyrus was buried in a simple gabled stone tomb outside his capital of Pasargadae in modern Iran. According to the historian Strabo, this inscription once graced the structure:

Passer by, I am Cyrus, the son of Cambyses, who founded the empire of Persia, and was king of Asia. Grudge me not therefore this monument.[364]

Cyrus' Tomb

---

[360] britishmuseum.org/explore/highlights/highlight_objects/me/c/cuneiform_nebuchadnezzar_ii.aspx, retrieved April 25, 2011.
[361] 2 Kings, chapter 24.
[362] biblearchaeology.org/post/2008/04/nebo-sarsekim-found-in-babylonian-tablet.aspx, retrieved April 25, 2011.
[363] Isaiah 45:1–3.
[364] wikipedia.org/wiki/Pasargadae, retrieved April 25, 2011.

Further confirmation that Cyrus was once king of Persia comes in the form of an inscription on a palace ruin, stating:

I Cyrus the king, an Achaemenid (Persian).[365]

Cyrus' Inscription

Darius the Great

Darius the Great was king of the Persian Empire from 522–486 BC. On the request of the Jews, he ordered a search of the records and recovered the decree to restore the Jerusalem temple,[366] the construction of which, had been discontinued. Darias the Great's tomb has been discovered at a site in Iran and is explicitly identified by an inscription.[367] Nearby Darius's tomb are three others which are thought to be those of the biblical characters: Xerxes, Artaxerxes and Darius II.

The tomb of Darius the Great

The Dead Sea Scrolls

These documents were held by a small Essene community who lived in the Judean desert on the western shore of the Dead Sea. They were written from about 200 BC to AD 70. They cover all the books of the Old Testament except those of Esther and Nehemiah. The Dead Sea Scrolls are discussed in more detail on page 123. However, they are included here as support for the integrity of the Bible in two major ways.

Firstly, they pre-date the oldest preserved written text of the Hebrew Bible by approximately 1,000 years, yet they are almost identical with the standard Hebrew

The Scroll of Isaiah

---

[365] wikipedia.org/wiki/Cyrus_the_Great, retrieved April 25, 2011.
[366] Ezra 6:1–12.
[367] wikipedia.org/wiki/Darius_I_of_Persia, retrieved April 30, 2011.

4 Can the Bible Withstand Scientific Scrutiny?

Masoretic text, which confirms the remarkable precision used in the copying of scripture. This gives believers great confidence that the Bible we have today is the same, with the exception of very minor details, to what was originally written.

The Shrine of the Book

Secondly, they give strong support to the unity of the authorship of Isaiah. Critics have claimed that the book had two authors: one, the original, wrote the first 39 chapters (which are basically about impending judgment), and later, another who completed the book with prophecies that were subsequently fulfilled. Liberal scholars claimed that the latter half of the book must have been written after the events because of its prophetic accuracy. Yet the Dead Sea Scrolls contain the entire book of Isaiah (this is on display at the *Shrine of the Book* in Jerusalem). A close examination shows no break between chapters 39 and 40. In fact, chapter 40 commences at the bottom of the chapter 39 column, thereby clearly demonstrating the unity of Isaiah.[368]

New Testament

The Pool of Siloam

Liberal scholars claimed that the Pool of Siloam never existed and that John's gospel[369] was pure allegory; the pool normally referred to by that name was built by Eudocia of Constantinople (AD 400–460) and could not have been the pool of Jesus' time. This liberal line of thinking was shown to be wrong in 2005, when a repair team, excavating a damaged sewer, uncovered two steps. Subsequent excavation revealed three groups of five stairs, each about 60 meters long, leading down to a pool, as shown.

This pool was built by King Hezekiah[370] and is about 200 meters from the other Pool of Siloam. Commenting on this discovery, James Charlesworth, a professor of New Testament at Princeton Theological Seminary, said:

To dismiss John as historically unimportant is absurd. Now it becomes clear that the gospel of John does have reliable historical information. We have found there is such a pool, precisely as John describes it.[371]

---

[368] C. R. Swindoll, *Insight's Archaeology Handbook,* Insight for Living, 2008, page 66.
[369] John 9:6-7.
[370] 2 Kings 20:20.
[371] *Christianity Today*, October, 2005.

4 Can the Bible Withstand Scientific Scrutiny?

The Pilate Inscription

The Bible was the only known source that affirmed Pontius Pilate as being the governor of Judea. Consequently, many doubted that he ever really held that position until 1961, when the Italian archaeologist Dr Frova uncovered a limestone block while he was excavating an ancient theater near Caesarea Maritima. It had inscribed on it a phrase in Latin, which is translated as *Pontius Pilate, Prefect of Judea*—which is how scripture describes him.[372]

The Pilate Inscription

The Ossuary (a receptacle for containing human bones) of Caiaphas the High Priest

Caiaphas the High Priest

Caiaphas was high priest for 18 years (AD 18–36). It is probable that he gained the position by marrying the daughter of Annas, head of a powerful high-priestly clan.[373] Caiaphas is infamous as the leader of the conspiracy to crucify Jesus. Dr Zvi Greenhut of the Israel Museum discovered his ossuary in November 1990.

At a meeting of the religious leaders, Caiaphas made this prophetic statement concerning Jesus:

Nor do you consider that it is expedient for us, that one man should die for the people and not that the whole nation should perish.[374]

Artemis Statue

During Paul's third missionary journey, he and fellow travelers stopped at Ephesus and argued persuasively about the kingdom of God. Acts 19:11 states:

And God wrought special miracles by the hands of Paul.

As a consequence, many people believed and rejected the worship of Artemis (the Greek name for the Roman goddess Diana), the goddess of fertility, and the silversmiths who made a living by making statues of Artemis felt the loss of sales and started a riot in order to have Paul and company taken from their midst.[375]

Many statues of Artemis have been discovered and one is shown here.

---

[372] Matthew 27:2, Luke 3:1 (Note, Prefect is a Latin word, Governor is its English equivalent).
[373] John 18:13.
[374] John 11:50.

4 Can the Bible Withstand Scientific Scrutiny?

The Tomb of Herod the Great Discovered

In May 2007, Professor Ehud Netzer announced that a team of archaeologists from the Hebrew University in Jerusalem had discovered the remains of the sarcophagus and mausoleum of Herod the Great, near the top of Mount Herodium, the cone-shaped hill he had created.[376]

This Herod is mentioned in the Bible as the king who ordered the death of all males under the age of two. Herod made his decree in order to take the life of the One who had been born King of the Jews, after the Maji, who had been warned in a dream, failed to return to him and tell him where he could find the Child.[377]

Mount Herodium (a Hebrew University of Jerusalem photograph)

A photograph of what is almost certainly Herod's sarcophagus

Jews Forced to Leave Rome

The forcing of the Jews to leave Rome during the reign of Claudius (AD 41–54)[378] was recorded by Suetonius (circa AD 70—a ter AD 130). In *The Life of Claudius* 25.4, we find the statement:

As the Jews were making constant disturbances at the instigation of Chrestus [a Latin name for Christ], *he expelled them from Rome.*

---

[375] Acts 19:23-27.
[376] israelnationalnews.com, retrieved December 1, 2008.
[377] Matthew 2:1–17.
[378] Acts 18:2.

4   Can the Bible Withstand Scientific Scrutiny?

This is plausibly a reference to the expulsion of Jewish Christians from Rome. The author of The Acts of the Apostles (commonly referred to as Acts), Luke, makes mention of this same expulsion, which occurred in AD 49 according to the fifth century church father Orosius. Acts 18:2 states:

And he [Paul] *found a certain Jew named Aquila, born in Pontus, who had recently come from Italy with his wife Priscilla (because Claudius had commanded all the Jews to depart from Rome); and he came to them.*

Aquila and Priscilla were converted to Christianity prior to meeting Paul.

Conclusion

Evidence has been presented that shows that the Bible is correct in all that it says, whether it is a cataclysmic event such as Noah's flood, or matters of science, agriculture, hydrology, cosmology or medicine. This is not the case for another ancient book (although not nearly as old as the Bible), the Koran. Finally, we have seen how archaeology has confirmed the historicity of the people, places and events mentioned throughout the Bible.

Our great God inspired the Bible and it is entirely reliable.

Chapter 5

The Bible and Prophecy

The validity of any faith-based theory or belief system may be affirmed by its ability to make accurate predictions. If it cannot do this, then there is no compelling reason to believe what it says about the future or the unprovable past.

As documented in the first chapter, the religions of Hinduism, Buddhism and Islam are all unable to do this.

The Bible is replete with detailed prophecies, and the unwavering accuracy of these prophecies affirms that the Bible is divinely inspired and is like no other book.

Prophesies of Isaiah 53 and Psalm 22

The Dead Sea Scrolls

The book of Isaiah was written about 700 years before the

Caves at Qumran

time of Jesus, and yet chapter 53 of this book very accurately predicts His linage and the purpose for His incarnation (in human form) and death in amazing detail.

Psalm 22, written about 1,000 years before Christ, gives a detail-by-detail description of our Lord's trial and crucifixion, even to the extent that soldiers gambled for His garment.

Many liberal scholars and critics of Christianity have said that because they make so many accurate predictions, the two chapters must have been written after the event. However, a Bedouin shepherd put an end to that line of thinking.

5   The Bible and Prophecy

In the year 1947, shepherds were minding sheep in the desert area around Qumran on the northwest shore of the Dead Sea, when one of the sheep went into a cave. Instead of climbing up and going in, one of the shepherds threw a stone to frighten the animal out, but the stone hit something, and instead of a thud noise, it went 'clunk'—the sound of pottery breaking. So he climbed in to investigate. This is one version of their discovery, others exist. The scrolls were not immediately recognized for their antiquity and at one stage, they were actually advertised in the *Wall Street Journal* on June 1, 1954 (see picture right).

What the shepherd discovered that day was one of the greatest biblical archeological treasure troves ever, which have become known as the Dead Sea Scrolls.

During the years following their discovery in 1947, between 825 and 870 documents were brought to light from eleven caves. They cover all of the books of the Hebrew Bible except for the books of Esther and Nehemiah. The scrolls were written during the period 250 BC to AD 70. The only scrolls dated as being written in the first century are the Temple Scroll, Genesis Apocryphon and Thanksgiving Hymns; all of the biblical writings discovered significantly pre-date Christ. The dating was carried out using paleography and the less accurate carbon-14 isotopic dating.[379] Interestingly, the most complete book is that of Isaiah, which has been accurately dated by paleography to between 125–100 BC, with the Psalms coming close behind. And of course, Isaiah 53 and Psalm 22 are there with the exact wording, apart from a few very minor exceptions, of the modern Hebrew Bible.

The Ancient Hebrew Research Center[380] compared Isaiah chapter 53[381] with that from the Masoretic text (AD 1,000).[382] Of the 166 Hebrew words that comprise the chapter, only 17 letters differ—10 letters are spelling differences, 4 are stylistic changes, and 3 letters are added for 'light' in verse 11.[383]

The Bible has not changed in any significant way over the thousands of years since it was originally written, even though it has been transcribed many times. **The text of the Bible can be trusted.**

---

[379] P. R. Davis, G. J. Brooks and P. R. Callaway, *The Complete World of the Dead Sea Scrolls*, Thames and Hudson, 2002, page 75.
[380] ancient-hebrew.org/31_isaiah53.html, retrieved April 10, 2011.
[381] Recorded on the Dead Sea Scrolls in Hebrew script (100 BC), top line.
[382] Bottom line, which is shown on the previous page.
[383] apologeticspress, retrieved July 12, 2008.

> **MISCELLANEOUS FOR SALE**
>
> **"The Four Dead Sea Scrolls"**
>
> Biblical Manuscripts dating back to at least 200 BC, are for sale. This would be an ideal gift to an educational or religious institution by an individual or group.
>
> Box F 206, The Wall Street Journal.

5 The Bible and Prophecy

Daniel's Prophecy of 70 Weeks

Over 60 Old Testament prophecies regarding the Messiah were fulfilled in the Person of Jesus of Nazareth.[384]

In chapter nine of his book, Daniel foretells a number of events.[385] One of these is the exact date, precise to the day, when 'Messiah the Prince' shall come. The point in Jesus' ministry when He presented Himself as the Messiah was when He accepted the worship of the people as He entered Jerusalem, four days before He was crucified. This occasion was foretold by Zechariah[386] and has become known as 'Palm Sunday.'

So what day was this in relation to our calendar? Much has been written regarding the time of Christ's crucifixion and resurrection. What is presented below is a view which is supported by historical data and harmonises Daniel's prophecy with Christ as the Passover Lamb.

The time of this event can be calculated by working back from the time of Christ's crucifixion, for which more information has been given. Although many dates have been proposed, April 3, AD 33, is the one favored by most scholars.

The reasons they give for this date are as follows: all gospels agree that Jesus died on the day before the Sabbath. Some scholars claim there may have been two Sabbaths in that week because the first day of the Feast of Unleavened Bread is a Sabbath and that Christ may have been crucified on a day other than Friday. However, there can be no doubt that Jesus rose on the first day of the week, a Sunday, and that it was the third day, inclusive, since His crucifixion. By the time of Taetullian (AD 160–220), the Greek word 'paraskeue,' was used in the gospels as the day of Christ's crucifixion and it was used to denote Friday. The third Bishop of Antioch, Ignatius, writing in the first century to the Trallians, makes it clear that Christ was crucified on the day of Preparation (Friday), was in the ground during the Sabbath and rose on the Lord's Day (Sunday).[387]

This fixed the crucifixion date as Nisan 14 (post-Exilic name; formerly Abib, Exodus 13:4, approximately our March/April), with the Passover commencing at moonrise that evening which signaled the start of a new day; Nisan 15. There appears to be a discrepancy in the gospels with Matthew, Mark and Luke stating that Jesus ate the Passover meal[388] and John stating that Jesus, knowing that Judas was about to betray Him, told him to leave the table and do what he had intended. Since Judas kept the money, some of the disciples thought that Jesus had sent him to buy what was needed for the feast, that is, the Passover.[389] This apparent contradiction has been successfully resolved by Sir Colin Humphreys in his book *The Mystery of the Last Supper*.[390]

---

[384] Refer to page 133.
[385] Daniel 9:24–27.
[386] Zechariah 9:9.
[387] For a thorough analysis of the days of Christ's crucifixion and resurrection, the reader is directed to bible.ca/d-3-days-and-3-nights.htm.
[388] Matthew 26:17-29; Mark 14:12-25; Luke 22:7-20.
[389] John 13: 1–29.
[390] Colin J Humpreys, *The Mystery of the Last Supper*, Cambridge University Press, 2011.

5 The Bible and Prophecy

Humphreys after establishing that the crucifixion took place on April 3, AD 33, provides convincing evidence that two calendars were operating at the time. Jesus celebrated the Passover with His disciples using the pre-exilic calendar of Moses on the Wednesday evening (Nissan 14) of April 1, AD 33 and John refers to the official Jewish calendar where Nissan 14 occurred Friday April 3, AD 33 with the Passover meal being eaten that evening on Nissan 15 which commenced at moonrise.

The crucifixion took place under the administration of Pontius Pilate, who held the position from AD 26–36. The only years that Nisan 14 occurs on a Friday during that period are the years 27, 33, 36 and maybe 30. Luke states that John the Baptist commenced his ministry in the fifteenth year of the reign of Tiberius,[391] thereby dating John's appearance to AD 29. As well, the Passover was celebrated on the first full moon of the spring. Only the dates of April 7, AD 30 and April 3, AD 33 satisfy these criteria for the time of Christ's crucifixion. Since John records three separate Passovers during Jesus' ministry,[392] the early date of AD 30 must be excluded, thereby leaving April 3, AD 33 as the time of Christ's crucifixion.[393]

However, there has been a problem with this later date—namely; Herod the Great was alive when Jesus was born. This is referenced by the fact that following a visit from the Maji, he ordered all babies under the age of two to be killed.[394] This implies that Jesus must have been born during the years of 6 or 5 BC, because the commonly accepted date for Herod's death is 4 BC. And Luke states that:

Jesus Himself began His ministry at about thirty years of age.[395]

This would be in keeping with what was required for a Levitical Priest.[396] Since Jesus' ministry lasted about three-and-a-half years, He could not have been born in 6–5 BC, commenced His ministry at the age of 30, ministered for three-and-one-half years and have been crucified as late as AD 33.

The evidence for believing Herod died in 4 BC mainly comes from the writings of Josephus (AD 37–103), a first century Jewish historian. However, Josephus was not always accurate or consistent and his chronologies should always be cross-checked.[397] Josephus states that Herod commenced his reign in 37 BC and that he reigned 34 years; elsewhere he states that Herod reigned 37 years[398] and that there was a lunar eclipse just before he died. Tradition has this event assigned to the eclipse of March 13, 4 BC. Further evidence for the 4 BC date of Herod's death comes from coins of the period, which show that his successors began their reign in 4–3 BC.

---

[391] Luke 3:1–2.
[392] John 2:23, 6:4, 13:1.
[393] C. J. Humphreys and G. Waddington, *The American Scientific Affiliation*, 1985, 37, pages 2–10; H. W. Hoehner, *Chronological Aspects of the Life of Christ,* Zondervan: Grand Rapids, 1977.
[394] Matthew 2:16.
[395] Luke 3:23.
[396] Numbers 4:3.
[397] M. Broshi, The Credibility of Josephus, *Journal of Jewish Studies 33*, Spring/Autum, 1982.
[398] J. P. Pratt, *The Planetarium*, 1990, 19 (4), pages 8–14.

5 The Bible and Prophecy

The argument of 4 BC for Herod's death is not as straight-forward as it seems. John P Pratt, in a well researched and referenced paper,[399] discusses the many problems associated with that year and claims the year of AD 1 to be much more in keeping with historical records and astronomical observations. For example, Josephus, who wrote almost 100 years after the event, mentions only one lunar eclipse. Furthermore, the eclipse of 4 BC happened in the middle of the night and would not have been observed by many. In contrast, the eclipse of December 29, 1 BC was clearly visible at sunset. As well, Pratt proposes that Herod's successors antedated their reigns, presumably to extend their lengths. This, Pratt suggests, is a factor of which Josephus was not aware. The later date for Herod's death means that the sixth century scholar Dionysius Exiguus, who set the Christian era of AD (Anno Domini; 'In the year of the Lord') and who had access to more records than are available today, was correct after all in calculating from 1 BC. The Dionysius Exiguus dating system is used to number the years of both the Gregorian and Julian Calendars (note, AD 1 follows 1 BC; there was no zero year).

Therefore, if Jesus was crucified on April 3, AD33, then his triumphant ride into Jerusalem would have taken place on March 30[400] of that year, which was five days before the Passover[401] if we count both Nisan 10 and 14 as was the Jewish practice of counting part of a day as one day.[402] The day, being a Monday, has become incorrectly known as 'Palm Sunday'. In complete harmony with the events of the Passover that require the lambs to be selected on Nisan 10, and then slaughtered four days (five Jewish days) later on Nisan 14 between the hours of 12 noon and 3 pm, Christ presented Himself as Messiah, the Passover Lamb[403] on Nisan 10 (Monday March 30, AD 33) and was slaughtered (crucified) on Nisan 14 (Friday, April 3, AD 33). He then died at 3 pm.

Before Daniel's prophecy is examined, it is of value to go back in time to when Jeremiah was warning Judah of their impending exile and that it would be Nebuchadnezzar, king of Babylon, who would bring this about.[404] In the same chapter,[405] Jeremiah goes on to say that they will serve the king of Babylon 70 years and he later repeats this warning with the added information that He, the Lord, will bring them back to this place after 70 years.[406] Although Jeremiah was severely criticised and thrown in a pit for his prophecy, he lived to see the first part of its fulfillment. At the time, Daniel would have been in his very early teens as he was taken to Babylon with the first wave of captives in 605 BC.

If we fast-forward about 69 years, Daniel is no longer a captive but a government official. Nebuchadnezzar has had a period of mental illness, thinking he was an ox and eating grass. He then recovered, gave praises to God, died and was followed by a succession of kings who only reigned for a short period before being assassinated. Finally Belshazzar comes to the throne, mocks God, Daniel reads the writing on the wall and it's all over for Belshazzar. The Medes and

---

[399] *Ibid.*
[400] In the year AD 33, Nisan 10 falls on Monday, March 30. cgsf.org/dbeattie/calendar/?roman=33.
[401] John 12:1-12.
[402] Colin J Humpreys, *The Mystery of the Last Supper*, Cambridge University Press, 2011, page 23.
[403] 1 Corinthians 5:7; John 1:29; 1 Peter 1:17.
[404] Jeremiah 25:9.
[405] Jeremiah 25:11.
[406] Jeremiah 29:10.

5 The Bible and Prophecy

the Persians are the world-power. Daniel writes in verse 1 of chapter 9 that Darius is in his first year as king, and at this time he reads from the prophet Jeremiah that the time of exile will be 70 years, and that this time is almost up. But God said through His prophet that He would bring them back when the people seek Him with all their hearts. So what does Daniel do? Verse 3 tells us:

Then I set my face toward the Lord God to make request by prayer and supplications, with fasting, sackcloth, and ashes.

Daniel prays from verse 3 to verse 19 and his answer comes in verse 20 when he is visited by the angel Gabriel, who tells him in a vision what is going to happen to his people.

Verse 24: *Seventy weeks are determined for your people and for your holy city, to finish the transgression, to make an end of sins, to make reconciliation for iniquity, to bring in everlasting righteousness, to seal up vision and prophecy and to anoint the Most Holy.*

Verse 25: *Therefore and understand, that from the going forth of the command to restore and build Jerusalem until Messiah the Prince, there shall be seven weeks and sixty-two weeks; the street shall be built again, and the wall, even in troublesome times.*

Verse 26: *And after the sixty-two weeks Messiah shall be cut off, but not for Himself; and the people of the prince who is to come shall destroy the city and the sanctuary. The end of it shall be with a flood and till the end of the war desolations are determined.*

Verse 27: *Then he shall confirm a covenant with many for one week; but in the middle of the week He shall bring an end to sacrifice and offering. And on the wing of abominations shall be one who makes desolate, even until the consummation, which is determined, is poured out on the desolate.*

The prophecy is contained in verse 24 and detailed in verses 25–27. The Hebrew word for 'week' means a period of seven; it can be seven days, seven weeks, seven months or seven years. There are four good reasons for believing the period, in this context, refers to years:

1. Daniel is talking about years in verses 1 and 2.

2. It is impossible to fit the events of verses 24 to 27 into days, weeks or months.

3. The only other place Daniel uses the word week where he does not mean years, he qualifies it by adding the word days (10:2–3).

4. The fact that verse 27 speaks of a covenant being broken at the halfway point of the seventieth seven agrees well with Daniel 7:25, 12:7 and Revelation 12:14.

Using 'year' for the word 'week', verse 24 tells us that six events are going to happen in 490 years and verses 25–27 state that these 70 lots of 7 years are in three parts: one of 7 x7 years; one of 62 x7 years and one 1 x7 years. The six events are:

- To finish the transgression.

- To make an end of sins.

- To make reconciliation for iniquity.

5 The Bible and Prophecy

- To bring in everlasting righteousness.
- To seal up the vision and prophecy.
- To anoint the Most Holy.

Therefore, after 70 weeks God will have dealt with sin and brought in a period of everlasting righteousness.

Verse 25 reveals when the Messiah will come. This is in two lots of time; one of seven weeks, followed by sixty two weeks, making a total of 69 weeks. This gives a total of 483 years.

The number of days in the Jewish year was 360. That is, twelve months of thirty days. This 360-day year is confirmed in Genesis chapter seven, where it states that the flood lasted 5 months; verse 11 states that it commenced on the 17th day of the second month and chapter 8, verse 4, says it finished on the 17th day of the seventh month, a total of exactly 5 months. And verse 24 of chapter seven states it lasted 150 days. Five months of thirty days equals 150 days. And again in Revelation 12:6, we read that the woman (Israel) will seek refuge for 1,260 days, with verse 14 stating it will last three-and-one-half years.

Again, 360 days per year for three-and-one-half years equals 1,260 days. Therefore, multiplying 483 years by the number of days in each year, we obtain a **total of 173,880 days.**

The time of the commencement of the 70 weeks of Daniel's prophecy is 'from the going forth of the commandment to restore and to build Jerusalem.' Four decrees are mentioned in scripture concerning the return of the people to Jerusalem. These are:

- The decree of Cyrus in 539 BC[407]
- The decree of Darius 1 in 519/518 BC[408]
- The decree of Artaxerxes 1 to Ezra in 457 BC[409]
- The decree of Artaxerxes 1 to Nehemiah in 444 BC[410]

Only the last decree could fulfill the statement, since it was the only one of the four concerned specifically with rebuilding the city. This decree was given in the twentieth year of Artaxerxes in the month of Nisan,[411] but exactly what day and year has been the source of discussion. Sir Robert Anderson (1841–1918) appears to have been the first person to have published a serious and scholarly analysis of this time in particular and Daniel's prophecy in general with his book *The Coming Prince*.[412] Anderson posited the 483-year countdown commencing March 14, 445 BC (Nisan 1, 445 BC) and culminating with Christ's triumphant entry into Jerusalem on April 6, AD

---

[407] 2 Chronicles 36:22, 23; Ezra 1:1–4.
[408] Ezra 6:1, 6–12.
[409] Ezra 7:11–26.
[410] Nehemiah 2:1–8.
[411] Nehemiah 2:1.
[412] Available in many reprinted editions.

32 (Nisan 10, AD 32). Anderson's date for the crucifixion of AD 32 is untenable, for it would mean Christ was executed on either a Sunday or Monday. Even though other errors have been found as well, Anderson did show the likelihood of the extreme accuracy of Daniel's prophecy and set the stage for others to refine his work.

One such man was Dr Harold Hoehner, Chairman of the New Testament Department at Dallas Theological Seminary, USA. In his book *Chronological Aspects of the Life of Christ*,[413] he builds on the foundation that Anderson laid and corrects some of his errors. For example, it is clear that Nehemiah uses the Jewish Trishri-to-Trishri (March to April) calendar, because he records[414] that he heard of Jerusalem's desolation in the Jewish month of Chislev (November/ December), which by the Julian calendar was the year 445 BC.[415] Later, he reports that permission was granted to restore the city.[416] This was in the Jewish month of Nisan (March/April), still in Artaxerxes' twentieth year, but the Gregorian calendar had clicked over to 444 BC. Nehemiah states that the decree was given in the month of Nisan. Since he does not include the day of the month, it is assumed that it is the first day. That first day of the month is signified by the first appearance of the new moon. The first occurrence of crescent visibility would have appeared at 10 pm, March 4, late enough to be missed. However, on March 5, 444 BC it would have been clearly visible to all.

To summarise, Daniel's prophecy states that Messiah the Prince shall come 173,880 days from the decree to rebuild Jerusalem. We have shown that this decree was given on March 5, 444 BC. Jesus, Messiah the Prince, entered Jerusalem on March 30, AD 33.

In order to find the number of days between March 5, 444 BC and March 30, AD 33, it is necessary to take the number of years between these dates (444 +33 = 477) and subtract 1 year, since only one year elapsed from 1 BC to AD 1, which gives a total of 476 years. To find the number of days in the Gregorian calendar, which is in use now, it is necessary to multiply 476 years by 365.2422 (number of Gregorian days in a year). The product of this, to the nearest day, is 173,855; this is the number of days from March 5, 444 BC to March 5, AD 33. An additional 25 days is added, bringing the number of days to March 30, AD 33. **This gives exactly 173,880 days, which reveals the extreme accuracy of Daniel's prophecy and the reliability of scripture.**

After the completion of the sixty-nine weeks and before the commencement of the seventieth week, two events were predicted to take place in the following order:

- The "cutting off" of the Messiah.
- The destruction of the city and the temple.

---

[413] H. W. Hoehner, *Chronological Aspects of the Life of Christ,* Zondervan: Grand Rapids, 1977.

[414] Nehemiah 1:1.

[415] S. H. Horn and L. H. Wood, The Fifth Century Jewish Calendar at Elephantine, *Journal of Near Eastern Studies*, XIII, January 1954, page 9; R. A. Parker and W. H. Dubberstein, *Babylonian Chronology 626 BC –AD 75*, Second Edition, Providence, 1956, page 32; H. H. Goldstein, *New and Full Moons, 1001 BC to AD 1651*, Philadelphia, 1973, page 47.

[416] Nehemiah 2:1.

5 The Bible and Prophecy

In line with Daniel's prophecy, Christ was crucified before the Roman general Titus destroyed the temple and the city in AD 70. The prophecy of Daniel 9:27 concerning the seventieth week and the six events listed is still future to us.

Prophecies Concerning the Messiah

After the fall of Adam and Eve, but before God cursed the earth and pronounced judgment on Adam and Eve, He spoke of how He would restore mankind back to Himself. He would do this through the *offspring of the woman* as stated in Genesis 3:15. From this first glimmer of light, the Bible builds up a large and specific range of prophecies regarding this One (Messiah) who was to come and restore the close and intimate relationship that God had with mankind before Adam had sinned. He, the Messiah, would accomplish this by becoming the only sacrifice acceptable to the Father for the forgiveness of sin, because He was, and is, without sin. One scholar has suggested that there are 300 prophecies recorded in the Old Testament concerning the coming Messiah.[417] All of these prophecies were completely fulfilled in the birth, life, ministry, death and resurrection of Jesus of Nazareth.

Below is a list of 60 prophecies concerning the Messiah.

Concerning His birth	Prophesied	Fulfilled
1. Born of the seed of woman	Gen 3:15	Gal 4:4
2. Born of a virgin	Isa 7:14	Mt 1:18-25
3. Seed of Abraham	Gen 22:18	Mt 1:1
4. Seed of Isaac	Gen 21:12	Lk 3:23-34
5. Seed of Jacob	Num 24:17	Lk 3:34
6. Seed of David	Jer 23:5	Lk 3:31
7. Tribe of Judah	Gen 49:10	Rev 5:5
8. Family line of Jesse	Isa 11:1	Lk 3:32
9. Born in Bethlehem	Mic 5:2	Mt 2:1-6
10. Herod kills the children	Jer 31:15	Mt 2:16-18

Concerning His nature	Prophesied	Fulfilled
11. He pre-existed creation	Mic 5:2	1 Pet 1:20
12. He shall be called Lord	Ps 110:1	Acts 2:36
13. Called Immanuel (God with us)	Isa 7:14	Mt 1:22-23
14. Prophet	Deut 18:18-19	Acts 3:18-25
15. Priest	Ps 110:4	Heb 5:5-6
16. Judge	Isa 33:22	Jn 5:22-23
17. King	Ps 2:6	Jn 18:33-37
18. Anointed by the Spirit	Isa 11:2	Mt 3:16-17
19. His zeal for God	Ps 69:9	Jn 2:15-17

Concerning His ministry	Prophesied	Fulfilled
20. Preceded by a messenger	Isa 40:3	Mt 3:1-3

---

[417] J. E. Hunter, *Let Us Go On To Maturity*, Zondervan Books, 14th Printing, 1978, page 13.

5 The Bible and Prophecy

	Prophesied	Fulfilled
21. To begin in Galilee	Isa 9:1-2	Mt 4:12–17
22. Ministry of Miracles	Isa 35:5-6	Mt 9:35; 11:4
23. Teacher of parables	Ps 78:1-4	Mt 13:34–35
24. He was to enter the temple	Mal 3:1	Mt 21:10–12
25. Enter Jerusalem on donkey	Zech 9:9	Mt 21:1–7
26. Stone of stumbling to Jews	Isa 28:16; Ps 118:22	1 Pet 2:6–8
27. Light to Gentiles	Isa 49:6	Acts 13:46–48

The day Jesus was crucified	**Prophesied**	**Fulfilled**
28. Betrayed by a friend	Ps 41:9	Jn 13:18-27
29. Sold for 30 pieces of silver	Zech 11:12	Mt 26:14-15
30. 30 pieces thrown in Temple	Zech 11:13	Mt 27:3-5
31. 30 pieces buys potter's field	Zech 11:13	Mt 27:6-10
32. Forsaken by His disciples	Zech 13:7	Mk 14:27-50
33. Accused by false witnesses	Ps 35:11, 20-21	Mt 26:59-61
34. Silent before accusers	Isa 53:7	Mt 27:12-14
35. Wounded and bruised	Isa 53:4-6	1 Pet 2:21-25
36. Beaten and spat upon	Isa 50:6	Mt 26:67-68
37. Mocked	Ps 22:6-8	Mt 27:27-31
38. Fell under the cross	Ps 109:24-25	Jn 19:17; Lk 23:26
39. Hands and feet pierced	Ps 22:16	Jn 20:24-28
40. Crucified with thieves	Isa 53:12	Mt 27:38
41. Prayed for enemies	Isa 53:12	Lk 23:34
42. Rejected by His own people	Isa 53:3	Jn 19:14-15
43. Hated without cause	Ps 69:4	Jn 15:25
44. Friends stood aloof	Ps 38:11	Lk 22:54; 23:49
45. People wag their heads	Ps 22:7; 109:25	Mt 27:39
46. People stare at Him	Ps 22:17	Lk 23:35
47. Clothing divided and gambled for	Ps 22:18	Jn 19:23-24
48. Became very thirsty	Ps 22:15	Jn 19:28
49. Gall and vinegar offered to Him	Ps 69:21	Mt 27:34
50. His forsaken cry	Ps 22:1	Mt 27:46
51. Committed Himself to God	Ps 31:5	Lk 23:46
52. Bones not broken	Ps 34:20	Jn 19:32-36
53. Heart broken	Ps 69:20; 22:14	Jn 19:34
54. His side pierced	Zech 12:10	Jn 19:34-37
55. Darkness over the land	Amos 8:9	Lk 23:44-45
56. Buried in rich man's tomb	Isa 53:9	Mt 27:57-60

His Resurrection and Ascension	**Prophesied**	**Fulfilled**
57. Raised from the dead	Ps 16:8-11	Acts 2:24-31
58. Begotten as Son of God	Ps 2:7	Acts 13:32-35
59. Ascended to God	Ps 68:18	Eph 2:8-10
60. Seated beside God	Ps 110:1	Heb 1:3-13

5 The Bible and Prophecy

Prophecies Concerning Cities

There are many prophecies concerning cities and people in the Bible. Space does not permit a thorough examination of them all, so a representative sample has been chosen.

Tyre

Several Old Testament prophets prophesied against Tyre. Some condemned the Tyrians for delivering the Israelites to the Edomites[418] and selling them as slaves to the Greeks.[419] Jeremiah prophesied against Tyre,[420] but it is Ezekiel's prophecy which was made between April 587 BC and April 586 BC,[421] that will be considered here, although all the others were fulfilled as well. In Ezekiel 26:3–21, six things are predicted to happen to the city of Tyre:

- Nebuchadnezzar will destroy the mainland of Tyre.[422]
- Many nations will be against Tyre.[423]
- Tyre will be made a bare rock, flat like the top of a rock.[424]
- Fishermen will spread their nets over the site.[425]
- Debris will be thrown into the water.[426]
- Tyre never will be rebuilt. That is, she will never again have prominence as a world trader, never be rich, prosperous and a world power as she once was.[427]

Nebuchadnezzar laid siege to mainland Tyre three years after the prophecy was pronounced, and after a 15-year siege (586–571 BC), Nebuchadnezzar broke the gates down. He found the city almost empty. The majority of the people had moved by ship to an island about one kilometer off the coast and fortified a city there. The mainland city was destroyed in 573 BC, as prophesied. Tyre remained on the island and was a powerful city for over two hundred years.

Alexander the Great, as part of his war on Persia, marched southward and called on each city to open its gates to him. Tyre refused and in 332 BC,[428] he blockaded the island city for 7 months, but Tyre held on. Possessing no fleet, he used the debris of the abandoned mainland city to build a causeway or 'mole' 60 meters (200 feet) wide across the straits, which separated the old and new cities.

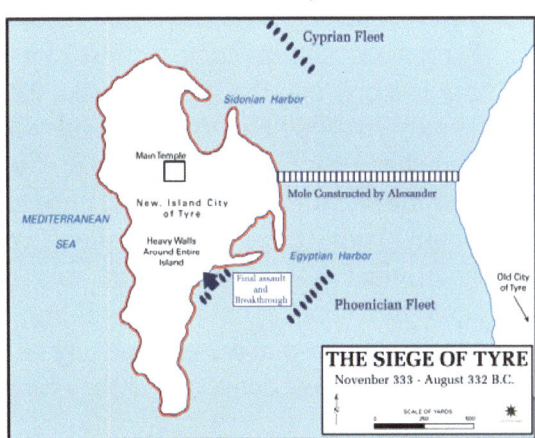

A map of the island city of Tyre showing the causeway (courtesy of the Department of History, United States Military Academy)

---

[418] Amos 1:9.
[419] Joel 3:5–6.
[420] Jeremiah 27:1–11.
[421] *The NIV Study Bible*, Zondervan, 1985, pages 1261-2.
[422] Ezekiel 26:7-8.
[423] Ezekiel 26:4.
[424] Ezekiel 26:4.
[425] Ezekiel 26:5.
[426] Ezekiel 26:12.
[427] Ezekiel 26:14.
[428] *The NIV Study Bible*, Zondervan, 1985, page 1262.

He then erected towers and war engines at the island end of the causeway (as shown). The people of Tyre continually raided the causeway with fire-ships, greatly retarding progress, until Alexander pressured conquered subjects to make ships for his operation. After attaining a superior naval force, Alexander finished the causeway, battered the walls of Tyre down, killed 10,000 of the inhabitants, and sold 30,000 into slavery.[429] Although Tyre continued to exist after Alexander, Ezekiel saw one nation after another coming against her like ocean waves on a beach.[430] Many nations did come against Tyre; the Persians, Macedonians, Ptolemies, Seleucids and Romans; in AD 638 the Arabs, and finally, in 1291, the Mameluke Muslims destroyed the city completely.

Philip Myers writes in his book:

Alexander the Great reduced Tyre to ruins in 332 BC. Tyre recovered in measure from this blow, but never regained the place she had previously held in the world. The larger part of the site of the once great city is now bare as the top of a rock; a place where fishermen now spread their nets to dry.[431]

Nina Jidejian writes:

The Sidonian port of Tyre is still in use today. Small fishing vessels lay at anchor there. An examination of the foundations reveals granite columns of the Roman period which were incorporated as binders in the walls by the Crusaders. The port has become a haven today for fishing boats and a place for spreading nets.[432]

The Ancient Port of Tyre with fishermen drying their nets from BibleArchaeology.org

All the prophecies of Ezekiel about Tyre have come true: Nebuchadnezzar destroyed the mainland city of Tyre; many nations came against Tyre; Alexander threw debris into the water to make the causeway, thereby enabling him to destroy the island city; he made her a bare rock; fishermen now spread nets over the site; the old city of Tyre has never been rebuilt. Today there is a city called Tyre, but it is not the original as this still lies bare, as shown by the photograph above; but rather buildings have been constructed around the original city. All six predictions have come true in the minutest detail.[433]

Tyre Ruins

---

[429] *Encyclopedia Britannica* (Compact Disc), 2000.
[430] Ezekial 26:3.
[431] P. Myers, *A General History for Colleges and High Schools,* Boston, Ginn and Company, 2003, page 55.
[432] N. Jidejian, *Tyre Through the Ages, Beirut,* Dar El-Mashreq Publishers, 1969, page 139.

5 The Bible and Prophecy

Sidon

Ezekiel (in chapter 28) made another prophecy concerning Tyre's sister city, Sidon:[434]

Verse 20: *Then the word of the Lord came to me, saying,*

Verse 21: *Son of man, set your face towards Sidon, and prophesy against her,*

Verse 22: *And say, thus says the Lord GOD; Behold, I am against you, O Sidon; I will be glorified in your midst: and they shall know that I am the LORD, when I executed judgments in her, and am hallowed in her.*

Verse 23: *For I will send pestilence upon her, and blood in her streets; and the wounded shall be judged in her midst by the sword against her on every side; then they shall know that I am the LORD.*

There are three predictions, which we shall investigate:

1. No mention of her destruction
2. Blood in the streets
3. Sword on every side

The prophecy against Sidon is very different from that concerning Tyre. It was foretold that Tyre would be destroyed, made bare like a rock and built no more. However there is no doom of extinction pronounced against Sidon. But in 351 BC the Sidonians, who had been vassals of the Persian king, Artaxerxes III, rebelled and successfully defended their city against his attacks. However, their king, Tennes, in order to save his own life, delivered up 100 of the town's principal citizens and then admitted Artaxerxes within the defences of the town where he had 600 citizens run through with the javelin. Sidon was then burnt to the ground either by the Persians or the Sidonians themselves and 40,000 people died. Tennes was later put to death by Artaxerxes.[435] Blood did indeed flow in the streets.

Sidon was rebuilt, captured by the Egyptians, then attacked and captured by the Greeks, followed by the Romans. In AD 636 it was taken by the Arabs. Sidon was destroyed by the Saracens in

Modern-day Sidon courtesy of The Full Wiki

---

[433] A well documented article on Tyre by Dr Paul Ferguson can be found at: biblearchaeology.org/post/2009/12/07Ezekiel-261-14-A-Proof-Text-For-Inerrancy-or-Fallibility.
[434] Ezekiel 28:20–23.
[435] wikipedia.org/wiki/Artaxerxes, retrieved August 28, 2008,

1249 and in 1260 it was destroyed again by the Mongols. In the seventeenth century the Ottoman Turks captured Sidon and retained it until World War 1, after which it became a French Mandate of Lebanon. It was recaptured by the British during World War 2. Sidon is now part of Lebanon.[436] Sidon has felt the sword at every side.

Samaria

The prophet Micah wrote in chapter 1, verses 1, 2 and 6:

The word of the LORD that came to Micah—which he saw concerning Samaria and Jerusalem. Hear, all you peoples! Listen, O earth, and all that is in it! Let the Lord GOD be a witness against you ... I will make Samaria a heap [of ruins] in the field, places for planting a vineyard; I will pour down her stones into the valley, and I will uncover her foundations.

Israel was divided after the death of King Solomon; the northern part became known as Israel and the southern part became known as Judah. This prophecy refers to the capital of the Northern Kingdom, Samaria, which was established by Omri.[437] Later the wicked King Ahab built his palace there.

After a succession of invasions, the Assyrian Empire succeeded in devastating Israel, the Northern Kingdom, and took most of its population captive in 722 BC.[438] The city was rebuilt and destroyed by Alexander the Great in 331 BC. It was rebuilt and destroyed again by John Hyrcanus in 108 BC. Pompey rebuilt the town in 63 BC and Augustus Caesar bestowed it upon Herod who expanded and renovated the city and named it 'Sebaste' (meaning 'Augustus') in his honor.[439]

Samaria (Sebastia) was finally and totally destroyed during the Maccabean wars. The modern village of Sebastia is located further down the Samaritan hills from the ancient city. As noted above, God had spoken through Micah almost 200 years earlier that He would uproot Israel from this good land which He had given to their fathers, and would scatter them beyond the [Euphrates] river. This, and many other details of the prophecies and historical account of the Assyrian invasions and resulting Israelite captivity, are verified by Assyrian records and other archaeological discoveries. The area is quite fertile and is now used for agriculture, including vineyards.

The site of Samaria courtesy of BiblePlaces.com

---

[436] wikipedia.org/wiki/Sidon, retrieved September 10, 2008.
[437] 1 Kings 16:23–24.
[438] 2 Kings 17:5–7, 15.
[439] Wikipedia.org/wiki/Sebastia, retrieved August, 2008.

Ashkelon

Ashkelon was a Philistine town, a little north of Gaza and on the coast. Amos (about 750 BC), Jeremiah (about 600 BC) and Zephaniah (about 620 BC) all prophesied against it, with the following predictions:

- The Philistines will not continue (Amos 1:8).
- Baldness shall come upon Gaza (Jeremiah 47:5).
- Desolation shall come upon Ashkelon (Zephaniah 2:4).
- Shepherds and sheep will dwell in the area of Ashkelon (Zephaniah 2:6).
- A remnant of the house of Judah will re-inhabit Ashkelon (Zephaniah 2:7).

Judgment fell upon Ashkelon precisely as predicted:

When this vast seaport, the last of the Philistine cities to hold out against Nebuchadnezzar finally fell in 604 BC, burnt and destroyed and its people taken into exile, the Philistine era was over.[440]

Modern-day Ashkelon

In 1270 the Mamluk Sultan Baybars ordered the citadel and the harbor at the site to be destroyed. As a result of this destruction, the site was abandoned by its inhabitants and fell into disuse.[441] For 700 years the once mighty city lay in ruins, becoming a grazing place for flocks of sheep, the area dotted with huts. Following the establishment of the state of Israel, the Jewish people recognised the splendid location of the old city, and now it has been transformed into a beautiful garden city in keeping with Zephaniah's prophecy.

The Philistines were 'cut off' from the face of the earth and the house of Judah re-inhabited Ashkelon.

Edom

Isaac had two sons; Esau and Jacob[442] whom God later named Israel. The descendants of Esau became the Edomites, and their main city, Petra, was built into the rock face in the mountains south-east of the Dead Sea, such as to render it almost impregnable. As the Children of Israel were coming out of the desert and heading towards the Promised Land, Moses asked the king of Edom to allow them to pass through since they were 'brothers.' The king refused and attacked them

---

[440] wikipedia.org/wiki/Ashkelon, 2008, retrieved June 23, 2011.
[441] *Ibid.*
[442] Gensis 25: 24-26.

when they tried[443] and for this action God held Edom to account as well as for the fact that the Edomites opposed Israel at every opportunity. God had Isaiah, Jeremiah, Obadiah[444] and Ezekiel pronounce many judgments on the Edomites.

- Edom will become desolate (Isaiah 34:13).
- They will never populate again (Jeremiah 49:18).
- They will be conquered by Israel (Ezekiel 25:14).
- They shall have a bloody history (Ezekiel 35:6, Isaiah 34:6–7).
- Wild animals will inhabit the area (Isaiah 34:13–15).

What has happened to Edom?

Petra ruins

According to Josephus[445] and 1 Maccabees 5:3, the Edomites were attacked and totally conquered by the Jews and were incorporated into the Jewish nation. From the fall of Jerusalem the Edomites completely disappeared from the pages of history.

When the Swiss traveler J L Burkhardt visited the area in 1812, he saw the place as a wild desert and even though the Edomites and their city Petra are mentioned several times in the Bible, many doubted their existence.[446] That is, until the splendidly preserved remains of Petra were discovered in the nineteenth century. One early traveler noted that the area was abounding with a variety of scorpions and vipers, to such an extent that the local Arabs avoided the place. As well, lions and leopards were often seen in the hills but never on the low land;[447] again, a complete fulfillment of prophecy.

---

[443] Numbers 20:14-21.
[444] The whole book of Obadiah is about the forthcoming destruction of Edom.
[445] *Antiquities* X II, 18, 1.
[446] wikipedia.org/wiki/Johann_Ludwig_Burckhardt, retrieved August 30, 2008.
[447] J. McDowell, *Evidence That Demands a Verdict,* Here's Life Publishers, 1979, pages 290–291.

5 The Bible and Prophecy

Nineveh and Babylon

These two cities are examined together because of their similarities. Both were extremely large and very well fortified. Nineveh was the capital of the Assyrian empire and Babylon was the capital of the Babylonian empire. Both, we are told in scripture, were places of great evil.

Nahum prophesied that Nineveh would be totally destroyed by flood (2:6) and burned (3:15). As for Babylon, Isaiah[448] and Jeremiah[449] foretold that it would be completely destroyed, never to be inhabited again, and that creatures would infest its ruins.

The fall of Nineveh is in line with scripture, for the *Babylonian Chronicle*[450] is clear that when the Assyrian army was on offensive maneuvers, there were several heavy downpours of rain that swelled the Tigris River, flooded part of the city and caused the walls to fall. Also, excavations have shown a course of pebbles and sand a few feet beneath the surface. When archeologists unearthed the site in the early 1800s, they found a layer of ash covering the ruins.[451] Encyclopedia Britannica states:

Nineveh suffered a defeat, from which it never recovered. Extensive traces of ash, representing the sack of the city by Babylonians, Scythians and Medes in 612 BC, have been found in many parts of the Acropolis.[452]

Babylon fell to Cyrus the Great in 539 BC, but the city still persisted and was captured by Alexander the Great in 331 BC. After Alexander's untimely death, a power struggle amongst his generals ensued and Babylon passed to the Seleucid dynasty in 312 BC. The city's importance was greatly reduced by the building of a new capital on the Tigris, called Seleucia. Babylon fell into disuse.[453]

Before 1840, both Nineveh and Babylon were thought to have never existed, so complete was their destruction, and many doubted or allegorised the Bible's statements concerning these two

Nineveh ruins

Babylonian ruins

---

[448] Isaiah 21: 1-10 and chapter 47.
[449] Jeremiah chapter 50.
[450] *Babylonian Chronicle,* No 21, 901.
[451] J. McDowell, *Evidence That Demands a Verdict,* Here's Life Publishers, 1979, page 301.
[452] Encyclopedia Britannia CD, International Version, Multimedia Edition, 1999.
[453] Ibid.

cities. When their ruins were discovered, archeologists were amazed at their enormous size, which demonstrated the power of the prophecies concerning the two cities.

Jerusalem's continual existence and enlargement

After prophesying the destruction of Judah, including Jerusalem, by the Babylonian king Nebuchadnezzar, Jeremiah goes on to state (in chapter 31) that Jerusalem will be rebuilt and never be demolished again.[454]

Verse 38: *Behold, the days come, says the LORD that the city shall be built for the LORD from the Tower of Hananel to the Corner Gate.*

Verse 39: *The surveyor's line shall again extend straight forward over the hill Gareb; then it shall turn toward Goath.*

Verse 40: *And the whole valley of the dead bodies and of the ashes, and all the fields as far as the Brook Kidron, to the corner of the Horse Gate toward the east, shall be holy to the LORD. It shall not be plucked up or thrown down anymore forever."*

The prophecy states that Jerusalem will be enlarged and will remain forever. In 1996 Jerusalem celebrated its 3,000-year anniversary. Historians and archeologists estimate that it was in mid-1,004 BC that King David defeated the Jebusites and claimed Jerusalem as the Hebrew capital, as recorded in 2 Samuel 5:6–14. Old Jerusalem still exists and has been enlarged into a modern city, as shown by the accompanying photograph taken from the Mount of Olives.

Modern Jerusalem

The Eastern or Golden Gate

Ezekiel's Prophecy (Chapter 44:1–3):

Then He brought me back to the outer gate of the sanctuary which faces toward the east, but it was shut. And the LORD said to me, "This gate shall be shut; it shall not be opened, and no man shall enter by it, because the LORD God of Israel has entered by it; therefore it shall be shut. As for the prince, because he is the prince, he may sit in it to eat bread before the LORD; he shall enter by way of the vestibule of the gateway, and go out the same way."

Ezekiel wrote this prophecy in about 580 BC in a vision he had from the Lord. And the gate he refers to is the Eastern Gate (East Gate or Golden Gate) in Jerusalem's wall. This was the one that was most used by Jesus and many others, because it led directly to the temple, as shown in the diagram on the next page.

---

[454] Jeremiah 31:38, 39, 40.

5 The Bible and Prophecy

The prophecy is:

1. The eastern gate was shut. It shall be shut. It shall not be opened. No man shall enter in by it.

2. The Prince shall sit in it and eat bread before the Lord. The Prince shall enter by way of the gate and go out by way of the gate.

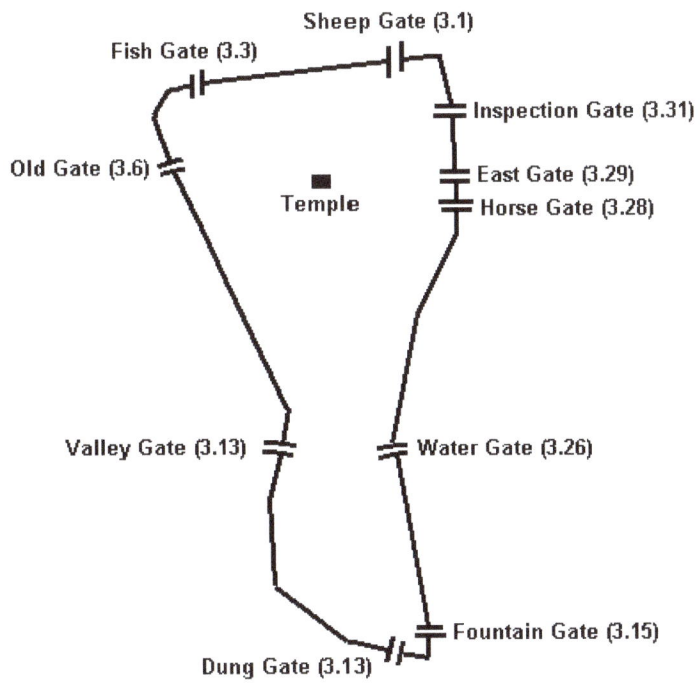

Jerusalem's wall and gates

Of course, the gate wasn't shut in Ezekiel's or Jesus' time, because it was used frequently. But Ezekiel's vision was future to him, and true to his vision the gate is now sealed. The walls of Jerusalem, including the Eastern gate, were razed by the invading Roman army in AD 70. However, the Eastern gate was rebuilt by the Byzantines in the sixth century and the Moslem leader Sultan Suleiman I had it sealed in 1541 in order to prevent the arrival of the Jewish Messiah, as revealed by the second part of Ezekiel's prophecy. But by doing so, he fulfilled the first part of the prophecy.

A 1530 painting of Suleiman 1

Jerusalem's Eastern Gate

Over the years the Muslims have contemptuously buried their dead in front of the Eastern Gate, as can be seen in the photograph. This stems from a misunderstanding of the Levitical law, which, they think, would prohibit the Messiah from coming into contact with the dead, thereby restraining Him from entering through this gate.

We know that Jesus will enter through this gate when He commences His Millennial Reign from Jerusalem for Ezekiel states at 43:4 and 7:

And the glory of the LORD came into the house by the way of the gate which faces toward the east. And He said to me, "Son of man, this is the place of My throne and the place of the soles of My feet, where I will dwell in the midst of the children of Israel forever.

There may have been occasions when men have tried to usurp the prophecy by opening the gate. On December 9, 1917, the Grand Mufti, the Arab leader of Jerusalem, ordered the gate to be opened. As the workmen picked up their sledge hammers, General Allenby's aeroplane flew over the city dropping leaflets, which told the Arabs to flee. This they did without a shot being fired and the gate remained closed.

Another fateful day was June 7, 1967. Jordan's King Hussein had made plans to open the Eastern Gate, possibly in order to disprove Bible prophecy. It was also on this day that Israel's Six Day War ended, with their troops capturing Jerusalem [455] and of course the gate was never opened.

Prophecies Concerning God's Chosen People and the Land

After God created mankind, things got off to a rocky start, and they have not changed. Adam and Eve rebelled against God and He removed them from His presence. Their descendants became very evil, to the extent that the Bible tells us:

-------*that every intent of the thoughts of his heart was only evil continually.*[456]

So God brought about a worldwide flood. The descendants of Noah's family, the only ones to survive the flood, attempted to usurp God and rejected His command to disperse, so God scattered the people by confusing their language. Finally, God raised Abraham and gave him a series of promises that concerned him and his descendants. The fulfillment of the promises was dependant only on God, and not on Abraham or his descendants.[457] As well, God gave him promises that concerned the possession of the land of Canaan by Abraham's descendants, the Jewish and Arab people, which were repeated many times to Abraham.[458] God repeated the promises, including those relating to the land, to Abraham's son Isaac and his descendants.[459] This time the promises became narrower, as they were only for Isaac's descendants, the Jews, and possibly some Arabs, rather than being for his half–brother, Ishmael, whose descendants became entirely the Arabs. God again repeated the same promise, this time narrowing it even further to Isaac's second son, Jacob,[460] whose name He later changed to Israel, and whose descendants became known as the Children of Israel, or Israelites. They are now known as the Jews. This latter name is derived from the members of Israel's major tribe; Judah.

There is no doubt that the land of Canaan, which was later named Palestine by the Romans after the second Jewish revolt in AD133–135, was given to the Jews as an unconditional and everlasting covenant by God. Implicit in the promise is that the people will remain separate, worship Him only, and not take on the customs and practices of the people around them. However, if they do reject God and taken on these practices, He will remove them from the land for a period of time. They did just this, and God had them exiled into Babylon for 70 years, after which He brought them back.

---

[455] These two reports come by way of *Shofar Ministries Newsletter*; shofarministries.net/newsletter0305.htm, retrieved September 2, 2008.
[456] Genesis 6:5.
[457] Genesis 12:1–3.
[458] Genesis 12:7; 13:14, 15, 17; 15:7; 15:18.
[459] Genesis 26:2–5.
[460] Genesis 28:13–15.

5 The Bible and Prophecy

On their return, they rebuilt Jerusalem and the Temple,[461] and 400 years after the completion of the Old Testament (or covenant), the promised and much-prophesised Messiah, the One who would put an end to temple sacrifices and initiate a new covenant (or testament), came. They rejected Him and as a consequence, God had them removed from the land again. However, the promise of the land was unconditional and everlasting. Their scattering started with the first Jewish uprising against their Roman occupiers, which was crushed with the destruction of Jerusalem and particularly the Temple, and the expulsion of the Jews in AD 70. The dispersion of the Jews from the land was complete when the second and final uprising was put down by the Romans in AD 135. As a consequence, there were few Children of Israel in the land from that time on.

During the following 1,813 years the Jews were persecuted in almost every country in which they lived. This culminated in the Holocaust, with which Adolf Hitler tried to eliminate them completely. Amazingly, on May 14, 1948, Israel was declared a state and God's chosen people began to re-inhabit the land. This seems to be a fulfillment of Isaiah's remarkable prophecy concerning Israel:

Before she goes into labor, she gives birth; before the pains come upon her, she delivers a son. Who has ever heard of such a thing? Who has ever seen such a thing? Can a country be born in a day or a nation be brought forth in a moment?[462]

Thus, Isaiah poses the rhetorical question: "*Can a nation be born in a day …*" Normally, the answer would be no. But when dealing with the supernatural history of Israel, the answer turned out to be yes.

God's promises to Abraham and to his descendants, made possibly 4,000 years ago, hold true today. His people have remained separate and clearly identifiable; despots have used this fact over the centuries to terrible effect. In defiance of historical precedents, the Jews have not blended in and become absorbed into other people groups. They have remained separate and unique.

Prophecies concerning their scattering

Just as the Israelites were to enter Canaan, the Promised Land, Moses outlined to them (as recorded in Deuteronomy) the blessings they would receive if they followed the Lord and worshipped Him only. However, if they did not follow the Lord, there would be consequences of this disobedience, which Moses went on to explain. The list is long and concludes with:

Then the LORD will scatter you among all peoples, from one end of the earth to the other, and there you shall serve other gods, which neither you nor your fathers have known—wood and stone. And among those nations you shall find no rest, nor shall the sole of your foot have a resting place; but there the LORD will give you a trembling heart, failing eyes, and anguish of soul.[463]

---

[461] Ezra, Nehemiah.
[462] Isaiah 66:7-8 (*New International Version*).
[463] Deuteronomy 28:64–65.

And again, in Leviticus:

I will scatter you among the nations, and draw out a sword after you; your land shall be desolate, and your cities waste.[464]

Throughout the Bible, the Jewish people were repeatedly commanded by God not to assimilate into the other nations by absorbing their customs, or their gods. Neither were they to marry foreigners from the people amongst whom they lived. They were to remain there as Jews, holding fast to their Judaic faith. This they did. These prophecies have been realised as the Jews inhabit every nation on earth, but have never found rest.

Prophecies concerning the return of the Jews

Isaiah records:

It shall come to pass in that day, that the Lord will set His hand again the second time to recover the remnant of His people... He will set up a banner for the nations, and will assemble the outcasts of Israel, and gather together the dispersed of Judah from the four corners of the earth.[465]

Note that the first time God brought the Jews back to their land was from Babylon. This event was so significant that two books of the Bible are devoted to it: Ezra and Nehemiah. The Exodus does not represent a return to the land for they were not established in the land as they were when they went into Babylonian exile and the emphasis of the account is on the exodus itself, hence the name of the book. Isaiah's prophesy refers to God bringing them back a second time from where they have been dispersed to every nation; the four corners of the earth. And this second exile started in AD 70 and was completed in AD 135 at the hands of the Romans.

Likewise Jeremiah wrote in about 590 BC:

But I will gather the remnant of My flock out of all countries where I have driven them, and bring them back to their folds; and they shall be fruitful and increase.[466]

Ezekiel records:

Therefore say, Thus says the Lord GOD: I will gather you from the peoples, assemble you from the countries where you have been scattered, and I will give you the land of Israel.[467]

Ezekiel also wrote:

Then say to them, Thus says the Lord GOD: Surely I will take the children of Israel from among the nations, wherever they have gone, and will gather them from every side and bring them into their own land; and I will make them one nation in the land, on the mountains of Israel; and one

---

[464] Leviticus 26:33.
[465] Isaiah 11:11–12.
[466] Jeremiah 23:3.
[467] Ezekiel 11:17.

5 The Bible and Prophecy

king shall be king over them all; they shall no longer be two nations, nor shall they ever be divided into two kingdoms again.[468]

When Ezekiel wrote his prophesy (between 593 and 571 BC), Israel was divided into two kingdoms. However, Israel was established again in 1948 as a united people; a sovereign nation.

Amos records:

I will bring back the captives of My people Israel; They shall build the waste cities and inhabit them; They shall plant vineyards and drink wine from them; They shall also make gardens and eat fruit from them. I will plant them in their land, And no longer shall they be pulled up from the land I have given them," Says the LORD your God.[469]

Again Jeremiah predicts the return of the Jews from *the ends of the earth*, to their homeland:

Behold, I will bring them from the north country, And gather them from the ends of the earth, Among them the blind and the lame, The woman with child And the one who labors with child, together;A great throng shall return there.[470]

These prophecies are very clear and specific. God, speaking through Isaiah, says that He will bring them back a second time; the first being from exile in Babylon. The second time could well refer to their return of 1948. And through Amos, God says that they will not be pulled out of their land any more.

Although many Jews returned to Israel after 1948, there have been obstacles preventing some Jews from emigrating. Two significant ones were the refusal of the Soviet Union to allow Russian Jews to return to their homeland and escape from the persecution they were experiencing. The fall of communism overcame this problem and by the mid 1990s, approximately one million Russian Jews had settled in Israel.

Further, a large group of Ethiopian Jews cohabitated harmoniously with their fellow countrymen, until Emperor Salassie's regime was replaced in 1974 by a committee within the military. From here Colonel Mengistu Haile Mariam rose to power and imposed a Marxist-Leninist dictatorship on the people. In the ensuing weeks, an estimated 2,500 Jews were killed and another 7,000 were made homeless. His policy of 'villagization' increased anti-Semitism greatly and by the early 1980s the practice and teaching of Hebrew was forbidden.

Pressure to allow Ethiopian Jews to emigrate to Israel was brought to bear on Mariam by both Israel and the United States, and between 1977 and 1984, 8,000 Jews came to Israel. Under the code name *Operation Moses*, the Israeli air force transferred some 8,000 Jews to Israel between November 21, 1984 and January 5, 1985. But still many more remained and another 800 people were air-lifted under the code name *Operation Joshua*. With the prospect of Eritrean and Tigrean rebels overthrowing the Mariam government and amid fears that of Ethiopian Jews maybe held hostage, Israel mounted a massive air-lift involving 34 aircraft flying non-stop for 36 hours, as a

---

[468] Ezekiel 37:21-22.
[469] Amos 9:14–15.
[470] Jeremiah 31:8. The whole of the prophecy is covered in verses 8-14.

5 The Bible and Prophecy

result of which 14,324 people were relocated to Israel. *Operation Solomon,* as it was called, transported more than twice the number of people as *Operations Moses* and *Joshua* combined. During the relocation, a world record for a single-flight passenger load was set on May 24, 1991, when an El Al 747 carried 1,122 passengers to Israel.

Operation Solomon, May 25, 1991(courtesy of http://www.zionism-israel.com/dic)

Prophecies concerning their name

Just before the Israelites were to enter the Promised Land, Moses addressed the whole congregation. He told them of the blessings they would receive if they worshipped God and Him only and kept His commandments and statutes. As well, Moses gave them a long list of curses which would befall them if they rejected God and worshipped the foreign and false gods of the pagans. Amongst the curses was the fact that God would disperse them throughout the world:

-- then I will cut off Israel from the land which I have given them; and this house which I have consecrated for My name I will cast out of My sight. Israel will be a proverb and a byword among all peoples.[471]

A 'proverb' is a saying, and the Hebrew word 'sheniynah', which the NKJV translates as 'byword', has the meaning of a jibe or taunt. The New International Version translates the passage as 'an object of ridicule amongst all people.' Matthew Henry, in his commentary, uses the phrase 'the most despicable people under the sun'[472] There is no doubt that the name 'Jew', in keeping with this prophecy, has become a word of derision.

Prophecies concerning their continual existence

The prophecy of Amos[473] has been realized in our time, as the Muslim Arab states have tried to 'pull [Israel] up from their land.' Consider the events since Israel was proclaimed a state by the United Nations.

1948

On the day that Israel declared its independence, the Arab League Secretary, General Azzam Pasha, declared 'jihad,' a holy war. He said:

This will be a war of extermination and a momentous massacre which will be spoken of like the Mongolian massacres and the Crusades.

The Mufti of Jerusalem, Haj Amin Al Husseini, stated:

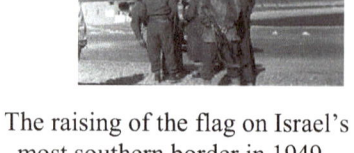

The raising of the flag on Israel's most southern border in 1949

---

[471] 1 Kings 9:7; Deuteronomy 28:37.
[472] *Matthew Henry's Commentary,* Marshall, Morgan and Scott, Volume 2, page 624.
[473] Amos 9:15.

5 The Bible and Prophecy

I declare a holy war, my Moslem brothers! Murder the Jews! Murder them all!

The armies of Lebanon, Syria, Jordan, Egypt and Iraq invaded the tiny new country with the declared intent of destroying it. However, the new Jewish state survived. In 1949 Israel signed armistice agreements with several Arab states, including Jordan, which annexed the area of Judea and Samaria, now known as the West Bank. From there they were to launch many attacks against the very vulnerable Jewish people.

1967

On May 15, 1967, Egyptian forces moved into the Sinai. On May 18, Egypt expelled the UN Peacekeeping forces from Israel's borders. On the 22nd, the Egyptians closed the Straits of Tiran to Israeli shipping. On the 25th, encouraged by Egypt; Syria, Jordan, Iraq and Saudi Arabia moved their troops to Israel's borders.

Nasser, backed by Arab states, kicks Israel into the Gulf of Aqaba. Pre-1967 War cartoon. Al-Jarida newspaper, Lebanon

Just after this, on May 26, President Nasser of Egypt declared:

Our basic goal is the destruction of Israel. The Arab people want to fight ... The mining of Sharm El Sheik is a confrontation with Israel.

Pacts were signed by Egypt with Jordan and Iraq on May 30 and June 4, thereby completing the encirclement of Israel.

On June 5, Israel launched a pre-emptive attack on Egypt and destroyed her air force in two hours. Israel issued an appeal to Jordan to stay out of the war. Jordan refused and opened a heavy artillery barrage on both west Jerusalem and the Tel-Aviv area that forced Israel to counterattack. By June 8, the Israel Defence Forces had defeated the Jordanian forces and captured the whole of the West Bank. On the morning of June 9, Israel attacked the Syrians on the Golan Heights and captured this strategic area.

In just six days, despite having been attacked from all sides and facing overwhelming odds against them, Israel had captured the entire Sinai Peninsula, the Gaza strip, the West Bank and the Golan Heights.

But this was not to be the end of Arab attempts to destroy the nation of Israel.

1973

On October 6, 1973—Yom Kippur, the Day of Atonement, the holiest day in the Jewish calendar, Egypt and Syria opened a coordinated surprise attack against Israel. On the Golan Heights approximately 180 Israeli tanks faced an onslaught of 1,400 Syrian tanks. Along the Suez Canal, fewer than 500 Israeli defenders were attacked by 80,000 Egyptians.

5 The Bible and Prophecy

At least nine Arab states, including four non-Middle Eastern nations, actively aided the Egyptian–Syrian war effort. A few months before the Yom Kippur War, Iraq transferred a squadron of Hunter jets to Egypt. During the war, an Iraqi division of some 18,000 men and several hundred tanks was deployed in the central Golan and participated in the October 16 attack against Israeli positions. Iraqi MiGs began operating over the Golan Heights as early as October 8, the third day of the war.

Besides serving as financial underwriters, Saudi Arabia and Kuwait committed men to battle. A Saudi brigade of approximately 3,000 troops was dispatched to Syria, where it participated in fighting along the approaches to Damascus. Also, violating Paris's ban on the transfer of French-made weapons, Libya sent Mirage fighters to Egypt (from 1971 to 1973, President Muammar Qaddafi gave Cairo more than $1 billion in aid to rearm Egypt and to pay the Soviets for weapons delivered).

Other North African countries responded to Arab and Soviet calls to aid the front-line states. Algeria sent three aircraft squadrons of fighters and bombers, an armored brigade and 150 tanks. Approximately 1,000–2,000 Tunisian soldiers were positioned in the Nile Delta. Sudan stationed 3,500 troops in southern Egypt, and Morocco sent three brigades to the front lines, including 2,500 men to Syria.

Thrown onto the defensive during the first two days of fighting, Israel mobilised its reserves and eventually repulsed the invaders and carried the war deep into Syria and Egypt. The Arab states were swiftly resupplied by sea and air from the Soviet Union, which rejected U.S. efforts to work toward an immediate cease-fire. As a result of a pleading telephone call from Israel's Prime Minister Golda Meir at 3am, President Nixon of the United States ordered an air lift of 22,000 tons of equipment, involving 566 flights. To pay for this infusion of weapons, Nixon asked congress for and received 2.2 billion dollars in emergency aid for Israel.

What makes Meir's telephone call more interesting is that, according to Grant McKay's *Against All Odds:*

An abandoned Syrian tank on the Golan Heights

Israel Survives, as Nixon sat on the side of his bed listening to Golda Meir, her words promoted him to recall his own mother's voice:

...as a young boy growing up, his mother had told him that one day he would be in a powerful position, and a situation would arise where Israel and the Jews needed his help. When it did, he was to help them.[474]

Two weeks later, Egypt was saved from a disastrous defeat by the UN Security Council, which had failed to act while the tide was in the Arabs' favor.

---

[474] Grant McKay, *Against All Odds: Israel Survives* (13-part documentary), American Trademark Pictures, 2005.

5 The Bible and Prophecy

Can anyone doubt that the hand of God is on Israel?

In order to complete this section on Prophecies Concerning God's Chosen People and the Land, it is necessary to briefly mention that many Bible scholars interpret the prophecies of Ezekiel,[475] Joel[476] and The Revelation[477] as foretelling an attack on Israel known as the Battle of Armageddon. This is prophesised to take place at the end of the Great Tribulation, by an overwhelming force coming predominantly from the north, and is still future to us. Some have suggested that this army could comprise a confederation of Russian and Muslim nations. The prophecy also states that when His people cry out to Him, God will step in, destroy these armies and save His people;

... then the nations shall know that I am the Lord, the Holy One in Israel.[478, 479]

A prophecy that did not come true

Voltaire

Francois-Marie Arouet (1694–1778), better known by his pen name Voltaire, was a French enlightenment writer, essayist, philosopher and deist. Voltaire is remembered for his sharp wit, philosophical writings and defence of civil liberties. He is also known for his dislike of Christianity and the Bible, in reference to which he made this statement:

In 100 years from my day there will not be a Bible in the earth, except the one that is looked upon by an antiquarian curiosity seeker.

Voltaire at 24, by Catherine Lusurier after Nicolas de Largillière's painting

Contrary to Voltaire's prediction, Bible sales have grown at an almost exponential rate. For example, the Guinness eBook of Records states that 2,500,000,000 (2.5 billion) Bibles have been sold since 1815, and the Bible has been translated into 2,233 languages.[480]

An appropriate epitaph to Voltaire's prophecy is found in the Quarterly Papers of the American and Foreign Bible Society:[481]

---

[475] Ezekiel 38, 39.
[476] Joel 2:30-32.
[477] Revelation 16:16.
[478] Ezekiel 39:7.
[479] A thorough discussion on this topic is contained in many books, including: John Ecob, *The Bible Prophecy Handbook,* Herald of Hope, 2003 (Available from Herald of Hope magazine, PO Box 4216, Marayong, NSW, 2148, Australia); Randall Price, *The Coming Last Days Temple,* Harvest House Publishers, 1999; Michael A. Redick, *Ready for His Return, How to live in the Light of Eternity*, Nosnuma Singapore, 2010.
[480] guardian.co.uk/books/2008/jun/18/harrypotter.news, retrieved April 11, 2011

A Bible Society was some years since established at Ferney, once the residence of Voltaire—the prince of infidels. This noble enterprise for the propagation of the Christian religion is said to have commenced by Baron de Stael, and a few zealous Christians in that place. In the history of Bible Societies, this is truly a memorial event. That the antidote should issue from the very spot where the poison of infidelity for so many years disseminated; and the advocates of Christianity should in that very place print and circulate the sacred volume, as a sufficient shield against misrepresentations sophistry which he had there assailed divine revelation, are the events which the brilliant Frenchman would have pronounced impossible.

Ferney, Voltaire's residence

"There" said a friend to Rev. A. Acworth, when in France, "this is the room where Voltaire's plays were acted, for the amusement of himself and his friends, but now converted into a repository for Bibles. Oh! That, that gifted infidel could have been there, to witness the result and repent of his ratiocinations respecting the downfall of Christianity. But, there is a point beyond which divine forbearance does not extend."

And again more recently, John Lennon of *The Beetles* fame made the following statement which was reported in the London *Evening Standard*: *Christianity will go. It will vanish and shrink. Jesus was alright, but His disciples were thick and ordinary.*[482]

John Lennon is now dead and *The Beetles* are just a faint memory in the minds of an older generation, but Christianity is expanding rapidly throughout Africa, South America and S E Asia.

Conclusion

It has been shown that time and time again; biblical prophecies have been fulfilled, demonstrating that the Bible can indeed be trusted.

Matthew 24:35:

Heaven and earth will pass away, but my words will by no means pass away.

---

[481] Quarterly Papers of the American and Foreign Bible Society, No 11, New York, July 1837, page 21-22 (Digitized by Google under the heading Bible Society at Ferney).
[482] Geofrey Blainey, *A Short History of Christianity*, Penguin Group, Australia, 2011, page 547. Quoting Lennon's interview in 1966; Bob Spitz, *The beetles: The Biography*, New York, 2005, page 615.

Chapter 6

Did Jesus Really Live, Die and Rise from the Dead?

Introduction

Right from Genesis 3:15, when God gave the first indication of the coming Messiah, the Bible provides an ever-revealing description of who this Man will be. He will be God incarnate. The scriptures give over 60 detailed prophecies about the Messiah and all were all completely fulfilled in the Person of Jesus of Nazareth.[483]

Very little information is given about His physical appearance in either the Old or New Testaments. Nothing is said about his size; tall, short, fat, thin or muscular; His hair, straight or curly; the shape of His face; the color of His eyes, etc. This may be for a reason. If we knew what He looked like, people would paint a picture or construct an image and worship that, thereby violating the second commandment. The first known images of Jesus appeared in the sixth century and are Christ Pantocrator (the Savior), the oldest surviving panel icon of Christ; the Veil of Veronica; and the Image of Edessa, which came to light in 525. This last image is that of a man's face on cloth. Legend has it that it is the image of Jesus. All show a man with long straight hair, a beard and a straight 'Nordic' nose. Most subsequent images of Jesus incorporate these features. Interestingly; nothing could be further from the truth. He would not have had long hair because the Jews of the day considered it effeminate for a man to wear his hair long. Paul makes this point in his first letter to the church at Corinth in 1 Corinthians 11:14–15:

Christ Pantocrator

Veil of Veronica

The Image of Edessa

Does not even nature itself teach you, that, if a man has long hair, it is a dishonor *to him? But if a woman has long hair, it is a glory to her: for her hair is given her for a covering.*

---

[483] See page 131-133.

6   Did Jesus Really Live, Die and Rise from the Dead?

However, being a practicing Jew, Jesus would have had a full beard. Of course, Jesus could have had any body or facial features He desired. He could have had, for example, deep penetrating eyes with a soft gentle voice such that women would like being around Him, or He could have been big and strong like King Saul gathering the respect of men. But scripture tells us in Isaiah 53:2 that:

… He had no beauty or majesty to attract us to him, nothing in his appearance that we should desire him [484]

So those paintings showing Jesus as a handsome man with a good crop of long dark hair and a strong jaw line are simply not true to life.

Did Jesus Really Live?

By way of introduction to this question, let us consider the story of John the Baptist. He was the son of Zechariah and Elizabeth, and Elizabeth was related to Mary the mother of Jesus. John was at the River Jordan and calling people to repent of their sins and be baptized. As Jesus approached him, he made the profound statement:

Behold the Lamb of God who takes away the sin of the world [485]

… and at Jesus' insistence he baptised Him. Later King Herod Antipas had John imprisoned because he criticized him for illegally and immorally marrying Herodias, who was already married to her uncle and Herod's brother, Herod Philip 1. During Herod's birthday celebration, Herodias' daughter Salome danced before Herod and his guests. Her dance was unquestionably lascivious and it so pleased Herod that he promised on oath to give her whatever she asked. Prompted by her mother, she said:

Give me John the Baptist's head here on a platter [486]

The king was distressed but because of his oath, made before his dinner guests, he consented.

Before Herod's birthday celebrations, John was languishing in prison with no expectation of being released. He seemingly had doubts as to whether Jesus whom he baptized was really the Christ, that is, the Messiah, the anointed One chosen by God, the One whom the prophets spoke of; so he sent his disciples to inquire of Jesus.

Jesus answered and said to them, "Go and tell John the things you have seen and heard: that the blind see, the lame walk, the lepers are cleansed, the deaf hear, the dead are raised, the poor have the gospel preached to them." [487]

In other words, Jesus said if you want to be assured that I am who I say I am, look at the

---

[484] Isaiah 53:2 (New International Version).
[485] John 1:29.
[486] Matthew 14:8.
[487] Luke 7:22.

evidence. His statement is still true today. So what is now before you, dear reader, is the evidence that Jesus of Nazareth was and is Jesus the Christ.

Extra-Biblical Writings Concerning Jesus of Nazareth

There are 5,656 New Testament manuscripts—some dating back to the second century and available today and in reasonable condition.[488] However, the inquirer may want additional evidence from non-Christian sources.

Hardly any writings have survived from early in the first century and according to E M Blaiklock in his book, *Jesus Christ: Man or Myth?*,[489] only a small amount of written work has been retained from the 50s and 60s. The writings that have survived are discussed below.

Thallus

Possibly the earliest non-Christian writer to refer to Jesus, is the man Thallus, a Greek historian, who was most likely a Samaritan. About AD 55, he wrote a three volume history of the Mediterranean world from before the Trojan War to about AD 50. Other historians such as Julius Africanus, who wrote a *History of the World* around AD 220, and the Hebrew historian Josephus, refer to his writings. Eusebius tells us that he wrote in Greek. Thallus details the crucifixion of Jesus but explains that the darkness that fell over the land at the time of His death[490] was not a supernatural miracle, but merely an eclipse.[491] His writings have been lost and we only know of them through the citations of other historians. For example, Julius Africanus writes:

Thallus in the third book of his histories explains away this darkness as an eclipse of the sun; unreasonably, as it seems to me.

The Passover is celebrated at the full moon in the month of Nisan and Christ was crucified at Passover time. It is not possible for there to have been a solar eclipse, because the moon must pass between the sun and the earth. A full moon occurs when the moon is fully illuminated by the sun and this only happens when the earth is between the sun and the moon.

FF Bruce states in his book, *The New Testament Documents: Are They Reliable?*:

Africanus stated his objection to the report arguing that an eclipse of the sun cannot occur during the full moon, as was the case when Jesus died at Passover time. The force of the reference to Thallus is that the circumstances of Jesus' crucifixion were known and discussed in the Imperial City as early as the middle of the first century. The fact of Jesus' crucifixion must have been fairly well known by that time, to the extent that unbelievers like Thallus thought it necessary to explain the matter of the darkness as a natural phenomenon.[492]

---

[488] R. E. Beacham and K. T. Bauder, *Only One bible?* Kregel Publications, Grand Rapids Michigan, 2,001, page 77.
[489] E. M. Blaiklock, *Jesus Christ: Man or Myth?* Anzea, 1983; Thomas Nelson, 1984.
[490] Matthew 27:45.
[491] wikipedia.org/wiki/Thallus, retrieved January 2011.
[492] F. F. Bruce, *The New Testament Documents: Are They Reliable?* Downers Grove, Intervarsity Press, 1981, page 113.

6   Did Jesus Really Live, Die and Rise from the Dead?

Mara Bar Serapion

Writing in the first century AD, Mara Bar Serapion, a Syrian writer, is believed to be the provider of one of the earliest non-Jewish, non-Christian references to Jesus. His letter to his son, who was in prison at the time, has been dated to sometime after AD 73. In it, he encourages his son in the pursuit of wisdom and points out that those who persecute wise men are overtaken by misfortune. To support his contention, he gives the examples of Socrates, Pythagoras and Christ.[493] F. F. Bruce cites this letter, even though it does not mention Jesus by name, as clear evidence of the historicity of Jesus.[494] The letter resides in the British Museum.

What advantage did the Athenians gain by putting Socrates to death? Famine and plague came upon them as a punishment for their crime. What advantage did the men of Samos gain for the burning of Pythagoras? In a moment their land was covered with sand. What advantage did the Jews gain from executing their wise king? It was just after that, that their kingdom was abolished. God justly avenged these three wise men: the Athenians died from hunger; the Samians were overwhelmed by the sea; the Jews, ruined and driven from their land, live in complete dispersion. But Socrates did not die for good; he lived on in the teaching of Plato. Pythagoras did not die for good, he lived on in the statue of Hera. Nor did the wise king die for good; he lived on in the teaching, which he had given.

Phlegon of Tralles (written AD 80?)

Phlegon was a first century Greek historian whose writings have been lost. However, they are referred to by Julius Africanus, who comments on Phlegon's documentation of the darkness that came over the earth at the time of Christ's crucifixion. As with Thallus, Phlegon puts it down to a solar eclipse, but also makes the point that it occurred during the reign of Tiberius Caesar and at the time of the Passover, and that there was a full moon, which, as stated before, makes a solar eclipse impossible.

The writings of Phlegon are also referred to by Origen in *Contra Celsum*, who wrote:

Phlegon mentioned the eclipse which took place during the crucifixion of the Lord Jesus Christ, and no other (eclipse) it is clear that he did not know from his source about any (similar) eclipse in previous times… And this is shown by the historical account itself of Tiberius Caesar.

From the above examples of non-biblical evidence, it is clear that none of the early writers doubted the historicity of Jesus' existence, His crucifixion and the darkness that fell over the land.

Flavius Josephus (AD 37–103)

Josephus was the son of a priest and was reared in traditional Judaism. He got caught up in the Jewish anti-Roman resistance movement and found himself in charge of the Jotapata fortress in Galilee. Though he refused to surrender until his life was guaranteed, it was his successful prophecy that Vespasian would become emperor that brought imperial favor. He received

---

[493] wikipedia.org/wiki/Mara_Bar-Serapion, retrieved April 11, 2011
[494] F. F. Bruce, *The New Testament Documents: Are They Reliable?*, Downers Grove, IL, Intervarsity Press, 1981.

6   Did Jesus Really Live, Die and Rise from the Dead?

Roman citizenship and was commissioned to write a history of the Jewish people, which he did in two compilations of writings, each consisting of many books: *History of the Jewish War* (against Rome) and *Antiquities of the Jews.*[495]

In *Antiquities of the Jews*, Josephus confirms the authenticity of John the Baptist and the fact that Herod had him executed:

Now some of the Jews thought that the destruction of Herod's army came from God, and that very justly, as a punishment of what he did against John, that was called the Baptist: for Herod slew him, who was a good man, and commanded the Jews to exercise virtue, both as to righteousness and to one another, and piety towards God.[496]

Another quotation from Antiquities confirms the authenticity of Jesus' brother James:

Festus was now dead, and Albinus was put upon the road; so he assembled the Sanhedrin of judges, and brought before them the brother of Jesus who was called Christ, whose name was James, and some others, and when he had formed an accusation against them as breakers of the law, he delivered them to be stoned.[497]

Josephus confirms the authenticity of the High Priest Annas who tried Jesus before His crucifixion:

But the younger Annas who, as we said, received the high priesthood, was of a bold disposition and exceptionally daring; he followed the party of the Sadducees who are severe in judgment above all of the Jews, as we have already shown.[498]

Josephus gives more information about Jesus in *Antiquities* which is consistent with scripture:

At this time there was a wise man called Jesus, and his conduct was good, and he was known to be virtuous. Many people among the Jews and the other nations became his disciples. Pilate condemned him to be crucified and to die. But those who had become his disciples did not abandon his discipleship. They reported that he had appeared to them three days after his crucifixion and that he was alive. Accordingly, he was perhaps the Messiah, concerning whom the prophets have reported wonders. And the tribe of Christians, so named after him, has not disappeared to this day.[499]

The most common form of the above verse actually says that Jesus was the Messiah and that He did appear to His disciples after returning to life on the third day. Consequently, it has been declared by many scholars to have been altered by Christians some time after the time of Josephus. The verse quoted above was found by Professor Schlomo Pines of the Hebrew

---

[495] wikipedia.org/wiki/josephus, retrieved June 15, 2011.
[496] Josephus, *Antiquities of the Jews*, Book 18, chapter 5, paragraph 2.
[497] *Ibid,* Book 20, chapter 9.
[498] *Ibid*, Book 20, chapter 9, paragraph 1.
[499] *Ibid*, Book 18, chapter. 3, paragraph 3.

6 Did Jesus Really Live, Die and Rise from the Dead?

University in 1972. It was written by the tenth century Melkite historian Agapius and could be the original.[500]

Cornelius Tacitus (circa AD 56–AD 117)

Tacitus was a senator and historian of the Roman Empire. He was governor of Asia in 112. His two major works are the *Annals* and the *Histories*, many portions of which have survived. Reporting on Emperor Nero's decision to blame Christians for the fire that destroyed Rome, Tacitus wrote:

Consequently, to get rid of the report, Nero fastened the guilt and inflicted the most exquisite tortures on a class hated for their abominations, called Christians by the populace. Christus, from whom the name had its origin, suffered the extreme penalty during the reign of Tiberius at the hands of one of our procurators, Pontius Pilatus, and a most mischievous superstition, thus checked for the moment, again broke out not only in Judea, the first source of the evil, but even in Rome, where all things hideous and shameful from every part of the world find their center and become popular. Accordingly, an arrest was first made of all who pleaded guilty; then, upon their information, an immense multitude was convicted, not so much of the crime of firing the city, as of hatred against mankind. Mockery of every sort was added to their deaths. Covered with the skins of beasts, they were torn by dogs and perished, or were nailed to crosses, or were doomed to the flames and burnt, to serve as a nightly illumination, when daylight had expired.[501]

Tacitus' statement tells us in rather unsympathetic terms that Christians derived their name from a historical person named 'Christus' (Latin form of the Greek Christ), and that this person suffered *the extreme penalty*, obviously referring to the Roman method of execution, which is crucifixion. Tacitus writes that this occurred during the reign of Tiberius and that He was sentenced by Pontius Pilate. This confirms what the Bible says about the death of Jesus.[502]

Gaius Plinius Caecilius Secundus (Pliny the Younger) (AD 61/63–ca AD 113)

Pliny the Younger was the Governor of Bithynia in Asia Minor. In AD 112 he wrote a letter to the Emperor Trajan asking for advice on how to deal with Christians. He explained that he had been killing men, women, boys and girls. He was putting to death so many, he wondered if he should continue executing all he found to be Christians, because:

This contagious superstition is not confined to cities only, but has spread its infection among the neighboring villages and country.

Medieval statue of Pliny the Younger on the façade of Cathedral of S. Maria Maggiore in Como

Further, he states that he forces them to curse Christ, which genuine

---

[500] P. L. Maier, *Eusebius The Church History,* Kregel Publications, 1999, page 378.
[501] Tacitus, *Annals,* XV 44; see Appendix 2.
[502] The full text of this part of Tacitus' writings is in Appendix 2 and is available online from: perseus.tufts.edu/hopper, retrieved April 11, 2011.

6 Did Jesus Really Live, Die and Rise from the Dead?

Christians cannot be made to do. In his letter he relates some information he has learnt about these people:

They affirmed the whole of their guilt, or their error, was, that they met on a stated day before it was light and addressed a form of prayer to Christ, as to a divinity, binding themselves to a common oath, not to do any wicked deeds, but never to commit any fraud, theft or adultery, never to falsify their word, nor deny a trust when they should be called upon to deliver it up; after which it was their custom to separate, and then reassemble to eat in common a harmless meal.[503]

This letter provides us with a number of insights into the practice and customs of early Christians. They had a fixed day for worship, they directed their worship to Christ, they adhered to a moral code which was consistent with Christ's teaching, and they gathered to share a common meal, possibly communion. Furthermore, true believers would prefer to be executed than to curse Christ.

Suetonius (Gaius Suetonius Tranquillus, circa 70–after 130)[504]

Suetonius was a friend of Pliny the Younger and he served under him for a period of time. He was a Roman historian and court official under Hadrian. His most important work is a surviving set of biographies on the lives of twelve successive Roman rulers from Julius Caesar to Domitian. In these writings, he makes two references to Christ:

In the *Life of Claudius* he wrote:

As the Jews were making constant disturbances at the instigation of Chestus [another spelling of Christus, or Christ] *he* [Claudius] *expelled them from Rome.*

Gaius Suetonius Tranquilius (illustration from the *Nuremberg Chronicle*)

In the *Lives of Caesars* he wrote:

Punishment by Nero was inflicted on Christians, a class of men given to a new and mischievous superstition.

In these two references Suetonius confirms that:

1. There was a Christian presence in Rome and that Claudius expelled them because they were *making constant disturbances*. This statement is in keeping with the departure from Rome by Priscilla and Aquila in AD 49.[505]

2. Christians were persecuted by Nero.

---

[503] The full text of Pliny's letter (courtesy of Project Gutenberg) and Trajan's reply are in Appendix 3.
[504] wikipedia.org/wiki/Suetonius, retrieved July 18, 2011.
[505] Acts 18.

6 Did Jesus Really Live, Die and Rise from the Dead?

Lucian of Samosata (AD 115–ca AD 180)

Lucian of Samosata was a well-known second century Greek Satirist. He claimed to have been born in Samosata, in the former kingdom of Commagene, which was absorbed by the Roman Empire and made part of Syria. He mocked the followers of Jesus for their ignorance and credulity, although he did credit Christians with a certain level of morality. He is considered important to Christians for giving insight into the historical Jesus as follows:

The Christians ...worship a man to this day ... the distinguished personage who introduced their novel rites, and was crucified on that account. It was impressed upon them by their original lawgiver that they were all brothers, from the moment they were converted, and deny the gods of Greece, and worship the crucified sage and live under his laws.[506]

Here Lucian tells us that the Christians worshipped a man who introduced novel rites and that He angered many of His contemporaries with His teaching to the extent that they crucified Him.

The Babylonian Talmud

The Talmuds and Tosefta are rabbinic commentaries on the Jewish scriptures and they contain references to Yeshu (Jesus). The writing most often cited as evidence of the Jesus of the Bible is the Babylonian Talmud, which was most likely compiled between AD 70 and 200.[507]

The following quotation was translated by Rabbi Dr I Epstein:

Babylonian Talmud, a complete set

On the eve of the Passover Yeshu was hanged. For forty days before the execution took place, a herald went forth and cried, "He is going forth to be stoned because he has practiced sorcery and enticed Israel to apostasy. Anyone who can say anything in his favor let him come forward and plead on his behalf." But since nothing was brought forward in his favor he was hanged on the eve of the Passover![508]

Here the Jewish Talmud confirms the time, the reason and the mode of Jesus' execution. The term 'Hanging' was often used by the Jews to describe crucifixion. Notice Paul[509] quotes from Deuteronomy 21:23 when he refers to Christ, *Cursed is everyone who hangs on a tree*. But the commentators have put their slant to His execution to give the impression of a fair trial.

---

[506] Lucian, *The Death of Peregrine*, 11–13, in *The Works of Lucian of Samosata*, trans. H. W. Flower, 4 volume, Oxford: Clarendon, 1949, cited by G. R. Habermas, *The Historical Jesus*, College Press, 1996, page 206.
[507] G. Habermas, *The Historical Jesus*, College Press, 1996, pages 202–203.
[508] I. Epstein, *Contents of the Soncino Babylonian Talmud*, The Soncino Press, London, 1935.
[509] Galatians 3:13.

6 Did Jesus Really Live, Die and Rise from the Dead?

Summary

The aforementioned evidence of the life and death of Christ presented from non-Christian sources can be condensed as follows:

1. Jesus' death by crucifixion was confirmed by Josephus, the Babylonian Talmud, Lucian and Tacitus, and alluded to by Mara Bar Serapion. The fact that this occurred under Pontius Pilate was stated by Tacitus and Josephus and under the reign of Tiberius Caesar by Phlegon and Tacitus.

2. The darkness that came during the crucifixion has been mentioned by Thallus, Phlegon and Africanus.

3. His worship by Christians who followed His teaching has been confirmed by Josephus, Lucian and Suetonius. Further, Pliny states that they worshipped Christ as deity.

4. The fact that He was a powerful and revered teacher was stated by the Babylonian Talmud and implied by Lucian and Pliny.

5. His performance of miraculous feats was indicated by Josephus and the Talmud.

6. That His followers were prepared to suffer the vilest of torture and death rather than reject Him has been confirmed by Tacitus and Pliny. That Christianity started in Judea was mentioned by Tacitus.

Only the extracts of Josephus can be open to question since they have been handed down by Christian scribes. The others were handed down through Roman and Greek scribes and are free from any allegations of tampering.

Extra-biblical sources confirm that the man described in the Bible as Jesus of Nazareth once walked this earth and was executed by crucifixion.

Did Jesus Really Die When He Was Crucified?

Having established that Jesus really lived and walked this earth, the next question is, "Did He really die at His crucifixion?"

Scourging

Before being nailed to the cross, Jesus was beaten by both the Jews and the Romans and possibly had His whiskers pulled from His face. Then Pilate had Him scourged. This form of punishment was normally carried out by the use of a short whip with several single or braided leather thongs of variable lengths, in which small lead balls and sharp pieces of bone were tied at intervals. A possible form of scourging (as depicted on the next page) has the man stripped of his clothing, with his hands tied to an upright post. The back, buttocks and legs were flogged either by two soldiers or by one who alternated positions. The severity of the scourging depended on the disposition of the soldiers and was intended to weaken the victim to a state just short of collapse or death. The Jews were prohibited by Levitical law from applying more than 40 lashes, so they gave 39 just in case they miscounted. However, the Romans were not so limited.

6   Did Jesus Really Live, Die and Rise from the Dead?

As the heavy and sharp whip was drawn across the body, it would cut through the skin and tear open the flesh. Successive lashes would cut deeper, severing blood vessels. Much blood would be lost through scourging and the victim would be left with a mass of shredded flesh, weeping and oozing blood. So cruel was the practice that women and Roman citizens were exempt.[510]

Jesus then had to carry the heavy horizontal bar of His cross. The prophet Isaiah[511] tells us that, at this stage, Jesus was so beaten that He was unrecognisable as a man. No wonder He could not carry His cross the whole distance to His place of execution.[512]

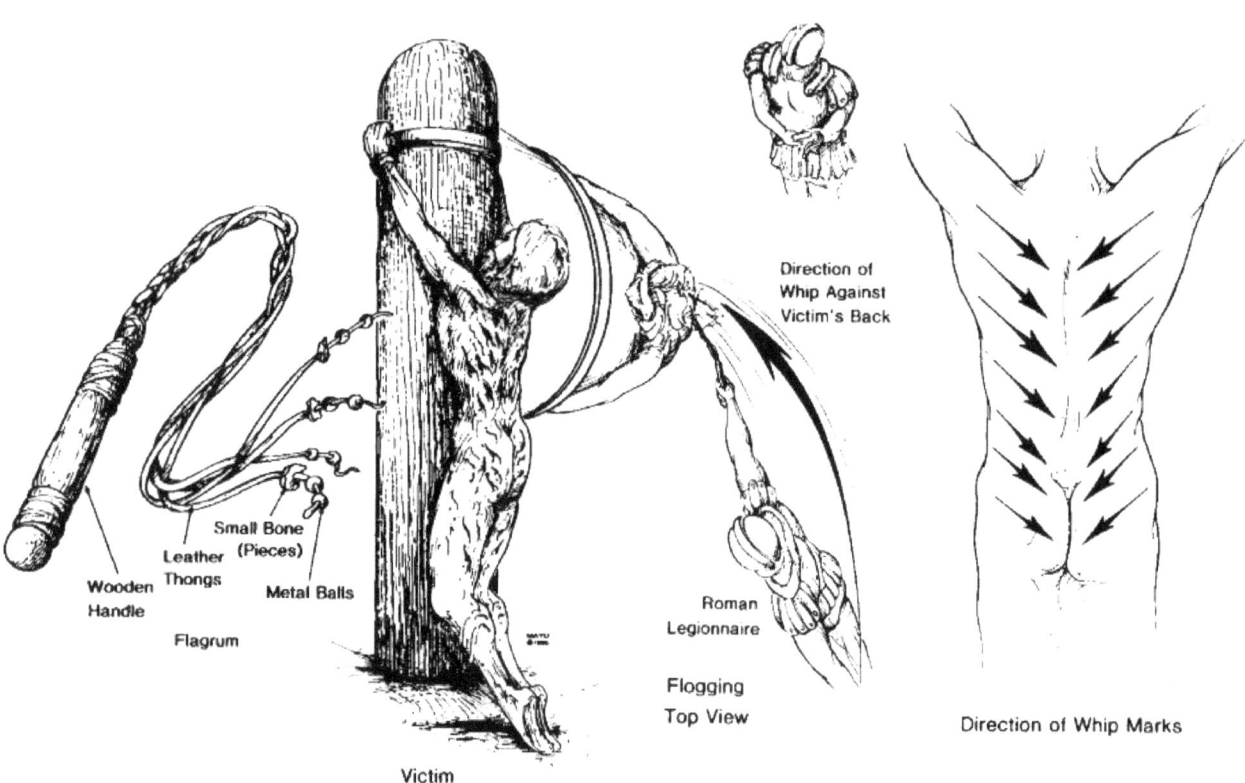

Crucifixion

Crucifixion is an ancient form of execution, which the Romans developed to an 'art'. None of the vital organs are damaged and the hapless victim is left to die in excruciating pain for up to four days, depending on how he was treated before being nailed to the cross.

The Position of the Nails

The general consensus by those who have investigated this topic is that the nails were hammered

---

[510] Encyclopedia Britannica Online, retrieved October 14, 2008; *Wycliffe Bible Dictionary,* Hendrickson, 1998.
[511] Isaiah 52:14.
[512] Luke 23:26.

through the wrists rather than the palms. The Greek word *cheir* that is translated as *hand* may have, in fact, included everything below the mid-forearm. Acts 12:7 uses this word to report chains falling from Peter's hands, although the chains would have been around his wrists.

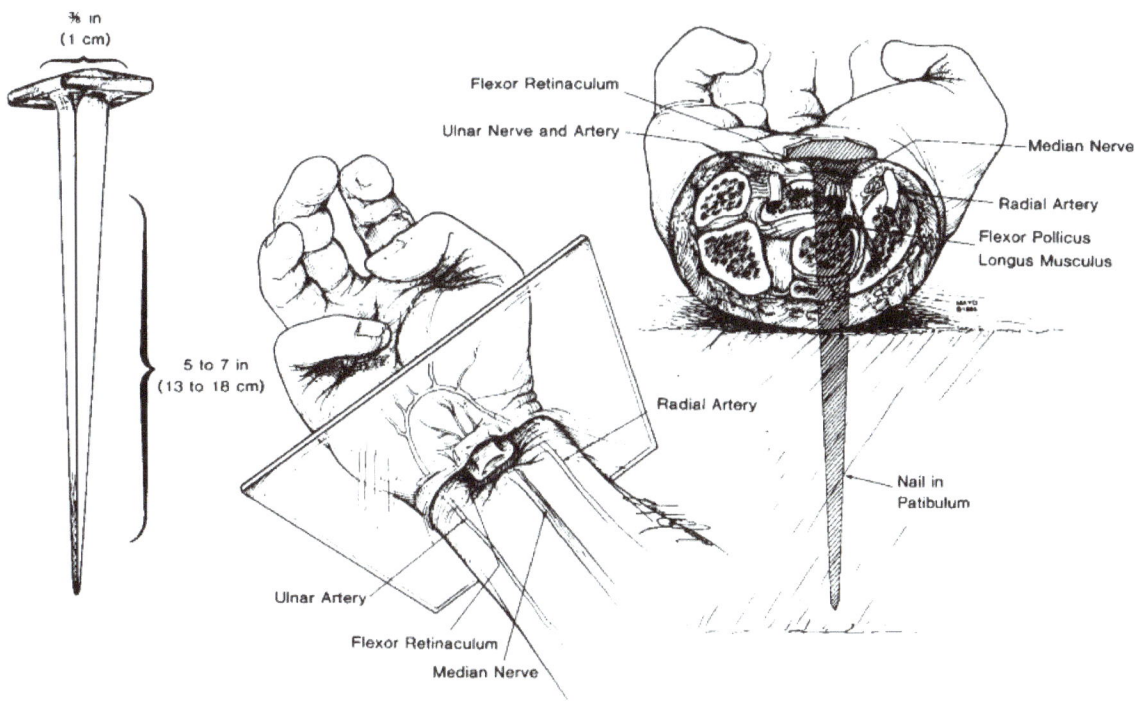

In order for the victim to breathe whilst hanging on the cross, thereby greatly extending the period of suffering, a nail or nails were driven through the feet. In 1968, the remains of a man were discovered in a burial cave at Giv'at ha-Mivtar, northeast of Jerusalem. An ossuary (bone-box) was discovered containing the skeletal remains of a man who had been crucified, evidence of which was a large nail, still in the heel bone (calcaneus). The nail was still in place because it had bent when driven through his ankle. The remains of an olive wood plank placed on his foot prior to the nail being driven in were found also, evidently acting as a

'washer' to prevent the victim from pulling his foot off the spike. With this mode of securing the feet, both feet would be nailed separately either side of the crucifixion pole as shown in the photograph.

6 Did Jesus Really Live, Die and Rise from the Dead?

Another idea for holding the feet in position was for one foot to be placed upon the other and a single nail driven through both feet. However, although this form of securing is commonly depicted (as in *Crucifixion of Jesus of Nazareth*, Marco Palmezzano's painting of about 1490—see adjacent image), there are no archeological specimens, to support it.

Mode of Death

Survival time on the cross generally ranged from a few hours to up to four days and this was dependent on the severity of the scourging. Even if the victim leveraged himself against the spike that had been nailed through the feet, breathing would still be very difficult and labored. The sufferer would die from any one, or most likely, a combination of, suffocation; shock; exhaustion as a result of his attempts to breathe; dehydration; pulmonary edema (water on the lungs); and congestive heart failure.

The Certainty of Jesus' Death

Joseph of Arimathea requested the body of Jesus from Pontius Pilate so that He could be interred. As well, the Jews did not want Jesus to remain on the cross, because they did not want bodies left on the cross during the Sabbath, which commenced at sundown that night, so they requested that Pilate would have His legs broken to hasten death. John, in chapter 19, verses 32–34, continues the story:

Then the soldiers came and broke the legs of the first and of the other who was crucified with Him. But when they came to Jesus and saw that He was already dead, they did not break His legs. But one of the soldiers pierced His side with a spear, and immediately blood and water came out.

The Roman soldiers, whose stock in trade was killing people and who were under pain of death themselves if they failed to carry out an order, on approaching Jesus could see that He was dead, probably because of the absence of breathing—which, as has been stated before, was very labored for a crucified person. Thus, they did not break His legs. In not doing so, they fulfilled the prophecy of Psalm 34:20 that not one of his bones would be broken, in keeping with Jesus as being the 'Passover Lamb.'[513] However, a soldier did thrust a spear up under His ribcage and into His heart and we are told blood and water issued forth.

---

[513] Exodus 12:46; Numbers 9:12.

6 Did Jesus Really Live, Die and Rise from the Dead?

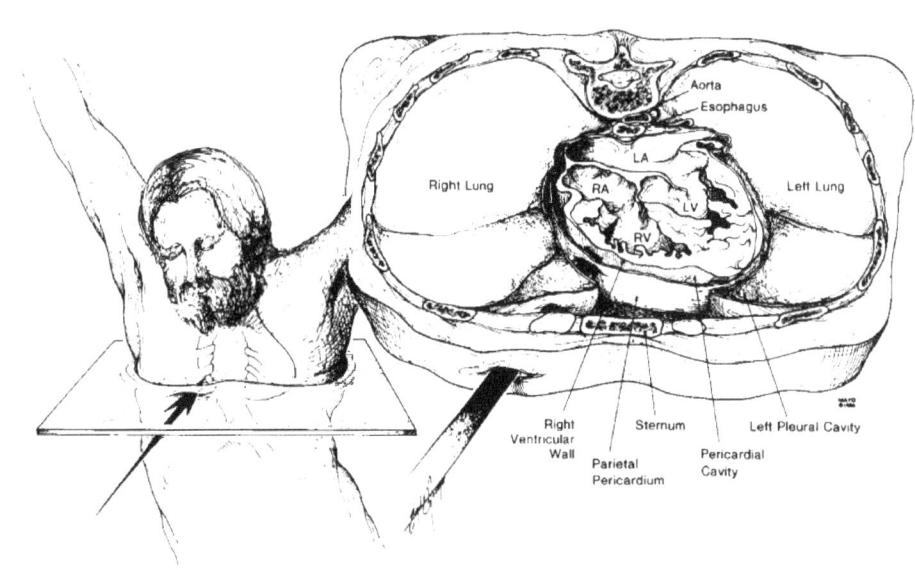

If any further confirmation of Jesus' death is required, surely this is it, as the spear would have penetrated His lungs as shown in the schematic opposite, thereby releasing the clear fluid which would have built up there because of His limited breathing. It would have then proceeded to pierce the pericardium (sac around the heart) where more clear liquid would be released. Finally, it would have penetrated the enlarged right ventricle of the heart releasing the accumulated blood.

The act of spearing Jesus was a fulfillment of Zechariah's prophecy of 12:10:

... and they shall look upon me whom they have pierced, and they shall mourn for him, as one mourns for his only son.

This point was not lost on John, who refers to it in chapter 19, verse 37.

A study on the likelihood of Jesus' death from crucifixion was published in the prestigious *Journal of the American Medical Association*.[514] A summary of this is presented below:

Jesus of Nazareth underwent Jewish and Roman trials, was flogged, and was sentenced to death by crucifixion. The scourging produced deep stripe-like lacerations and appreciable blood loss, and it probably set the stage for hypovolemic shock, as evidenced by the fact that Jesus was too weakened to carry the crossbar (patibulum) to Golgotha. At the site of crucifixion, his wrists were nailed to the patibulum and, after the patibulum was lifted onto the upright post (stipes), his feet were nailed to the stipes. The major pathophysiologic effect of crucifixion was an interference with normal respiration. Accordingly, death resulted primarily from hypovolemic shock and exhaustion asphyxia. Jesus' death was ensured by the thrust of a soldier's spear into his side. Modern medical interpretation of the historical evidence indicates that Jesus was dead when taken down from the cross.[515]

There can be no doubt that Jesus died.

---

[514] *Journal of the American Medical Association*, vol. 255 No. 11, March 21, 1986.
[515] W. D. Edwards, W. J. Gabel and F. E. Hosmer, *On the physical death of Jesus Christ*, JAMA, Vol. 255 No. 11, March 21, 1986.

6 Did Jesus Really Live, Die and Rise from the Dead?

Did Jesus Really Rise From the Dead?

If you want to disprove Christianity, disprove the resurrection. If you can do this, then Christianity crumbles. The apostle Paul says similarly in 1 Corinthians 15:14:

And if Christ be not risen, then our preaching is futile and your faith is also in vain.

He makes the point further in verses 15–18 and concludes in verse 19:

If in this life only we have hope in Christ, we are of all men most to be pitied.

Albert Henry Ross was skeptical regarding the resurrection of Jesus, and set out to analyse the sources and to write a short paper entitled *Jesus – the Last Phase,* to demonstrate the apparent myth. In compiling his notes, he came to be convinced of the truth of the resurrection, and set out his reasoning in the book *Who moved the stone?,* which he wrote under the pseudonym Frank Morison. It was first published in 1930 and it has led many people to Christianity.[516]

Josh McDowell set out to disprove Christianity by disproving the Christ's resurrection. He states:

After more than 700 hours of studying this subject, I have come to the conclusion that the resurrection of Jesus Christ is either one of the most wicked, vicious, heartless hoaxes ever foisted on the minds of human beings—or it is the most remarkable fact of history.[517]

He concluded the latter and became a Christian. Since then he has written life-changing books on the subject, and is one of the most quoted apologetics' authors. Now, let us consider some of the evidence for Christ's resurrection.

Evidence for the Resurrection

1. **The tomb was secured**. Pilate ordered the tomb to be guarded at the insistence of the Jews:[518]

    "Sir, we remember, while He was still alive, how that deceiver said, 'After three days I will rise.' Therefore command that the tomb be made secure until the third day, lest His disciples come by night and steal Him away, and say to the people, 'He has risen from the dead.' So the last deception will be worse than the first."

    Pilate's response to this request is recorded as:

    You have a guard; go your way, make [it] as secure as you know how."

    His answer can be interpreted in either of two ways;[519] Pilate consenting to their request in providing a Roman guard or telling the Jews to use their own guard which would have been the Temple guard. The latter interpretation has the advantage of being more in keeping with

---

[516] http://en.wikipedia.org/wiki/Albert_Henry_Ross.
[517] leaderu.com/everystudent/easter/articles/josh2.html, retrieved April 12, 2011.
[518] Matthew 27:63–64.
[519] http://creation.com/joseph-of-arimathea.

the guards being bribed to say that His disciples stole His body during the night while they were asleep.[520] In any event, the tomb was guarded to make it secure.

2. **The large stone was removed**. Archaeological evidence suggests that this stone would have weighed two tons. The normal procedure was for the stone to be rolled along a v-shaped groove, and once the body was interred, it would be rolled into place and wedged there in order to prevent the grave from being robbed. It would have taken many men to perform this task.

A first century tomb at Jerusalem

3. **The tomb was empty**. This is the greatest evidence of the risen Savior. No body has ever been produced. It would have been very easy for the Jews to disprove the resurrection by simply producing His body. No one has been able to do this in 2,000 years.

4. **The graveclothes were intact.** The tomb was not totally empty, for when the disciples looked where Jesus had lain:

   [They] *saw the linen cloths lying there, and the face cloth, which had been on Jesus' head, not lying with the linen cloths but folded up in a place by itself.*[521]

   In fact, the clothes were possibly set hard since they consisted of strips of linen saturated with a mixture of about 34 kilograms (75 pounds) of myrrh and aloes.[522] Indeed, this embalming procedure would make it very difficult, if not impossible, for anyone to remove the body and reconstitute the bandages.

5. **His resurrection was unexpected.** According to the gospel narratives, none of Jesus' followers expected Him to rise from the dead. Luke wrote that when Jesus appeared to them in a room with the doors closed:

   ...they were terrified and frightened, and supposed they had seen a spirit.[523]

   Jesus comforted them by telling them not to be afraid because it really was Him, and He invited them to look at His hands and feet where the nails had pierced. He assured them that He was not a spirit but real flesh and blood.[524] The disciple Thomas (Doubting Thomas) was not present and when told of the incident, he refused to believe that Jesus had risen from the dead[525] until one week later when Jesus actually stood before him. At this point, Thomas no longer doubted and made his great confession, for now he knew that Jesus was alive and recognized His divinity with his statement:

---

[520] Matthew 28:13-14.
[521] John 20:6-7 (*English Standard Version*).
[522] John 19:39–40.
[523] Luke 24:37.
[524] Luke 24:37-41.
[525] John 20:24-28.

6 Did Jesus Really Live, Die and Rise from the Dead?

My Lord and my God.[526]

6. **The testimony of a hostile witness.** As compelling evidence as the above may be, even more compelling is the testimony of a hostile witness: in this case Saul of Tarsus, who despised Jesus and persecuted His followers.[527] However, when the risen Christ appeared to him on the road to Damascus, he believed with a passion and became one of the greatest proponents and propagators of Christianity.

7. **Those who saw the resurrected Christ were still alive.** Paul states in chapter 15 of his first letter to the church at Corinth that Jesus appeared to 500 witnesses at the one time and if anybody doubted this, most of these witnesses were still alive and he or she could quickly obtain confirmation.

8. **Jesus' post-resurrection appearances.** In all, there were 11 recorded post-resurrection appearances of Jesus over a forty-day period and at various times of the day. We can count twelve if we include Paul's conversion on the road to Damascus.

Event	Date	Matthew	Mark	Luke	John	Acts	1 Corinthians
At the empty tomb	Early Sunday morning	28:1–10	16:1–8	24:1–12	20:1–9		
To Mary Magdalene at the tomb	Early Sunday morning		16:9–11		20:11–18		
To two travelers on the road to Emmaus	Sunday at midday			24:13–32			
To Peter in Jerusalem	During Sunday			24:34			15:5
To ten disciples in upper room	Sunday evening			24:36–43	20:19–25		
To eleven disciples in upper room	One week later		16:14		20:26–31		15:5
To seven disciples fishing on Sea of Galilee	One day at daybreak				21:1–23		
To eleven disciples in Galilee	Some time later	28:16–20	16:15–18				
To more than 500	Some time later						15:6
To James	Some time later						15:7
At the Ascension on the Mt of Olives	Forty days after the resurrection					1:3–8	

9. **Two of Jesus' brothers did not believe in His Messiahship** during his earthly life[528] and yet after His resurrection they both became believers, each wrote a book (James and Jude) and spent the rest of their lives proclaiming the 'good news.'

10. **Being prepared to die for what they believed.** If more evidence is needed, it can be found in the form of His disciples who, by spreading the gospel, risked their lives. Extra-biblical writings tell that all of them (except John) lost their lives for the sake of Christ. This is even more compelling when their cowardly behavior at the time of Christ's arrest is taken into

---

[526] John 20:28.
[527] Acts 7:51-8:1; 8:3; 22:4-5.
[528] John 7:1–5.

account. Of all people, it was the disciples and the women with them who would have known if Jesus had risen from the dead, and on the basis of His resurrection, they willingly gave their lives. Would you give your life for something that you knew was a lie?

11. **The Nazareth Inscription.** Further evidence comes in the form of a marble tablet known as the Nazareth Inscription. It was acquired by Wilhelm Fröhner (1834–1925) to form part of his collection of ancient inscriptions and manuscripts. It was labeled: *This Marble was sent from Nazareth in 1878.* Since 1925 it has been in the Bibliothèque nationale, Paris, displayed in the Cabinet des Médailles[529]

The Nazareth Inscription Translation from the Koine Greek text by Clyde E. Billington:[530]

1. EDICT OF CAESAR
2. It is my decision [concerning] graves and tombs--whoever has made
3. them for the religious observances of parents, or children, or household
4. members--that these remain undisturbed forever. But if anyone legally
5. charges that another person has destroyed, or has in any manner extracted
6. those who have been buried, or has moved with wicked intent those who
7. have been buried to other places, committing a crime against them, or has
8. moved sepulcher-sealing stones, against such a person, I order that a
9. judicial tribunal be created, just as [is done] concerning the gods in
10. human religious observances, even more so will it be obligatory to treat
11. with honor those who have been entombed. You are absolutely not to
12. allow anyone to move [those who have been entombed]. But if
13. [someone does], I wish that [violator] to suffer capital punishment under
14. the title of tomb-breaker.

Michael Green[531] cites the inscription as a secular source of early origin that bears testimony to Jesus' empty tomb:

It is an imperial edict, belonging either to the reign of Tiberius (A.D. 14-37) or of Claudius (A.D. 41-54). And it is an invective, backed with heavy sanctions, against meddling around with tombs and graves! It looks very much as if the news of the empty tomb had got back to Rome in a garbled form. (Pontius Pilate would have had to report: and he would obviously have said that the tomb had been rifled). This edict, it seems, is the imperial reaction.

Clyde Billington of Northwestern College (Minnesota) has dated it to AD 41, and interpreted it as evidence for the historicity of Christians preaching the resurrection of Jesus within a decade of His crucifixion since it seems to apply specificall to Jewish burials from the early first century (*moved bodies, moved sepulcher-sealing stones,* whereas Gentiles either cremated or buried their dead in coffins).[526]

---

[529] wikipedia.org/wiki/Nazareth_Inscription
[530] *The Nazareth Inscription: Proof of the Resurrection of Christ?* Clyde E. Billington, in *Artifax*, Spring, 2005.
[531] Michael Green, *Man Alive*, Leicester: IVP, 1968, page 36.

6   Did Jesus Really Live, Die and Rise from the Dead?

This is what others who have undertaken serious investigation into the resurrection have concluded:

In a letter to Rev E. L. Macassey, Former British High Court judge, Sir Edward George Clarke, offered the following perspective:

As a lawyer I have made a prolonged study of the evidences for the first Easter. To me the evidence is conclusive, and over and over again in the High Court I have secured the verdict on evidence not nearly so compelling. As a lawyer I accept it unreservedly as the testimony of men to facts that they were able to substantiate.[532]

Thomas Arnold, Professor of History at Oxford University and author of a three-volume history on ancient Rome, wrote:

I have been used for many years to study the history of other times, and to examine and weigh the evidence of those who have written about them; and I know of no fact in the history of mankind which is proved by better and fuller evidence of every sort, to the understanding of a fair inquirer, than that Christ died and rose again from the dead.[533]

J. N. D. Anderson, in the words of Armand Nicholi of the Harvard Medical School,[534] is a scholar of international repute, eminently qualified to deal with the subject of evidence. He is one of the world's leading authorities on Muslim law, Dean of the Faculty of Law at the University of London, Chairman of the Department of Oriental Law at the School of Oriental and African Studies, and Director of the Institute of Advanced Legal Studies at the University of London. In Anderson's text, *Christianity: The Witness of History*, he supplies the standard evidences for the Resurrection and asks:

How, then, can the fact of the resurrection be denied?

Anderson further emphasises,

*Lastly, it can be asserted with confidence that men and women disbelieve the Easter story **not because of the evidence but in spite of it***.[535]

Jesus said the same thing, as is recorded in Luke's gospel:

If they do not listen to Moses and the Prophets, they will not be convinced even if someone rises from the dead.[536]

There can be no doubt that Jesus of Nazareth is Jesus the Christ and that He rose from the dead, thereby demonstrating that He was fully man and is fully God.

---

[532] christianity.co.nz/res-3.htm, retrieved July 2, 2011.
[533] Thomas Arnold, *Christian Life, Its Hopes, Its Fears, and Its Close*, 6th Ed, London, 1859, pages 15-16.
[534] *Christianity Today*, March 29, 1968.
[535] J. N. D. Anderson, *Christianity: The Witness of History*, Tyndale Press, London, 1970, page 105.
[536] Luke 16:31 (*New International Version*).

Chapter 7

Summary

Initially we looked at the other major religions to see if there was any truth in them.

The Hindus believe that all people and animals, including insects, are involved in an endless cycle of reincarnation, whereby the form in which a person or creature returns to life depends on how the previous life was lived. There is absolutely no evidence to support this concept and it is difficult to understand how an animal or insect can rise up the ladder by being good.

Buddhism was initiated by an Indian Prince named Siddhartha Gautama, who later became known as The Buddha. He taught that desire is at the root of human suffering, and this can be avoided by following his four noble truths and his eight-fold path to obtain a state called *Nirvana*, whereby a person can escape from desire and, essentially, convince him/herself that he does not exist. There is absolutely no evidence to support this position, and, in fact, normal life experiences confirm that desire and suffering are integral parts of being human.

Islam was started by a man named Muhammad, who claimed to have received divine revelation while sitting in a cave. His followers wrote his biography about these revelations 125 years after his death and what was written was revised a further 200 years thereafter; these writings have become known as the Hadiths. The Koran consists of a collection of writings purportedly from Muhammad (although it has been claimed he was illiterate) and parts of it are based on the Bible (which predates the Koran by up to 2,000 or more years as some books were written pre-1,500 BC). The Koran contains many scientific errors (see page 111) and contradictions with respect to the Bible (see page 9).

A common feature of the cults is that they deny the Lordship and Deity of Christ and are based on the fallible teachings of the person who started the cult.

We have found that there is a lack of scientific evidence to support the Theory of Evolution. Even the foundational Big Bang Theory has been shown by way of the Hubble telescope to be inconsistent with what is observed and the idea of the universe being formed from an explosion; that is, disorder going to order, is a clear violation of the Second Law of Thermodynamics. The chance formation of life through random chemical collisions is impossible, and even if some of the chemicals of life were formed, they would break down rather than build up to even bigger molecules. The field of genetics represents another huge problem for Darwinists as they require mechanisms for adding about three billion nucleotides (pieces of information) to a bacterium's DNA (genes) to change it into a human. They say they had billions of years for all of this to happen, yet there be an abundance of evidence that supports a young earth, including soft tissue and red blood cells in 'Jurassic' period fossils that are claimed to be many millions of years old.

Finally, there is an absence of fossils of 'intermediate' species, without which Darwin said his theory would collapse; as well, there are many 'living fossils', which have not changed over their period of existence.

Contrary to evolution, biblical creation is consistent with what is observed and measured now. We see design in every aspect of nature; from a hive of bees working together for the common good, to

7 Summary

the mind-boggling fact that one fertilised human egg cell has enough genetic information to instruct itself to form a complete human being with thousands of kilometers of blood vessels and 100 billion precisely-ordered brain cells, each with up to 10,000 connections. That makes an incomprehensible 1,000-trillion connections[537]—each of them perfectly ordered. These give us the ability to plan, design, love … and experience and exhibit our emotions in all their many forms.

One scientist has commented that in order to tell the difference between what man has made and what God has made, one only needs to examine it closely. As magnification increases, what man has made becomes less precise. But what God has made becomes ever more complex and intricate.

When we examined the Bible under the microscope of modern science, we found that it could withstand this close scrutiny. Although written thousands of years ago, the Bible tells us that the heavens are being 'stretched out'; the earth is round, and suspended in space. There is strong evidence of Noah's flood and that all representatives of the animal kingdom could have fitted in the ark. Blood clotting factors reach their maximum concentration on the eighth day after birth, an ideal time for circumcision, as per God's directive to Abraham.

We have seen that, when it comes to prophecy, the Bible is one hundred percent accurate. At least 60 detailed and descriptive prophecies concerning the coming Messiah were all completely fulfilled in the Person of Jesus of Nazareth. As well, prophecies concerning the future of towns, cities and nations have come to pass, even in the minutest detail, and those that haven't are still future to us. Archeological discoveries have provided evidence that the people and places mentioned in the Bible once existed.

All of this means that the Bible is indeed trustworthy in all areas where it can be tested, whether in the fields of astronomy, chemistry, physics, hydrology, medicine or prophecy. Consequently, we can safely conclude that it can be trusted in areas where it cannot be tested empirically, such as Adam and Eve's rejection of God and the consequential fall into sin of all humanity.

The Bible tells us that,

… all have sinned and fall short of the glory of God.[538]

This being the case, the Bible is replete with the sin of even its most prominent characters. Abraham took his wife's servant girl Hagar to have his child, even though God had told him that his wife Sarah would produce an heir for him.[539] Jacob deceived his father into giving him the blessing instead of his brother Esau.[540] God refused Moses entry into the Promised Land because he disobeyed His instructions by striking the rock instead of speaking to it. As well, he took God's glory for himself.[541] King David, whom God described as being, *a man after His own heart,*[542] committed adultery and deception, and ordered the murder of a faithful soldier in order to cover his

---

[537] *New Scientist*, 24/31 December, 2011, page 30
[538] Romans 3:23.
[539] Genesis 15:4; 16:1–4.
[540] Genesis 27.
[541] Numbers 20:9–12.
[542] 1 Samuel 13:14, Acts 13:22.

7 Summary

crime.[543] The disciple Peter denied Christ three times[544] and the great apostle Paul was so distressed by his own sinful nature that he stated:

O wretched man that I am! Who shall deliver me from this body of death?[545]

And again:

This is a faithful saying and worthy of all acceptances, that Christ Jesus came into the world to save sinners, of whom I am chief.[546]

We can trust the Bible when it says that God is holy and His anger burns against this sin,[547] and that the penalty for sin is death, both physical and spiritual.[548] Spiritual death is a separation from God. Adam died spiritually when he sinned and God cast him out from His presence.[549] He was physically alive but spiritually dead. Similarly, those who reject Christ are spiritually dead and once they die physically, the separation from God is permanent;[550] the eternal abode of unsaved people is Hell and ultimately the Lake of Fire, where they will endure everlasting punishment.[551]

We can trust the Bible when it says that God's love is so great that He sent His only begotten Son whom He loved, the Lord Jesus Christ, (God the Son) to pay the penalty on our behalf through His sacrificial death on the cross. When He cried:

It is finished[552] (paid in full)

as He hung on the cross, His work was completed and no other payment for our sin is required, or in fact, can be made. In other words, Jesus took our penalty for sin upon Himself and suffered its accompanying punishment. In return for our sin, He bestowed His righteousness on all who believe, which makes us alive spiritually[553] and enables us to enter into heaven.[554]

As the Bible states:

For God so loved the world, that he gave his only begotten Son, that whoever believes in him should not perish, but have everlasting life.[555]

---

[543] 2 Samuel 11.
[544] Matthew 26: 69–75.
[545] Romans 7:24
[546] 1 Timothy 1:15.
[547] Exodus 32: 10, 11, 12, 19; 2 Kings 22:13.
[548] Genesis 2:17; Romans 6:23.
[549] Genesis 3:23–24.
[550] Luke 16:19-31.
[551] Luke 16:23; Revelations 20:14.
[552] John 19:30.
[553] Colossians 2:13.
[554] 2 Corinthians 5:21; Romans 8:1.
[555] John 3:16.

7 Summary

That if you confess with your mouth the Lord Jesus, and believe in your heart that God has raised him from the dead, you will be saved.[556]

For by grace you have been saved through faith, and that not of yourselves; it is the gift of God, not of works, lest anyone should boast.[557]

When the Philippian jailer asked: *Sirs, what must I do to be saved?* Paul answered:

Believe in the Lord Jesus, and you will be saved—you and your household.[558]

Therefore, all who accept His gift, through faith, will have eternal life with Him. At death the believer will pass directly into the presence of Jesus.[559] **Praise God!**

Of all the leaders of the various religions who are worshipped, only one has been able to rise from the dead. There fore,

Confucius' tomb
Occupied

Buddha's tomb (The Tooth Sanctuary) **Occupied**

Muhammad's tomb
Occupied

only He has the power to give eternal life to those who believe in Him.

Jesus' tomb (the Garden tomb)
Empty

Please consider the following:

For those who do not know the Lord; Jesus will not go away; you cannot remain neutral.

He is calling you today—He wants none to perish—but to *not accept* Him is to *reject* Him:

---

[556] Romans 10:9.
[557] Ephesians 2:8-9.
[558] Acts 16: 30-31.
[559] John 8:51; 11:26; Acts 7:54-60; 2 Corinthians 5:8; Philippians 1:23; 1 Corinthians 15:51-55.

7   Summary

He who is not with me is against me.[560]

I urge you: do not let the sun go down without accepting Jesus as your Savior. Death, as we see on our television news services every night, can come quickly and without warning. It is only a heartbeat away. Then it will be too late.

You can accept Jesus right now with a simple, heartfelt prayer asking for Jesus to reign in your heart, confessing and repenting of your sins, and asking for forgiveness based on His work on the cross. The actual words are not so important; God sees what is in your heart.

Here is a sample of how you could pray:

Lord Jesus, I realise that I have rebelled against you and I'm not worthy to get into heaven on my own merit. I believe you died for me and that your death paid for my sins and restores my relationship with God. I acknowledge you as my Lord, Savior, and Friend. Thank you for your gift of eternal life, which I accept by faith. I pray this through your holy name. Amen.

Next steps:

Talk to a Christian friend or pastor, find a Bible study group and look around for a Bible-believing church that honors Jesus. Other Christians are now your brothers and sisters in Christ—get to know your family!

---

[560] Luke 11:23

Appendix 1

A Summary of the Bible

The Bible is made up of the Old Testament (before Christ)—39 books; and the New Testament (after Christ)—27 books; making a total of 66 books.

It starts with the account of how God did His work of creation. Included in this is a lovely garden in which He placed a man and a woman, Adam and Eve, whom He had created. They were allowed to eat all of the fruit from the garden except the fruit from the Tree of Knowledge of Good and Evil; for if they did, they would surely die. They did. And through the temptation of Satan, sin entered the world and they were expelled from God's presence (known as spiritual death)–and the process which would lead to physical death commenced.

However, God desired to have a close and intimate relationship with all mankind for God had created them in His image. He promised to re-establish this relationship through someone He would send; a Messiah, that is, God's anointed One.[561] As the Bible unfolds, the nature of this person becomes clearer until He is finally revealed as Jesus of Nazareth, God's Son, at the commencement of the New Testament.

After Adam and Eve were expelled, they obeyed God's direction to 'be fruitful and multiply' and the population grew rapidly. The people became evil to such an extent that,

every imagination of the thoughts of his heart was only evil continually.[562]

As a consequence, God brought on a worldwide flood which destroyed all land based creatures. Since Noah was the only righteous man, God saved him and his family and all of the animals on board the Ark. After the flood mankind multiplied and become prideful so God divided them by 'confusing their language.'[563] As the population grew, God chose one man, Abraham, through whom He would establish a people for Himself. Abraham's son was Isaac and his son was Jacob whom God renamed Israel; his descendants became known as the Children of Israel. God said He would bless and prosper these people if they kept His laws and worshipped only Him. This is basically the old covenant or testament.

The book of Genesis ends with the Children of Israel, only about 70 people, going to Egypt for food, and Jacob dying there. They increase in number dramatically, with Jacob's 12 sons giving rise to the 12 tribes of Israel. When God calls Moses to lead them out of Egypt 430 years later, they have grown into a nation of about two million people. During their wanderings in the desert, which are described in the books of Exodus, Leviticus, Numbers and Deuteronomy, God gives those laws by which they should live, including the Ten Commandments.[564] Joshua then leads them into the Promised Land (Canaan), which they conquer and settle. Here the books of Joshua, Judges, 1 and 2 Samuel, 1 and 2 Kings and 1 and 2 Chronicles describe how the people lived, their

---

[561] Genesis 3:15.
[562] Genesis 6:5.
[563] Genesis 11:7.
[564] Exodus 20.

Appendices

cycles of embracing and rejecting God and the roles their kings played. During this period the kingdom is divided, and after many warnings from God through the prophets against their rejection of Him, the Assyrians take the Northern Kingdom into captivity and the people are subsumed into the foreign culture, never to be heard of again. Two hundred and thirty six years later, the Southern Kingdom known as Judah, (hence the name "Jew") is taken into captivity by the Babylonians. However, God through His prophets tells them it will only be for seventy years. After this time some of the people return and rebuild Jerusalem and the Temple, which is described in the books of Ezra and Nehemiah.

The prophets through whom God spoke are Isaiah, Jeremiah (who wrote Lamentations), Ezekiel and Daniel, collectively known as Major Prophets because they wrote a lot; and the Minor Prophets, who wrote less, namely: Hosea, Joel, Amos, Obadiah, Jonah, Micah, Nahum, Habakkuk, Zephaniah, Haggai, Zechariah and Malachi. The books of Ruth, Esther and Job tell particular stories of their times. Psalms are songs and Proverbs are wise sayings, both were mainly written by King David and his son King Solomon. Ecclesiastes and Song of Songs (also called Song of Solomon) were written by King Solomon.

A period of four hundred years elapsed between the Old Testament and New Testament. The prophets mentioned above give descriptive information about the future Person (Messiah) who will restore the relationship with mankind that God once had with Adam and Eve. Over sixty clear, prophetic statements regarding this Person were completely fulfilled in the person of Jesus of Nazareth.

The New Testament starts with the four gospels of Matthew, Mark, Luke and John, which describe Jesus' birth, ministry, crucifixion and resurrection.

The book of Acts (written by Luke is mainly about the growth of the early church through Peter and Paul) commences with Jesus' ascension back to heaven, the birth of the church and how the gospel message (good news) was taken to the then known world.

The apostle Paul started many churches and wrote the books of Romans, 1 and 2 Corinthians, Galatians, Ephesians, Philippians, Colossians, 1 and 2 Thessalonians, 1 and 2 Timothy, Titus and Philemon. The author of Hebrews is unknown; James, a brother of Jesus wrote the book bearing his name; Peter wrote the books of 1 and 2 Peter; and John wrote 1, 2 and 3 John as well as the Revelation and his gospel, already mentioned. Another brother of Jesus wrote Jude. The last book of the Bible, The Revelation, gives an account of what will happen in the future and is written in a dramatic style.

The New Testament or covenant replaces the former or old one to the extent that it brings in a new relationship between God and mankind. In the New Testament, God does not require anything from mankind except to believe in Jesus and in His payment, through His death on the cross, for the forgiveness of sins,[565] in order to have that original relationship with God restored and to be with Him for all eternity.

---

[565] John 3:16.

Appendix 2 (Refer to Chapter 6)

Tacitus' Comments on Nero's Treatment of Christians

This text is based on the following book:

Complete Works of Tacitus. Tacitus, A J Church, W J Brodribb, S Bryant; Edited for Perseus. (New York: Random House, 1942). Reproduced online from Perseus Tufts.

XLIV. Such indeed were the precautions of human wisdom. The next thing was to seek means of propitiating the gods, and recourse was had to the Sibylline books, by the direction of which prayers were offered to Vulcanus, Ceres, and Proserpina. Juno, too, was entreated by the matrons, first, in the Capitol, then on the nearest part of the coast, whence water was procured to sprinkle the fane and image of the goddess. And there were sacred banquets and nightly vigils celebrated by married women. But all human efforts, all the lavish gifts of the emperor, and the propitiations of the gods, did not banish the sinister belief that the conflagration was the result of an order. Consequently, to get rid of the report, Nero fastened the guilt and inflicted the most exquisite tortures on a class hated for their abominations, called Christians by the populace. Christus, from whom the name had its origin, suffered the extreme penalty during the reign of Tiberius at the hands of one of our procurators, Pontius Pilatus, and a most mischievous superstition, thus checked for the moment, again broke out not only in Judæa, the first source of the evil, but even in Rome, where all things hideous and shameful from every part of the world find their center and become popular. Accordingly, an arrest was first made of all who pleaded guilty; then, upon their information, an immense multitude was convicted, not so much of the crime of firing the city, as of hatred against mankind. Mockery of every sort was added to their deaths. Covered with the skins of beasts, they were torn by dogs and perished, or were nailed to crosses, or were doomed to the flames and burnt, to serve as a nightly illumination, when daylight had expired.

Nero offered his gardens for the spectacle, and was exhibiting a show in the circus, while he mingled with the people in the dress of a charioteer or stood aloft on a car. Hence, even for criminals who deserved extreme and exemplary punishment, there arose a feeling of compassion; for it was not, as it seemed, for the public good, but to glut one man's cruelty, that they were being destroyed.

Appendices

Appendix 3 (Refer to Chapter 6)

Pliny the Younger's Letter to Emperor Trajan

XCVII66

To THE EMPEROR TRAJAN

IT is my invariable rule, Sir, to refer to you in all matters where I feel doubtful; for who is more capable of removing my scruples, or informing my ignorance? Having never been present at any trials concerning those who profess Christianity, I am unacquainted not only with the nature of their crimes, or the measure of their punishment, but how far it is proper to enter into an examination concerning them. Whether, therefore, any difference is usually made with respect to ages, or no distinction is to be observed between the young and the adult; whether repentance entitles them to a pardon; or if a man has been once a Christian, it avails nothing to desist from his error; whether the very profession of Christianity, unattended with any criminal act, or only the crimes themselves inherent in the profession are punishable; on all these points I am in great doubt. In the meanwhile, the method I have observed towards those who have been brought before me as Christians is this: I asked them whether they were Christians; if they admitted it, I repeated the question twice, and threatened them with punishment; if they persisted, I ordered them to be at once punished: for I was persuaded, whatever the nature of their opinions might be, a contumacious and inflexible obstinacy certainly deserved correction. There were others also brought before me possessed with the same infatuation, but being Roman citizens, I directed them to be sent to Rome. But this crime spreading (as is usually the case) while it was actually under prosecution, several instances of the same nature occurred. An anonymous information was laid before me containing a charge against several persons, who upon examination denied they were Christians, or had ever been so. They repeated after me an invocation to the gods, and offered religious rites with wine and incense before your statue (which for that purpose I had ordered tube brought, together with those of the gods), and even reviled the name of Christ: whereas there is no forcing, it is said, those who are really Christians into any of these compliances: I thought improper, therefore, to discharge them. Some among those who were accused by a witness in person at first confessed themselves Christians, but immediately after denied it; the rest owned indeed that they had been of that number formerly, but had now (some above three, others more, and a few above twenty years ago) renounced that error. They all worshipped your statue and the images of the gods, uttering imprecations at the same time against the name of Christ. They affirmed the whole of their guilt, or their error, was, that they met on a stated day before it was light, and addressed a form of prayer to Christ, as to a divinity, binding themselves by a solemn oath, not for the purposes of any wicked design, but never to commit any fraud, theft, or adultery, never to falsify their word, nor deny a trust when they should be called upon to deliver it up; after which it was their custom to separate, and then reassemble, to eat in common a harmless meal. From this custom, however, they desisted after the publication of my edict, by which, according to your commands, I forbade the meeting of any assemblies. After receiving this account, I judged it so much the more necessary to endeavor to extort the real truth, by putting two female slaves to the torture, who were said to officiate' in their religious rites: but all I could discover was evidence of an absurd and extravagant superstition. I deemed it expedient, therefore, to adjourn all further proceedings, in order to consult you. For it appears to be a matter highly deserving your consideration, more especially as great numbers must be involved in the danger of these prosecutions, which have already extended, and are still likely to extend, to persons of all ranks and ages, and even of both sexes. In fact, this contagious superstition is not confined to the cities only, but has spread its infection among the neighboring villages and country. Nevertheless, it still seems possible to restrain its progress. The temples, at least, which were once almost deserted, begin now to be frequented; and the sacred rites, after along intermission, are again revived; while there is a general demand for the victims, which till lately found very few purchasers. From all this it is easy to conjecture what numbers might be reclaimed if a general pardon were granted to those who shall repent of their error.

XCVIII

TRAJAN TO PLINY

You have adopted the right course, my dearest Secundus, in investigating the charges against the Christians who were brought before you. It is not possible to lay down any general rule for all such cases. Do not go out of your way to look for them. If indeed they should be brought before you, and the crime is proved, they must be punished; with the restriction, however, that where the party denies he is a Christian, and shall make it evident that he is not, by invoking our gods, let him (notwithstanding any former suspicion) be pardoned upon his repentance. Anonymous informations ought not to he received in any sort of prosecution. It is introducing a very dangerous precedent, and is quite foreign to the spirit of our age.

Index

A

Adam and Eve 83
Adam's rib 109
Agate Springs 98
Ager, Derek 92, 95
Ahab 116, 136
Aisha 8
Alexander the Great 133, 134, 136, 139
Amino Acids 22, 23, 24, 25
Ammonite Fossils 98, 99
Amulet Scroll 114
Ancient Hebrew Research Center 124
Anderson, Sir Robert 129, 130, 168
Anglerfish 75, 76
Anthropocentric 50, 57
Antiquities of the Jews 155
Apemen 83
Apostasy 10
Archaeology 90, 113, 119
Archaeopteryx 31
Armageddon 12, 149
Arnold, Professor Thomas 168
Artaxerxes 118, 129, 130, 135
Artemis 120
Ashkelon 137
Ashley Beds 98
Ashton, John 22, 51
Athanasius 15
Australopithecus 85

B

Babylon 116, 117, 139
Babylonian Chronicle 139
Babylonian Talmud 158, 159
Bacteria 43
Baker, Mary 12
Barkay, Gabriel 114
Baybars, Mamluk Sultan 137
Behe, Michael 50
Belshazzar 116
Biblical Creation 55

Big Bang Theory 18, 19
Biochemical Predestination 22
Blaiklock, E M 153
Blood 109
Blood clotting 49, 107
Bombardier Beetle 75
Brahman (Brahma) 3, 4, 5
Bruce, F F 154
Buddha 6, 7, 8
Buddhism 2, 6
Burkhardt, J L 138

C

Caiaphas 120
Capillary action 60
Carbon-14 .... 63, 64, 71, 124
Carter, Dr Robert W 62
Carthage 15
Castes 4
CFTR protein 25
Chapman, Robert 16
Charlesworth, James 119
Chemical evolution 22, 23
Chirality 26
Christ Pantocrator 151
Christ's blood 109
Christadelphians 13
Christian Science 12, 13
Christianity 2, 13, 14
Chromosomes 45, 80, 110
Church of Jesus Christ of Latterday Saints
    (Mormon Church) 11
Circumcision 107, 108
Clark, Graeme 50
Clarke, Sir Edward George 168
Claudius 121, 122, 157
Clement of Alexandria 14
Coal 63, 72, 92, 96
Coelacanth 33, 34
Comets 58, 66, 67, 113
Contra Celsum 154
Cornelius Tacitus 156

Cosmological argument 55
Courtenay-Latimer, Marjorie 33
Cro-Magnon Man 84
Crucifixion 160
Cults 2, 11
Cyrus Cylinder 117
Cyrus Inscription 117, 118
Cyrus the Great 117, 139
Cyrus's tomb 117

D

Daniel's Prophecy 125
Darius the Great 118
Darwin, Charles 20, 79, 81
Darwin's Theory of Evolution 20
Darwin's Tree of Life 21
David Inscription 114
Dawkins, Richard 27, 46, 53, 78
Dead Sea Scrolls 118, 119, 123, 124
Denton, Michael 50
Design, Evidence of 74
Dionysius Exiguus 127
DNA 44, 73

E

Earth's magnetic field 69
Eastern Gate 140, 141, 142
Eddington, Sir Arthur 40
Edessa, image of 151
Edom 137, 138
Edwards, W D 163
Epstein, I 158
Eudocia of Constantinople 119
European Ice Core Project (GRIP) 64
Evolution from Space 27

F

Feathered dinosaur 29
Feduccia, Dr Alan 31
Finkel, Irving 117
First Cause Argument 55
First Law of Thermodynamics 39
Flat Gaps 94
Fossils graveyards 97
Fossils, Age of 40

Four Noble Truths 7
Francois-Marie Arouet 149
Fruit flie 47

G

Gabel, W J 163
Gaius Plinius Caecilius Secundus 156
Gaius Suetonius Tranquillus 157
Galaxies 66
Gautama, Siddhartha 6, 169
Genes 44, 80
Genetically inherited characteristics 79
Genetics 62, 79, 81
Gilgamesh Epic 91
Giraffes 82
Gobi Desert 98
God's Chosen People 142
Golden Gate 140
Gould, Dr Stephen Jay 33
Great Unconformity 92
Greenhut, Zvi 120

H

Habermas, Gary R 158
Haeckel's stages of human embryos 30
Hebrew Masoretic text 119
Helium in zircons 70
Hemochromatosis 46
Hendrick, Captain 33
Herod the Great's tomb 121
Hezekiah's Tunnel 115
Hinduism 2, 3
Hippo 15
History of the Jewish War 155
Hobbit 85
Hoehner, Harold 130
Homo pongoides 30
Hosmer, F E 163
Hoyle, Fredrick 20, 27
Hubble telescope images 102
Huibers, Johan 99
Human eye 76
Humphreys, Russell 3, 65
Hydrologic cycle 106
Hydrothermal vent 57

I

Ibn Abd Allah 8
Ice Core Dating 64
Ichthyosaur 96
Ignatius 125
Intelligent Design 23, 49, 50
Irreducible complexity 74
Islam 2, 8

J

Java Man 84
Jehovah's Witnesses 12
Jerusalem 140
Jihad 11
Johnson, Phillip 51
Josephus, Flavius 154
Justin Martyr 14

K

Karma 4, 7
Kenyon, Dr Dean 22
Koran 9, 111
Krishna 5
Kuiper Belt 67

L

Latent heat of vaporization 61
Lennox, Dr John C 47
Living fossils 33, 34, 35
Lucian of Samosata 158
Lysenko, Tromfim 81

M

Macassey, Rev E L 168
Macreadie, Dr Ian 47
Mara Bar Serapion 154
Marcus, Dr John 22
Marshall, Dr George 78
Maury, Matthew 106
Mecca 8
Mendel, Gregor Johann 79
Milky Way Galaxy 59
Miller, Stanley 23
Mitochondrial Eve 62

Moabite Stone 116
Montceau-les Mines 98
Morris, Professor Brian 108
Muhammad 8
Müller cells 78
Muller, Dr H J 47
Mutations 46

N

Natural Selection 48
Nazareth Inscription 167
Neanderthals 83
Nebraska Man 84
Nebuchadnezzar 116
Nineveh 139
Noah's Ark 99
Noah's Flood 90
Noble, David 35
Nucleic Acids 28
Nucleotides 45

O

Operation Joshua 145
Operation Moses 145
Operation Solomon 146
Oscillating theory 20

P

Path of Devotion 4
Path of Duties 4
Path of Knowledge 4
Patterson, Dr Collin 32
Peking Man 85
Penzias, Dr Arno 18
Peppered Moth 48
Pharaoh Shishak 114
Phlegon of Tralles 154
Physical constants 59
Pilate Inscription 120
Piltdown man 30, 84
Polonium-210 69
Polystrate Fossils 95
Pool of Siloam 119
Pratt, John P 127

Q

Quimby, Phineas 12
Qumran caves 124

R

Radiohalos 69
Radiometric dating 62
Rapid burial 96
Reservoir Effect 62
Retina 76
Russell, Charles Taze 12
Russell, Dr Rex 108

S

Samarian Ostracon 113
Sanford, Dr John 50
Schweitzer, Dr Mary 40, 72
Scourging 159
Second Law of Thermodynamics 39
Sedimentary rock 92
Sennacherib 15, 115, 116
Shiite 9
Sickle Cell Anemia 25, 46
Sidon 135
Single Cells 29
Smalley, Professor Richard 51
Smith, Joseph 11
Smith, Professor J L B 33
Smriti 4
Spentner, Dr Lee 48
Steady State theory 20
Strata 68, 93, 95
Stratified layers 94
Suleiman I 141
Sunni 9
Supernova 73
Surface tension 60
Sweet pea experiment 79

T

Taylor Prism 115
Tertullian 14
Thallus 153
The Merneptah Stele 114
Theory of Evolution 17
Thomas, John 13
Time 104
Transitional Forms 29
Trinity of Creation 56
Tyrannosaurus rex 40
Tyre 133

U

Upanishads 3
Upper Carboniferous 92
Urey, Dr Harold 23
Urey/Miller Experiment 23
Ussher, Bishop 61

V

Vedas 3
Veil of Veronica 151
Vishnu 5
Voltaire 149

W

Wald, George 52
Water 60
Watson, Dr Lyall 86
Wickramasinghe, Dr 27
Wollemi Pines 35
Wood, Bernard 86

Y

Y-Chromosome Adam 62
Young earth, evidence for 65

Z

Zircons 70

www.ingramcontent.com/pod-product-compliance
Lightning Source LLC
Chambersburg PA
CBHW041543220426
43665CB00002B/18